Studying Shakespeare

A CASEBOOK

EDITED BY

JOHN RUSSELL BROWN

MACMILLAN

First published 1990 by
THE MACMILLAN PRESS LTD
Houndmills, Basingstoke, Hampshire RG21 2XS
and London
Companies and representatives
throughout the world

ISBN 0–333–31941–9 paperback

A catalogue record for this book is available
from the British Library.

Printed in Hong Kong

Reprinted 1991, 1992, 1994

CONTENTS

ACKNOWLEDGEMENTS

The editor and publishers wish to thank the following for permission to use copyright material:
Bernard Beckerman, essay on 'Explorations in Shakespeare's Drama', *Shakespeare Quarterly*, 29 (1978), pp. 133–45, by permission of the Folger Shakespeare Library; John Russell Brown, extract from *Discovering Shakespeare: A New Guide to the Plays*, (1981), pp. 75–91, by permission of Macmillan, London; Rosalie L. Colie, extract from *Shakespeare's Living Art*, (1974), pp. 14–27, by permission of Princeton University Press. Copyright © 1974 by Princeton University Press; Jonathan Dollimore, extract from *Radical Tragedy: Religion, Ideology and Power in the Drama of Shakespeare and His Contemporaries*, (1984), pp. 189–203, by permission of Harvester Press Ltd; E.A.J. Honigmann, extract from *Shakespeare: Seven Tragedies, The Dramatist's Manipulation of Response*, (1976), pp. 4–15, by permission of Macmillan, London: Grigori Kozintsev, extract from *King Lear: The Space of Tragedy – The Diary of a Film Director*, trans. by Mary Mackintosh (1977), Heinemann Educational, by permission of VAAP, Moscow; Alexander Leggatt, essay on 'The Extra Dimension: Shakespeare in Performance', *Mosaic*, X, No. 3, Spring (1977), pp. 37–49, by permission of *Mosaic*; Maynard Mack, essay on 'Rescuing Shakespeare', Occasional Paper No. 1 (1979), Oxford University Press in association with the International Shakespeare Association, by permission of the author; Norman Rabkin, extract from *Shakespeare and the Problem of Meaning*, (1981), pp. 1–32, by permission of The University of Chicago Press. Every effort has been made to trace all the copyright holders but if any have been inadvertently overlooked the publishers will be pleased to make the necessary arrangement at the first opportunity.

GENERAL EDITOR'S PREFACE

The Casebook series, launched in 1968, has become a well-regarded library of critical studies. The central concern of the series remains the 'single-author' volume, but suggestions from the academic community have led to an extension of the original plan, to include occasional volumes on such general themes as literary 'schools' and genres.

Each volume in the central category deals either with one well-known and influential work by an individual author, or with closely related works by one writer. The main section consists of critical readings, mostly modern, collected from books and journals. A selection of reviews and comments by the author's contemporaries is also included, and sometimes comment from the author himself. The Editor's Introduction charts the reputation of the work or works from the first appearance to the present time.

Volumes in the 'general themes' category are variable in structure but follow the basic purpose of the series in presenting an integrated selection of readings, with an Introduction which explores the theme and discusses the literary and critical issues involved.

A single volume can represent no more than a small selection of critical opinions. Some critics are excluded for reasons of space, and it is hoped that readers will pursue the suggestions for further reading in the Select Bibliography. Other contributions are severed from their original context, to which some readers may wish to turn; indeed, if they take a hint from the critics represented here, they certainly will.

A. E. DYSON

INTRODUCTION

This casebook is unlike others on Shakespearian topics. It does not focus attention on one particular play or group of plays. Rather, it examines how Shakespeare can best be studied and provides instruction and discussion about method. Students of any play-text should find guidance and stimulus here for their own work.

Nor does this book open with reprints of early critical assessments and move forward chronologically to the present day. In Part 1 there are accounts of the critical approaches in use from Shakespeare's time to our own. Its first section, with some extended quotations, tells the story until the very beginning of the twentieth century, but the second is more discursive and concentrates on the first twenty-five years after the Second World War. The third section introduces the accounts of critical method and research which comprise the main part of the book. All the articles and chapters from books which are chosen for reproduction date from after 1970; they are arranged according to subject and not date of writing, and they cover as far as possible, within limitations of space, the full spectrum of what has been published.

NOTE ON TEXTS

In this Casebook all references to Shakespeare are to the edition of the complete works by Peter Alexander, first published in 1951.

PART ONE

1 EARLY RESPONSES

A publisher recommending *Troilus and Cressida* to purchasers is the
first to tell others how to study. He repeats the conventional wisdom
of the times – this was in 1609 – that a comedy should display the
'actions of our lives' and so comment on them, but he argues that
Shakespeare outreached other dramatists for the 'dexterity and
power of wit'; and if this needs 'labour' to appreciate, then the effort
will be well rewarded:

A Never Writer, to an Ever Reader.
News.

Eternal reader, you have here a new play, never staled with the stage, never
clapperclawed with the palms of the vulgar, and yet passing full of the palm
comical; for it is a birth of your brain[1] that never undertook anything
comical vainly. And were but the vain names of comedies changed for the
titles of commodities, or of plays for pleas, you should see all those grand
censors, that now style them such vanities, flock to them for the main grace
of their gravities – especially this author's comedies, that are so framed to
the life that they serve for the most common commentaries of all the actions
of our lives, showing such a dexterity and power of wit that the most
displeased with plays are pleased with his comedies. And all such dull and
heavy-witted worldlings as were never capable of the wit of a comedy,
coming by report of them to his representations, have found that wit there
that they never found in themselves and have parted better witted than
they came, feeling an edge of wit set upon them more than ever they
dreamed they had brain to grind it on. So much and such savoured salt of
wit is in his comedies that they seem, for their height of pleasure, to be
born in that sea that brought forth Venus. Amongst all there is none more
witty than this; and had I time I would comment upon it, though I know
it needs not, for so much as will make you think your testern[2] well bestowed,
but for so much worth as even poor I know to be stuffed in it. It deserves
such a labor as well as the best comedy in Terence or Plautus. And believe
this, that when he is gone and his comedies out of sale, you will scramble
for them and set up a new English Inquisition. Take this for a warning,
and at the peril of your pleasure's loss, and judgment's, refuse not, nor like
this the less for not being sullied with the smoky breath of the multitude;
but thank fortune for the 'scape it hath made amongst you, since by the
grand possessors'[3] wills I believe you should have prayed for them rather
than been prayed. And so I leave all such to be prayed for, for the state of
their wits' healths, that will not praise it. *Vale.*

'Wit', the key word in this preface, had a wide range of meanings from sound judgement, wisdom and intelligence, through power of imagination and invention and on to verbal acuity and energy of mind, and foolishness. Conjunction with the 'height of pleasure' situates the present usage among the least pedantic and the most superhuman; promise of an 'English Inquisition' mocks the zeal of scholarship and reinforces the godlike qualities of the dramatist's wit.

From the beginning, then, study seemed both necessary and demanding for the reader of Shakespeare's plays. When the first folio collected edition was prepared in 1623, John Heminge and Henry Condell, two Sharer-members of the King's Men, signed an Epistle 'To the great variety of readers' which acknowledged again that study was appropriate and repeated readings of the text recommended:

From the most able to him that can but spell – there you are numbered. We had rather you were weighed, especially when the fate of all books depends upon your capacities, and not of your heads alone, but of your purses. Well! It is now public, and you will stand for your priviledges we know: to read, and censor. Do so, but buy it first – that doth best commend a book, the Stationer says. Then, how odd soever your brains be or your wisdoms, make your licence the same, and spare not. Judge your sixpen'orth, your shilling's worth, your five shillings' worth at a time, or higher – so you rise to the just rates – and welcome. But whatever you do, buy.

Censure will not drive a trade or make the jack go: and though you be a Magistrate of wit, and sit on the stage at Blackfriars or the Cockpit[4] to arraign plays daily, know these plays have had their trial already and stood out all appeals, and do now come forth quitted rather by a Decree of Court than any purchased letters of commendation.[5]

It had been a thing, we confess, worthy to have been wished that the author himself had lived to have set forth and overseen his own writings. But since it hath been ordained otherwise and he by death departed from that right, we pray you do not envy his friends the office of their care and pain, to have collected and published them; and so to have published them as, where before you were abused with divers stolen and surreptitious copies, maimed and deformed by the frauds and stealths of injurious impostors that exposed them, even those are now offered to your view cured and perfect of their limbs, and all the rest absolute in their numbers as he conceived them. Who, as he was a happy imitator of Nature, was a most gentle expresser of it. His mind and hand went together, and what he thought, he uttered with that easiness that we have scarce received from him a blot in his papers.

But it is not our province, who only gather his works and give them you, to praise him. It is yours that read him. And there we hope, to your divers capacities, you will find enough both to draw and hold you, for his wit can no more lie hid than it could be lost. Read him therefore, and again and again. And if then you do not like him, surely you are in some manifest danger not to understand him. And so we leave you to other of his friends whom, if you need, can be your guides. If you need them not, you can lead yourselves and others. And such readers we wish him.

John Heminge.
Henry Condell.

Textual problems, an appeal to the performance qualities of the plays and the assumption that Shakespeare is wittier than his readers – these are concerns that were to be echoed time and again by those who write about studying the plays. Less common is the assumption that those who 'can but spell' are fit students and the wish that every reader will join in the guidance of others.

Publication in four folio editions, followed by editions by Nicholas Rowe the dramatist in 1709 and 1714, by Alexander Pope the poet in 1723 and 1728, and by a long procession of others, men-of-letters and scholars, has provided the ground for the English (and International) Inquisition foreseen in the epistle of 1609. By 1675, when Edward Phillips published his literary companion, *Theatrum Poetarum*, his assessment of Shakespare fitted into conventional critical terminology, but as if to the surprise of the writer:

William Shakespear [*sic*], the Glory of the English Stage, whose nativity at Stratford-upon-Avon is the highest honour that town can boast of, from an actor of tragedies and comedies, he became a Maker, and such a Maker that though some others may perhaps pretend to a more exact decorum and economy, especially in tragedy, never any expressed a more lofty and tragic height, never any represented Nature more purely to the life; and where the polishments of Art are most wanting, as probably his learning was not extraordinary, he pleaseth with a certain wild and native elegance; and in all his writings hath an unvulgar style, as well as his *Venus and Adonis*, his *Rape of Lucrece* and other various poems, as in his dramatics.

Pope expressed surprise outright, in the Preface to his edition:

The power over our passions was never possessed in a more eminent degree, or displayed in so different instances. Yet all along, there is seen no labour, no pains to raise them; no preparation to guide our guess to the effect, or be perceived to lead toward it. But the heart swells, and the tears burst out, just at the proper places. We are surprised, the moment we weep; and yet upon reflection find the passion so just, that we should be surprised if we had not wept, and wept at that very moment.

How astonishing is it again, that the passions directly opposite to these, laughter and spleen, are no less at his command! that he is not more a master of the Great, than of the Ridiculous in human nature; of our noblest tendernesses, than of our vainest foibles; of our strongest emotions, than of our idlest sensations!

Studies such as Pope's gave open way to bardolatory and hyperbole. The application of ordinary measures of judgement served little beyond augmenting wonder – even when Shakespeare was found wanting. So Pope continued:

It must be owned that with all these great excellencies, he has almost as great defects; and that as he has certainly written better, so he has perhaps written worse, than any other. But I think I can in some measure account for these defects, from several causes and accidents; without which it is hard to imagine that so large and so enlightened a mind could ever have been susceptible to them. That all these contingencies should unite to his disadvantage seems to me almost as singularly unlucky, as that so many various (nay contrary) talents should meet in one man, was happy and extraordinary.

The main culprit, in Pope's view, was Shakespeare's audience, the 'populace' that had insisted on easy pleasures; and then the players, who pandered to its tastes. For the student, this had one particular consequence:

To judge . . . of Shakespeare by Aristotle's rules is like trying a man by the Laws of one country, who acted under those of another. He writ to the people; and writ at first without patronage from the better sort, . . . without assistance or advice from the learned, . . . without that knowledge of the best models, the Ancients, to inspire him with an emulation of them. . . .

By the time the plays came to be edited by Samuel Johnson (1765) – essayist, poet, novelist, etymologist, dramatist, biographer, critic and editor, leader of literary London – a new study had begun, the task of placing Shakespeare in his own time in the theatre, thought and politics of the Elizabethan age, Editions became more learned, footnotes lengthened and the distinguishing features of the Elizabethan stage began, very slowly, to be recovered. Johnson's Preface put it like this:

Every man's performances, to be rightly estimated, must be compared with the state of the age in which he lived, and with his own particular opportunities; and though to the reader a book be not worse or better for the circumstances of the author, yet as there is always a silent reference of human works to human abilities, and as the enquiry, how far man may extend his designs, or how high he may rate his native force, is of far greater dignity than in what rank we shall place any particular performance, curiosity is always busy to discover the instruments, as well as to survey the workmanship, to know how much is to be ascribed to original powers, and how much to casual and adventitious help. The palaces of Peru or Mexico were certainly mean and incommodious habitations, if compared to the houses of European monarchs; yet who could forbear to view them with astonishment, who remembered that they were built without the use of iron?

The English nation, in the time of Shakespeare, was yet struggling to emerge from barbarity.

Yet despite Shakespeare's barbarism, Johnson read and studied the plays with learned attention. Like others of his own time, he recommended that the texts should be searched for their depiction of 'common humanity' and the 'instruction' derived from Shakespeare's 'wisdom'. He also recommended that he should be compared to other authors:

Shakespeare is above all writers, at least above all modern writers, the poet of Nature; the poet that holds up to his readers a faithful mirror of manners and of life. His characters are not modified by the customs of particular places, unpractised by the rest of the world; by the peculiarities of studies or professions, which can operate but upon small numbers; or by the accidents of transient fashions or temporary opinions: they are the genuine progeny of common humanity, such as the world will always supply, and observation will always find. His persons act and speak by the influence of those general passions and principles by which all minds are agitated, and the whole system of life is continued in motion. In the writings of other poets a character is too often an individual; in those of Shakespeare it is commonly a species.

It is from this wide extension of design that so much instruction is derived. It is this which fills the plays of Shakespeare with practical axioms and domestic wisdom. It was said of Euripides, that every verse was a precept; and it may be said of Shakespeare, that from his works may be collected a system of civil and oeconomical prudence. Yet his real power is not shown in the splendor of particular passages, but by the progress of his fable, and the tenor of his dialogue; and he that tries to recommend him by select quotations, will succeed like the pedant in Hierocles, who, when he offered his house to sale, carried a brick in his pocket as a specimen.

It will not easily be imagined how much Shakespeare excels in accommodating his sentiments to real life, but by comparing him with other authors. It was observed of the ancient schools of declamation, that the more diligently they were frequented, the more was the student disqualified for the world, because he found nothing there which he should ever meet in any other place. The same remark may be applied to every stage but that of Shakespeare. The theatre, when it is under any other direction, is peopled by such characters as were never seen, conversing in a language which was never heard, upon topics which will never arise in the commerce of mankind. But the dialogue of this author is often so evidently determined by the incident which produces it, and is pursued with so much ease and simplicity, that it seems scarcely to claim the merit of fiction, but to have been gleaned by diligent selection out of common conversation, and common occurrences.

It was left to a political pamphleteer and one-time Under-Secretary of State, Maurice Morgann, to concentrate study on one of Shakespeare's characters. But he did not try to make general deductions about Humanity; he treated Falstaff, from the two Henry IV plays, as if he were a very distinct individual, and taking the advice of Heminge and Condell he read the text again and again until he believed he might have understood Shakespeare's hidden intention. His *Essay on the Dramatic Character of Sir John Falstaff*, written in 1774 and published in 1777, is the first sustained attempt to discover in Shakespeare's writings more than meets the eye, to insist on relating any one verbal statement to the 'impression' of a character in action and any one part of a play to the whole as it develops in the course of performance or reading. This student takes pleasure in apparent contradictions and in what is latent and obscure:

It must, in the first place, be admitted that the appearances in this case are singularly strong and striking; and so they had need be, to become the ground of so general a censure. We see this extraordinary character, almost in the first moment of our acquaintance with him, involved in circumstances of apparent dishonour; and we hear him familiarly called coward by his most intimate companions. We see him, on occasion of the robbery at Gads-Hill, in the very act of running away from the Prince and Poins; and we behold him, on another of more honourable obligation, in open day light, in battle, and acting in his profession as a soldier, escaping from Douglas even out of the world as it were; counterfeiting death, and deserting his very existence; and we find him on the former occasion, betrayed into those lies and braggadocioes, which are the usual concomitants of cowardice in military men, and pretenders to valour. These are not only in themselves strong circumstances, but they are moreover thrust forward, pressed upon our notice as the subject of our mirth, as the great business of the scene: no wonder, therefore, that the word should go forth that Falstaff is exhibited as a character of cowardice and dishonour.

What there is to the contrary of this, it is my business to discover. Much, I think, will presently appear; but it lies so dispersed, is so latent, and so purposely obscured, that the reader must have some patience whilst I collect it into one body, and make it the object of a steady and regular contemplation.

(ed., Oxford, 1972, pp. 145–6)

Morgann began by reminding his readers that in 'real' life character is intuited from 'impressions' more than from statements of fact appealing directly to the 'understanding'. So the argument comes back to Falstaff and to Shakespeare:

It is not to the *courage* only of Falstaff that we think these observations will apply: no part whatever of his character seems to be fully settled in our minds; at least there is something strangely incongruous in our discourse and affections concerning him. We all like Old Jack; yet, by some strange perverse fate, we all abuse him, and deny him the possession of any one single good or respectable quality. There is something extraordinary in this: it must be a strange art in Shakespeare which can draw our liking and good will towards so offensive an object. He has wit, it will be said; chearfulness and humour of the most characteristic and captivating sort. And is this enough? Is the humour and gaiety of vice so very captivating? Is the wit, characteristic of baseness and every ill quality capable of attaching the heart and winning the affections? Or does not the apparency of such humour, and the flashes of such wit, by more strongly disclosing the deformity of character, but the more effectually excite our hatred and contempt of the man? And yet this is not our feeling of Falstaff's character. When he has ceased to amuse us, we find no emotions of disgust; we can scarcely forgive the ingratitude of the Prince in the new-born virtue of the King, and we curse the severity of that poetic justice which consigns our old good-natured delightful companion to the custody of the warden, and the dishonours of the Fleet.

(*Ibid.*, pp. 148–9)

Morgann was specific about how to study Shakespeare:

It may be proper, in the first place, to take a short view of all the parts of Falstaff's character, and then proceed to discover, if we can, what impressions, as to courage or cowardice, he had made on the persons of the drama: after which we will examine, in course, such evidence, either of persons or facts, as are relative to the matter; and account as we may for those appearances, which seem to have led to the opinion of his constitutional cowardice.

(*Ibid.*, p. 151)

Because Morgann advanced the notion that 'Shakespeare has made certain impressions, or produced certain effects, of which he has thought fit to conceal or obscure the cause', he stands at the beginning of much reading and rereading of the text – in a more sleuth-like manner than was envisaged by the actors who recommended the first folio edition to the 'great variety of readers'.

But while some students delved with care into the depths of Shakespeare's text, others used his words to awaken their own imaginations and weave dreams for their own satisfaction. The sonnet 'On sitting down to read *King Lear* once again', written by John Keats in 1818, opposes the study of Shakespeare to indulgence in romance and celebrates an intense and personal involvement with the drama from which he hopes to emerge with a flight of his own imagination:

> O GOLDEN tongued Romance, with serene lute!
>   Fair plumed Syren, Queen of far-away!
>   Leave melodizing on this wintry day,
> Shut up thine olden pages, and be mute:
> Adieu! for, once again, the fierce dispute
>   Betwixt damnation and impassion'd clay
>   Must I burn through; once more humbly assay
> The bitter-sweet of this Shakespearian fruit:
> Chief Poet! and ye clouds of Albion,
>   Begetters of our deep eternal theme!
> When through the old oak Forest I am gone,
>   Let me not wander in a barren dream,
> But, when I am consumed in the fire,
> Give me new Phoenix wings to fly at my desire.

Romantic poets and critics and the best actors of their time believed that they had unlocked the secret of Shakespeare. Wordsworth wrote that no one before his own generation had appreciated the plays 'justly'.[6] Coleridge asserted that:

Providence has given England the greatest man that ever put on and put off mortality, and has thrown a sop to the envy of other nations by inflicting upon his native country the most incompetent critics . . . His critics among us during the whole of the last century have neither understood nor appreciated him; for how could they appreciate what they could not understand?[7]

When de Quincey wrote the entry for Shakespeare in the *Encyclopædia Britannica* of 1838, a covering letter sent to the editor explained:

You will not complain of want of novelty, which was in this case quite reconcilable with truth – so deep is the mass of error which has gathered about Shakespeare.[8]

William Hazlitt took issue with Dr Johnson, arguing that Shakespeare did not portray general Nature and could be appreciated only by recognizing the individuality and originality of his inventions. He argued that the famous earlier critic

> was not only without any particular fineness of organic sensibility, alive to all the 'mighty world of ear and eye', . . . but without that intenseness of passion, which, seeking to exaggerate whatever excites the feelings of pleasure or power in the mind, and moulding the impressions of natural objects according to the impulses of imagination, produces a genius and a taste for poetry.
>
> (Preface, *Characters of Shakespeare's Plays*, London, 1817)

Shakespeare had to be studied so that he kindled the reader's imagination: the reality of Hamlet, argued Hazlitt, was 'in the reader's mind':

> It is *we* who are Hamlet . . . We have been so used to this tragedy that we hardly know how to criticize it any more than we should know to describe our own faces.
>
> (ed. Oxford, 1916; pp. 85–6)

Students became proud of their humility before Shakespeare's vast powers, as Matthew Arnold's Sonnet of 1849 attests:

> OTHERS abide our question. Thou art free.
> We ask and ask: Thou smilest and art still,
> Out-topping knowledge. For the loftiest hill
> That to the stars uncrowns his majesty,
> Planting his steadfast footsteps in the sea,
> Making the Heaven of Heavens his dwelling-place,
> Spares but the cloudy border of his base
> To the foil'd searching of mortality:
> And thou, who didst the stars and sunbeams know,
> Self-school'd, self-scann'd, self-honour'd, self-secure,
> Didst walk on Earth unguess'd at. Better so!
> All pains the immortal spirit must endure,
>   All weakness that impairs, all griefs that bow,
>   Find their sole voice in that victorious brow.

The poet became more important than his characters or his plays. Edward Dowden's *Shakspere, a Critical Study of his Mind and Art* (London, 1875) traces the 'spiritual' life of the writer:

To come into close and living relation with the individuality of a poet must
be the chief end of our study – to receive from his nature the peculiar
impulse and impression which he, best of all, can give . . . We endeavour
to pass through the creation of the artist to the mind of the creator.

(pp. 2–3)

Unfortunately, Dowden had Matthew Arnold's penchant for out-
topping panegyric and mortal concerns; when he reached the 'great'
tragedies he claimed that

the imaginative fervour of Shakspere was at its highest, and sustained itself
without abatement. There was no feverish excitement in his energy, and
there was no pause.   (p. 223)

But more pedestrian study also flourished. R. G. Moulton's
*Shakespeare as a Dramatic Artist: a Popular Illustration of the Principles of
Scientific Criticism* (London, 1885) made constant and precise reference
to only a few texts. Its preface scorned generalities; other critics
located Shakespare's 'greatness' in his deep knowledge of 'human
nature', assuming that:

to the technicalities of Dramatic Art, he [was] at once careless . . . and too
great to need them.

Moulton proposed to

interpret a complex situation, not by fastening attention on its striking
elements and ignoring others as oversights and blemishes, but by putting
together *with business-like exactitude* all that the author has given, weighing,
balancing and standing by the product.

Moulton wanted to '*investigate* patiently' to discover a 'scheme' which
would 'give point' to every detail of a text (p. 25, editor's italics);
he wished to distinguish literary species and not make broad
qualitative judgements. After such a rallying cry, it is disappointing
that Moulton's 'dramatic' and 'technical' criticism rested chiefly on
character analysis and the dynamics of plot; even so, he led many
students onto firmer ground.

Indeed, industry began to replace perception, and students of
Shakespeare spared no pains and no lengths. The first volume of
the *New Variorum Edition* of the plays appeared in Philadelphia in
1871; it aimed at giving *all* variant readings and emendations,
together with a deep swathe of previous criticism and elucidation..

Sir Sidney Lee spent twenty years collecting material and sifting evidence for his *Life of William Shakespeare* (London, 1898) in which the plays were considered in the chronological sequence of his life and in the context of theatrical and political history. Lee continued to work on this study after publication, the final revision appearing in 1925.

At the beginning of the twentieth century A. C. Bradley's *Shakespearean Tragedy* (London, 1904) exemplifies the best in the study of the plays. The book is dedicated 'To My Students' and its Introduction sums up the full range of approaches that had been used until that time, adding a special plea for a theatrical understanding of character in action and in the inner movements of thought and being:

. . . I propose to consider the four principal tragedies of Shakespeare from a single point of view. Nothing will be said of Shakespeare's place in the history either of English literature or of the drama in general. No attempt will be made to compare him with other writers. I shall leave untouched, or merely glanced at, questions regarding his life and character, the development of his genius and art, the genuineness, sources, texts, inter-relations of his various works. Even what may be called, in a restricted sense, the 'poetry' of the four tragedies – the beauties of style, diction, versification – I shall pass by in silence. Our one object will be what, again in a restricted sense, may be called dramatic appreciation; to increase our understanding and enjoyment of these works as dramas; to learn to apprehend the action and some of the personages of each with a somewhat greater truth and intensity, so that they may assume in our imaginations a shape a little less unlike the shape they wore in the imagination of their creator. For this end all those studies that were mentioned just now, of literary history and the like, are useful and even in various degrees necessary. But an overt pursuit of them is not necessary here, nor is any one of them so indispensable to our object as that close familiarity with the plays, that native strength and justice of perception, and that habit of reading with an eager mind, which make many an unscholarly lover of Shakespeare a far better critic than many a Shakespeare scholar.

Such lovers read a play more or less as if they were actors who had to study all the parts. They do not need, of course, to imagine whereabouts the persons are to stand, or what gestures they ought to use; but they want to realise fully and exactly the inner movements which produced these words and no other, these deeds and no other, at each particular moment. This, carried through a drama, is the right way to read the dramatist Shakespeare; and the prime requisite here is therefore a vivid and intent imagination. But this alone will hardly suffice. It is necessary also, especially to a true conception of the whole, to compare, to analyse, to dissect. And such readers often shrink from this task, which seems to them prosaic or even a desecration. They misunderstand, I believe. They would not shrink if they remembered two things. In the first place, in this process of comparison and analysis, it is not requisite, it is on the contrary ruinous, to set imagination aside and to substitute some supposed 'cold reason'; and it is only want of practice that makes the concurrent use of analysis and of poetic perception difficult or irksome. And, in the second place, these dissecting processes, though they are also imaginative, are still, and are meant to be, nothing but means to an end. When they have finished their work (it can only be finished for the time) they give place to the end, which is that same imaginative reading or re-creation of the drama from which they set out, but a reading now enriched by the products of analysis, and therefore far more adequate and enjoyable.

(pp. 1–2)

NOTES

1. i.e., of Shakespeare.

2. i.e., your sixpence (slang).

3. i.e., either the King's Men, the actor's company, or the persons who commissioned this play for a private performance.

4. Two 'private' Jacobean theatres, in contrast to the 'public' playhouses, such as the Globe.

5. i.e., the quality of the plays is attested by applause for their performance, not by what has been written about them.

6. 'To Robert Peele', *Letters*, ed. E. de Selincourt (1938), V.3.

7. From a lecture as reported by J.P. Collier, 1811–12; quoted from *Coleridge's Writings on Shakespeare*, ed. Terence Hawkes (New York, 1959), pp. 88–9. See also *Lectures 1808–1819*, ed. R. A. Foakes (London, 1987), i. 354–55.

8. *Works*, ed. D. Masson (Edinburgh, 1890), iv. 17,n.

2 THE POST-WAR CONSENSUS

As criticism pulled itself back into activity after the Second World War, a huge growth in higher education and the development of libraries, institutes and research teams, together with new journals and more numerous performances of Shakespeare's plays, brought a great surge in Shakespeare studies and a general agreement about how to undertake them. Critics and scholars were so busy 'extending the boundaries of knowledge' that they had little time to ask why professional lifetimes were being spent in this pursuit. Each cultivated a particular brand of study and assumed that everything was working together towards some distant clarification. At conferences all differences were respected and enjoyed, while casebooks and other anthologies brought various viewpoints together in shapely collages. In 1971 an unprecedented World Shakespeare Congress celebrated a common achievement; theatre archaeology and textual studies raised some controversy, but dissent about appropriate critical approaches was polite or humorous, or in other ways muted. Discussion revealed a broadly-based consensus about how to study Shakespeare.

Some years earlier a schism could have been detected between those who studied each play, or part of a play, closely for its own sake, often out of historical context, and others who strove to understand Shakespeare as his contemporaries would have done. But peace broke out and the dispute served only to divide study into two main branches. It had become evident that close analysis of language involved a careful placing of words in time, while a consideration of plays as reflections of the life and thought of Shakespeare's day turned often enough upon a very particular use of key words. Besides, the two sides were united by a common desire to explain (or interpret) the plays, to identify their meanings. The following book-titles, listed chronologically, appeared between 1947 and 1970 and belong to both parties in the outgrown debate; they indicate how students were encouraged to pluck the heart out of Shakespeare's plays, to know what he thought about major issues and how these ideas were expressed in the plays: *As They Liked It –*

that sounds open-minded, but there is yet a subtitle – *An Essay on Shakespeare and Morality; An Interpretation of Shakespeare; Shakespeare's Doctrine of Nature; The Wheel of Fire: Essays in Interpretation of Shakespeare's Sombre Tragedies* (revised edition); *Shakespeare's World of Images* – again a wider aim, but again a subtitle – *The Development of his Moral Ideas; The Meaning of Shakespeare; Shakespearian Tragedy and the Elizabethan Compromise; Shakespeare and the Allegory of Evil; Dramatic Providence in 'Macbeth': a Study of Shakespeare's Tragic Themes of Humanity and Grace; The Question of 'Hamlet'; The Shakespearean Ethic; Justice and Mercy in Shakespeare; Shakespeare and Christian Doctrine; Shakespeare and the Reason* . . .

The pursuit of Shakespeare's meaning, the conceptual unity behind a changing drama, was pioneered by Wilson G. Knight in *The Wheel of Fire*, first published in 1930. An introduction to his second book, *The Shakespearean Tempest* (London, 1932), proclaimed a new mode of study:

While we view the plays primarily as studies in character, abstracting the literary person from the close mesh of that poetic fabric into which he is woven, we shall . . . end by creating a chaos of the whole. If, however, we give attention always to poetic colour and suggestion first, thinking primarily in terms of symbolism, not 'characters', we shall find each play in turn appear more and more amazing in the delicacy of its texture, and then, and not till then, will the whole of Shakespeare's work begin to reveal its richer significance, its harmony, its unity.

Knight published a chart showing the 'real lines of force in Shakespeare', how the 'basic symbols of tempest and music in vital opposition unify Shakespeare's world'. Key words, taken out of poetic and dramatic context, are arranged on the page, with 'Bright' at the top and 'Dark' at the foot; in between are music, tempests, battles, cannon, drums, silence. Across the page run 'Royalty' and 'Love', 'Warrior Honour' and 'Religious Grace', or 'Weird Women', 'Ghosts' and 'Madness'.

For Wilson Knight, action as well as character was of secondary concern:

To receive the whole Shakespearian vision into the intellectual consciousness demands a certain and very definite act of mind. One must be prepared to see the whole play in space as well as in time. It is natural in analysis to pursue the steps of the tale in sequence, noticing the logic that connects them, regarding those essentials that Aristotle noted: the beginning, middle, and end. But by giving supreme attention to this temporal nature of drama we omit what, in Shakespeare, is at least of equivalent importance. A Shakespearian tragedy is set spacially as well as temporally in the mind. By this I mean that there are throughout the play a set of correspondences which relate to each other independently of the time-sequence which is the story: such are the intuition-intelligence opposition active with and across *Troilus and Cressida*, the death-theme in *Hamlet*, the nightmare evil of *Macbeth*. This I have sometimes called the play's 'atmosphere.'

(*The Wheel of Fire*, 2nd ed., London, 1949, p. 3)

The idea behind a play became the prime object of a student's search and research. L. C. Knights's *Some Shakespearean Themes* (London, 1959) identified several concepts such as 'Time', 'Nature', and 'Appearance and Reality' in a number of plays. *King Lear* was summed up like this:

our seeing has been directed towards . . . nothing less than *what man is*. The imaginative discovery that is the play's essence has thus involved the sharpest possible juxtaposition of rival conceptions of 'Nature'.

(p. 117; author's italics)

Some critics were more interested in Wilson Knight's 'atmosphere' than in themes, and studied Shakespeare's 'Imagery' as a distinct part of his artifice. Taking their cue from the criticism of short poems and a new awareness of linguistic ambiguity, the verbal texture of the plays was closely examined. The first in this line was Caroline Spurgeon who published *Shakespeare's Imagery and What It Tells Us* (London, 1935) as an attempt to reconstruct the mind of Shakespeare; so she reported that he disliked dogs but loved outdoor sports, that he was short of cash in the middle of his life and so forth. But her descriptions of dominant metaphors and similes in each individual work had greatest influence: the prevalence of beast images in many social plays, cosmic, global and mythic images in *Antony and Cleopatra*, images of corruption in *Hamlet* and so forth. W. H. Clemen's *The Development of Shakespeare's Imagery* (1936; tr., London, 1951) and I. A. Richards's *Practical Criticism* (London, 1929) and *Principles of Literary Criticism* (London, 1924) together helped to establish this form of study – although the chief concern of Richards was with short poems. W. W. Empson's *Seven Types of Ambiguity* (London, 1930) had discussed Shakespeare as a poet alongside untheatrical writers, such as Donne, Herbert, Marvell, Keats and early T. S. Eliot, but his *Structure of Complex Words* of 1951 analyses the use of significant words in single plays, as the imagists had discussed their dominant images: 'fool' in *Lear*, 'honest' in *Othello*, 'sense' in *Measure for Measure*. M. M. Mahood's *Shakespeare's Word-Play* (London, 1957) showed this kind of study in a highly developed form.

Perhaps the most influential book among those seeking to place Shakespeare in his historical context and to discover Elizabethan meanings in the plays was E. M. W. Tillyard's *Shakespeare's History Plays* (London, 1944). A year earlier Tillyard had published *The Elizabethan World Picture*, in which Tudor historians and homiletic propagandists speak for themselves and present a view of politics and society, and now he proceeded to show how the plays expressed this

universally held and still comprehensible scheme of history: a scheme fundamentally religious, by which events evolve under a law of justice and under the ruling of God's Providence, and of which Elizabeth's England was the acknowledged outcome.

(pp. 320–1)

Advice to the student was uncompromising:

Shakespeare's Histories with their constant pictures of disorder cannot be understood without assuming a larger principle of order in the background.

(p. 319)

Other books followed by other scholarly critics, notably a group arguing for Christian values in the plays and many that stressed conservative issues of order, inheritance, honour and loyalty. Students were warned that realistic notions of character were out of place; they should look for symbols of Christ or God, Virginity, Patience, Disorder and the like.

Warning voices were raised against too strict identification between character and concept, and too simplistic a notion of what 'an Elizabethan audience' might assume. Robert Ornstein's *The Moral Vision of Jacobean Tragedy* (Madison, Wisc., 1960) in title and organization is within the 'meaning-seeking' tradition but not easily so. In a critical opening chapter, Ornstein warned that we cannot 'know' the cultural background of the plays: an 'intellectual montage' of ideas that is 'perfectly accurate in every detail' would be perfectly misleading in its impression of static homogeneity; it is one thing to know what was in the books that dramatists and some of their audiences read, and quite another to know what they were able or willing to read in them. Ornstein refused to mark the boundaries or landmarks of an imaginary and theatrical world with measures appropriate to an intellectual one:

> within the drama there is no pattern of intellectual resolution, nor a continuing interest in specific ethical questions.
>
> (p. 45)

He looked for a 'positive note', but often could not find one. He began to consider what a play *does*:

> to attempt to define Hamlet's character by weighing his motives and actions against any system of Renaissance thought is to stage *Hamlet* morally without the Prince of Denmark, i.e., without the *felt impression* of Hamlet's moral nature. . . .
> Only if we surrender ourselves to the *moods* of the individual plays . . . can we 'know' the ethics of the tragedies.
>
> (pp. 235 and 46, editor's italics)

In an article in *Shakespeare Quarterly* (1960), Clifford Leech argued that if Keats was right in supposing that a great poet lives by sensations rather than thought and is therefore able to live in uncertainties, were critics not foolish to look for a 'meaning' in Shakespeare:

> we cannot legitimately regard the plays as we regard non-dramatic writings. We may certainly find in the verbal texture of a play a measure of coherence that will give us aesthetic satisfaction as we read. . . But we must not in the theatre expect or demand a rigid adherence to a formulated pattern, however strongly that may seem to emerge from a reading of the text.[1]

With more or less tact, historical criticism was the prevailing mode. In *The Business of Criticism* (Oxford, 1959), Helen Gardner defined what should be done:

> The critic or scholar has a different function from that of the artist or original thinker. One of his uses is to help to preserve the creative thought of his own day from provincialism in time, by keeping alive and available to his own age what is neglected or disparaged by those absorbed in the preoccupations of the hour. His humble task is to protect his betters from the corruption of fashions.
>
> (p. 156)

But the critic's function is also to offer the appropriate key and to

display, as Wilson Knight had done, the unity of conception that is
not apparent without careful analysis and research:

Asking the relevant historical questions and trying to learn a writer's
language are means to an end. They subserve the aim of discovering the
peculiar virtue of the individual work, play, poem, or novel. This means
recognizing its true subject or imaginative centre, the source of the work's
unity and of its whole tone. If we do not thus recognize the subject, feel the
unity, and respond to the tone, we have not understood what we have read,
or else the work is unsatisfying in itself.

(p. 62)

A broad sweep of scholarly endeavour supported the attempt to
reveal the 'true centre' of Shakespeare's plays. Physical characteristics of the playhouses, critical attitudes towards dramatic genres
prevalent in the Renaissance, the literary and dramatic sources
which Shakespeare used, monumental iconography, civic pageants,
folk ceremonies, topical references in the playtexts, language, grammar and rhetoric were all studied with renewed enthusiasm in order
to discover what they contributed to the shaping of the plays, and
to explain them.

One further line of study may also be distinguished in the post-
war period – an attempt to consider the theatrical life of the plays,
as distinct from their literary values. As early as 1927, and continuing
until 1947, Harley Granville-Barker wrote a series of *Prefaces* to
individual plays which brought a new precision and range to the
study of Shakespeare as a dramatic artist. He was concerned, in the
first place, to discover how to stage the productions of the plays and
this concentrated his attention on style and structure as well as on
older issues of character and plot. His books were acclaimed widely,
but they were not used as models for study because no one else was
expert in so many tasks as Barker – he was director, actor, dramatist,
theatre manager and scholar – and few could argue with such clarity
and grasp of practical issues. Only slowly did performance studies
begin to be established as an approach to an understanding of the
plays, and then most were based more on accounts of performances
(or their stage histories) and a re-examination of stage directions
and references to performance in the texts of the plays, than on a
direct study of rehearsal, production and performance.

In the 1960s, however, as critics began to be more concerned with
theatrical practice and the art of acting – and all the uncertainties

and freedoms which these involved – new questions were being asked about the nature of literary texts and their relationships to authors, readers and audiences. From both these sides conventional approaches came under attack. The theatrical critic argued that the task was to 'become an explorer . . . never knowing for sure what is *in* Shakespeare's plays waiting to be realized'.[2] Critics, following both the linguist, Ferdinand de Saussure (1857–1913) and the philosopher, Ludwig Wittgenstein (1889–1951), said much the same about all verbal texts: we cannot easily know what happens when any particular words are written, still less when they are spoken and heard, as they are in drama. Linguists, philosophers and critics sustained a long debate about language and communication, examining what words do for author, reader and hearer, without their author's authority or permission. Jacques Derrida's *Writing and Difference* (Paris, 1967) was not published in an English translation until 1978, but its argument that texts are never accurate, limited or reducible to a single interpretation began very soon to infect criticism of literature, Shakespeare's works included. The free play that is inherent in language, once this has been recognized, means that a critic will be hard pressed to claim that it is possible to probe unerringly to a single 'true subject or imaginative centre'. Once attention has been paid to Derrida, all critical approaches have to be reassessed.

Of course everyone has known, from Shakespeare's day and before, that words are 'wanton' (*Twelfth Night*, iii.i.15) and that a hearer may 'mistake the truth totally' (*Tempest*, ii.i.54), but linguists have thrust these matters to the forefront and provided new means to consider them. There has been no sudden explosion forcing everyone still alive to run for cover, but from roundabout 1970 critics have changed pitch or stance carefully and new lines of study have been opened up. Sounds of battle can be heard in critical writing and anyone interested in Shakespeare's plays should reconsider how to study them.

NOTES

1. 'The "Capability" of Shakespeare', *Shakespeare Quarterly*, xi (1960), 123–36.
2. J. R. Brown, 'The Theatrical Element of Shakespeare Criticism', *Reinterpretations of Elizabethan Drama*, ed. Norman Rabkin (New York, 1969), p. 194.

3 CONTROVERSY

If human language is intrinsically unreliable, how is it possible to consider the meaning of a work as complicated as a Shakespeare play? Critics live with this uneasiness and are still intent on unravelling the text to reveal its central truth. Norman Rabkin's study of criticism of *The Merchant of Venice* heads the present selection of writings which are engaged in this task, more or less confident in the possibility of success. But like the others, this essay does not point to one detachable meaning. Indeed Professor Rabkin proposes a kind of study that accepts 'disagreement' about the meaning of a work of art as a most significant fact about its nature. He calls for a new approach 'to consider the play as a dynamic interaction between artist and audience, to learn to talk about the process of our involvement rather than our considered view after the aesthetic event'.

Maynard Mack's lecture on 'Rescuing Shakespeare' begins with a survey of the critical approaches of recent years that leads to a reconsideration of how historical perspectives can illuminate the texts. But he does not address Elizabethan statements of belief or definitions of right and wrong in politics or society. He suggests that students should consider how people lived, rather than what some single-minded people thought about specific issues. By considering family life, with the help of recent historical studies, and Shakespeare's reflection of that, a new sense of the tensions within the plays can be gained and details of the text awaken more lively images of lived experience. This is not to push the plays into a museum of the past, but to help them quicken our own responses to the purposes and limitations of family life, marriage, inheritance, and the role of women in society. While reshaping an historical approach, Professor Mack also demonstrates what Terry Eagleton has claimed:

The problems which Shakespeare confronts are in some ways very much the problems which concern us, and we cannot examine these problems as they are present in his plays except through the focus of our own experience, as we cannot fully understand our own experience except through an understanding of Shakespeare.

Shakespeare and Society (London, 1967), p. 99

The last part of that statement may seem very extreme – that Shakespeare is needed to teach us about ourselves – but some critics find their understanding so much enhanced by this study that it seems to them to be no exaggeration. In some way, Shakespeare's works have entered our common pursuit of the truth of things.

Jonathan Dollimore also brings the past into the reckoning, but following the diagnoses of Lawrence Stone's *The Causes of the English Revolution, 1529–1642* (London, 1972), he looks for signs of subversion in the text of *King Lear*. His critique is also informed by writings of Louis Althusser, Roland Barthes, Derrida and Michel Foucault, so that he seeks the affirmation which 'determines the noncentre otherwise than as loss of the centre' (Derrida, *Writing and Difference*, p. 292). Edmund and not King Lear, Lear's madness and not his apparent sanity or his piteous experience or the awakening of his pity, are those parts of the play that represent the energies of subversion, signs of the changes in society that were to break out in civil war. He sees the play as a 'critique of the entire contemporary structure of authority', not a study of a great hero; 'man is decentred not through misanthropy but in order to make visible social process and its forms of ideological misrecognition'.

Rosalie Colie's concern is with the study of form and Shakespeare's use of the dramatic genres current in the theatre of his time. And again the student is warned not to look only for conformity; Shakespeare's 'interest in the traditional aspects of his art' she argues 'lay precisely in their problematic nature, not in their stereotypical force'. Because genres encompass the shaping of whole plays, in studying them we reach out to meanings which are different from 'literary' ones, and involve 'moral and social situations larger than the containments of a single play or poem'.

E. A. J. Honigmann pays attention to 'impressions' rather than either design or statement. He shows that conflicting messages are sent out from the play regarding the image of life that it presents. He argues that we should not look for 'complete' statements about character and, taking the word from Shakespeare, he suggests that in the course of a play the tragic heroes are 'stretched' to reveal more about their natures 'in a swirl of conflicting impressions'.

The next essay, by the editor, is included to give practical guidance on what authority any text might have as representing what Shakespeare wrote; this is by no means a constant from play to play, or between one aspect of a text and another. Here also is some account of how to seek out the meanings of words which are no longer current in speech or writing, and how to begin to visualise and hear the play in performance from a study of the printed words.

Two essays follow which address the theatrical life of the plays. Alexander Leggatt considers how seeing performances can become a useful part of the critical study of a text, while Bernard Beckerman advises on how to study a text so that it reveals its dramatic energies. Both critics assume that the task of a student is to contact the play in a far more complex way than is appropriate for a poem or novel: Professor Beckerman writes of 'living into' a text, not in order to 'secure data or determine theme', but to 'sense vibrations in the text'; Professor Leggatt seeks the means of 'building a fully conceived life around the dialogue, giving the text an extra dimension'.

The last passage reprinted is the shortest and comes from a film director, not a student in ordinary senses of that word. It is included to suggest the extent to which a Shakespeare play can claim its readers: the imaginary begins to seem real; past personal experience rises again in the mind; a need to 'go back to school' coexists with a sense of totally new experience, like beginning 'to live all over again'.

Every new form of criticism is not included here. No search would be complete, and no space enough to accommodate all varieties; besides, the aim of this casebook is not to be all-inclusive. Those essays chosen for re-presentation mark the main roads that are being constructed into the terrain. They use earlier expertise as well as the novel, and they point towards consolidation as well as new discoveries. Nor do they include purely theoretical studies of criticism; those would at least double the size of the book and are of less immediate interest to the student who is concerned primarily with Shakespeare's plays. Some introductory books on critical theory are listed in the Select Bibliography at the end of the volume, together with semiotic and feminist studies which are also not represented among the essays except incidentally. For these other omissions some further apology is needed; limitations of space is one reason but the other main reason is that so far insufficient progress has been made to believe that these lines of work have reached their full measure of success. Throughout this casebook, the process of selection has been difficult; the chosen essays are ones that should lead readers into libraries on their own searches.

The whole book has one further limitation which should be mentioned: it is written only by English and American critics. No one whose first language is other than English has been represented and even the introductory surveys have been given the same focus. This is regrettable at a time when the value of bringing different expectations and sensibilities to the texts has become increasingly obvious. But the reasons for this exclusion are different from those for other omissions: first, the readership of this volume will be mainly English-speaking and to introduce other voices, even in translations, in sufficient range would entail complicated presentation; secondly, the range of response across the nations is so diverse and interesting that it merits fuller consideration than a sample or two in such a volume as this could offer.

PART TWO

Critical Approaches

Norman Rabkin   Meaning and *The*
Merchant of Venice   (1981)

Literary criticism, as even the popular press reports, is in crisis.
Only a generation ago the war between an academic establishment
committed to historical and philological studies and a guerrilla band
of New Critics waving the banner of exegesis seemed to have been
resolved by a permanent consensus, and until very recently, at least
in the United States, critical energies have been devoted with little
self-questioning to perfecting the technology of interpretation. Only
yesterday it was widely assumed that the critic's job was to expound
the meaning of literary works. Today, under an extraordinarily swift
and many-fronted attack, that consensus is in ruins. The reader-
response theories argued in various ways by such critics as Stanley
Fish and Norman Holland call into question the power of an
imaginative work to elicit a uniform response from its audience;
Jacques Derrida and his deconstructive allies see language and art
as so intractably self-reflexive as to be incapable of analyzable
significance; Harold Bloom argues that all reading is misreading,
that one reads well only to find oneself in the mirror.[1] For such
critics it is hopeless to talk about plays or poems as if they 'mean'
anything, a mistake to believe as not only the New Critics but the
establishment they replaced did that one could speak for a community that looked out on the same world.

   The crisis of confidence has belatedly reached Shakespeare criticism in an aggressive analysis by Richard Levin.[2] Levin attacks the
self-aggrandizing approaches to literary criticism taken by a variety
of writers who have learned that in order to get their articles and
books published they must possess the key that everyone else has
missed, the secret hidden from all previous critics and scholars. 'One
of the most striking features of current criticism of the drama of
the English Renaissance', he observes, 'has been its remarkable
proliferation of reinterpretations or 'new readings' which, if they
were accepted, would radically alter our traditional views of a great
many of these plays – views held, so far as we can tell, by virtually
all spectators and readers down to the present time' (p. ix). A
'reading,' he argues, has a number of characteristics: it is *'an
interpretation of a single literary work,' 'a complete interpretation of the*

meaning of the work,' 'an interpretation of the real as distinguished from the apparent meaning of the work,' 'a justification of the work,' 'a justification of a thesis about the work'; it is *'close,' 'new,'* and *'a tour de force'* (pp. 2–5). The readings Levin attacks 'come from the mainstream of academic criticism of English Renaissance drama' (p. 10). They fall into three main groups: thematic ('thematists very frequently disagree on what central theme any given play is about, yet never question the assumption that it must be about a central theme') (pp. 7–8), ironic (a play means something other than what it seems to mean), and historical (whether an attempt to find King James in *Measure for Measure* or to explain the play by exploring its Zeitgeist or by examining contemporary marriage laws and customs). There are shrewd exposés of some familiar critical gambits: treating deficiencies or flaws of plays as intentional or at least significant virtues (one recalls Fredson Bowers' embarrassing jeer at Delmore Schwartz's critical arabesque on the virtues of 'soldier Aristotle', which he didn't recognize as a typo for 'solider Aristotle', in 'Among School Children'); engaging in 'Fluellenism', a method by which one can see the identity shared by any two or more items, and one used by its nominal inventor to prove the similarity between Henry V and Alexander the Great by demonstrating that both Monmouth and Macedon had rivers, and the rivers had salmon in them; claiming as ironic every apparently straightforward moral statement or apparently decent character; recognizing 'Christ figures' in every shadow; seeing every play as about the writing of plays.

Much of the book is a chamber of horrors – aisles of readings each proclaiming its unique virtue ('my theme can lick your theme', as Levin puts it); juxtaposed assertions that plays are tracts, arguments, debates, proofs, analyses, statements, commentaries, critiques, meditations, demonstrations, etc.; knee-jerk refusals to take anything, especially the ending of a play, to mean what it says; preposterous claims for implausible interpretations based on shaky historical 'proofs'. Bad criticism is a scandal that all of us know and frequently lament. Levin has done a service by bringing it out of the closet, and his debunking, like much of the criticism to which I alluded at the outset, deserves attention.

But bad criticism is not the real problem. Consider a few of the names Levin lists, in bland alphabetical sequence, along with others more obviously deserving of the same contemptuous treatment: Peter Alexander, Don Cameron Allen, W. H. Auden, Jonas Barish,

Josephine Waters Bennett, Muriel Bradbrook, Cleanth Brooks, John
Russell Brown, Jackson Cope, John Danby, Madelaine Doran,
Francis Fergusson, Northrop Frye, Harold C. Goddard, G. B.
Harrison, R. B. Heilman, G. K. Hunter, Gabriele Bernhard Jackson,
R. J. Kaufmann, Frank Kermode, Alvin Kernan, G. Wilson Knight,
L. C. Knights, Robert Knoll, Clifford Leech, J. W. Lever, Harry
Levin, Barbara K. Lewalski, Laurence Michel, Winifred Nowottny,
Eleanor Prosser, A. P. Rossiter, D. A. Traversi, Virgil K. Whitaker,
Glynne Wickham, J. Dover Wilson. All of these critics are demonstrated to be guilty of the excessive claims that Levin finds in his
worst examples. No single reader would bestow equal praise on all
the critics named above, but few readers would fail to find among
them some they most admire. And that is the problem I want to
address. Not why there is so much bad criticism: there has always
been a lot of it, and the institutional rules of the academic game
insure its proliferation. Much more importantly: why is much of the
best criticism vulnerable to attacks like Levin's, so that the kinds of
theoretical rejection of critical study I mentioned at the outset have
been able to find so ready an audience? Unlike Fish and Holland, I
shall not conclude that the nature of literature and of individual
response to it rules out descriptions of literary works that come
close to being definitive; unlike Levin, I do not want to replace
interpretation with banal suggestions that instead of looking for
'readings' critics should accept a play as a 'literal representation of
particular human actions' (p. 202) or that they need only engage
in more dialogue with one another. I am going to insist that literary
works mean, and that there are ways in which we can talk about
their meanings. But in order to do so I must try to show what in
our best criticism has made it so easy to attack.

1

My test case is *The Merchant of Venice*. I have chosen it, first of all,
because it is an acknowledged success which has retained its
popularity on and off the stage. Second, it has been a centre of as
much controversy as any of Shakespeare's plays has aroused, and
the controversy has led good critics to real and crucial problems.
Third, though as I shall indicate there are still those who argue
what I take to be idiosyncratic interpretations, in recent years many

of the critics have reached a consensus on the play and in so doing have produced invaluable insights. And finally, for all of its virtues much of the best criticism leaves us with the sense that it has somehow failed to come to grips with or has even in some way denied the existence of essential qualities of the play.

The power of *The Merchant of Venice* has moved actors and audiences, critics and readers to interpretations opposed so diametrically that they seem to have been provoked by different plays. Most disagreements have centred on character. On stage Shylock has run a course between Macklin's savage monster and Irving's martyred gentleman; critical descriptions of Shylock range from a 'malevolence . . . diabolically inhuman'[3] whom Shakespeare 'clearly detested' to a 'scapegoat', an instinctively generous man who reminds his tormentors of the wickedness which they possess in greater measure than he.[4] Inevitably Portia has aroused responses similarly at odds, seeming to many the epitome of the romantic heroine, to some virtually a saint, and to others no more than a 'callous barrister' with a trump card up her sleeve; Jessica is an ideal portrait of the Christian convert and a 'dishonest and disloyal father-hating minx', Antonio a model of Christian gentleness and an underground Shylock, Bassanio a romanticized lover and a heartless money-grubber. Similarly Portia's use of the law to defeat Shylock has been seen by some as a brilliant and just device, by others as a malicious and unnecessary piece of conniving.[5]

A typical contention flourishes about the scene in which Shylock, provoked to swear vengeance by his daughter's defection and her plundering of his household, learns from Tubal that one of Antonio's ships is lost. To suggest the complexity of our responses to Shylock at this point I need only remind the reader that he justifies his savage commitment to revenge by claiming it as the mechanical and therefore normal human response to injury, and that the claim, thus reflecting an impoverished sensibility, is the climax of his moving appeal to universal brotherhood: 'I am a Jew. Hath not a Jew eyes? . . .' From moment to moment, even simultaneously, we respond to signals of Shylock's injured fatherhood, of his role as heavy father, of his lighthearted mistreatment at the hands of the negligible Salerio and Solanio, of his motiveless malignity, and we try hopelessly to reduce to a single attitude our response to his self-defining scorn for Antonio, whose combination of generosity, passivity, sensibility, and spitting hatred has itself already led us to mixed feelings.

SHY. I thank God, I thank God. Is it true, is it true?

TUB. I spoke with some of the sailors that escaped the wrack.

SHY. I thank thee, good Tubal; good news, good news! – Ha, ha! – heard in Genoa?

TUB. Your daughter spent in Genoa, as I heard, one night, fourscore ducats.

SHY. Thou stick'st a dagger in me – I shall never see my gold again. Fourscore ducats at a sitting! Fourscore ducats!

TUB. There came divers of Antonio's creditors in my company to Venice that swear he cannot choose but break.

SHY. I am very glad of it; I'll plague him, I'll torture him; I am glad of it.

TUB. One of them showed me a ring that he had of your daughter for a monkey.

SHY. Out upon her! Thou torturest me, Tubal. It was my turquoise; I had it of Leah when I was a bachelor; I would not have given it for a wilderness of monkeys.

(III.i.90–106)

More clearly evocative of laughter at Shylock's obsessions and speech mannerism than other parts of the scene, these lines nevertheless engage us in a kaleidoscopic shift of emotion and touch us at the end. At this point in Shakespeare's career his ability to create characters with authentic voices and to effect mercurial changes in his audience's emotions leaped beyond what he had been able to do earlier, and he seems to have become interested in shifting sequences of this kind. For in the exactly contemporary *1 Henry IV* the same thing happens repeatedly, most memorably perhaps when Falstaff's comic defence of himself as he plays Prince Hal in the 'play extempore' moves through a climatic series of imperatives – 'banish Peto, banish Bardolph, banish Poins' – and an outrageous series of epithets – 'sweet Jack Falstaff, kind Jack Falstaff, true Jack Falstaff, valiant Jack Falstaff' – to a suddenly no longer funny repetition of the fact of his age with which he began his speech – 'old Jack Falstaff' – and to the heartbreakingly repeated 'banish not him thy Harry's company, banish not him thy Harry's company' and the climax, 'banish plump Jack, and banish all the world', culminating both the imperative and the comic epithet, and followed by Hal's response, mysteriously appropriate from both the player and the role he plays as Henry IV, 'I do, I will' (II.iv.450–63). No one, I believe, misses the emotional complexity of that moment. But at the corresponding moment in *The Merchant of Venice* critic after critic, rather than acknowledging the welter of our responses, insists that this scene reveals a clear and simple truth about Shylock's martyred humanity or his comic villainy.[6]

Such radical disagreements between obviously simplistic critics testify to a fact about their subject that ought to be the point of departure for criticism. Instead, critics both bad and good have constructed strategies to evade the problem posed by divergent responses. Some blame Shakespeare, suggesting that his confusion accounts for tension in the work and its audience. Others appeal to a narrow concept of cultural history which writes off our responses as anachronistic, unavailable to Shakespeare's contemporaries because of their attitude toward usury or Jews or comedy. Still others suggest that, since the plays are fragile confections designed to display engaging if implausible characters, exegetical criticism is misplaced. Though all of these strategies attract modern practitioners, they have lost ground before the dominant evasion, the reduction of the play to a theme which, when we understand it, tells us which of our responses we must suppress. The ingenious thematic critic, so adroitly delineated by Richard Levin, is licensed to stipulate that 'in terms of the structure of the play Shylock is a minor character' and can be ignored,[7] or that the action is only metaphorical and does not need to be examined as if its events literally happened,[8] or that Shylock is only a Jew, or a banker, or a usurer, or a man spiritually dead, or a commentary on London life, never a combination of these;[9] or that *The Merchant of Venice* is built on 'four levels of existence' corresponding to Dante's divisions – 'Hell (Shylock), Purgatory proper (Antonio) and the Garden of Eden (Portia-Bassanio), and Paradise';[10] or that the play is exclusively about love, or whatever, and, insofar as it doesn't fit the critic's formulation, it is flawed.[11]

2

My chief concern here, as I said above, is not with such dismal stuff but rather with a less obviously procrustean kind of criticism which, accepting the play as a whole, attempts to account for its unity without expelling characters or issues or plot. The new consensus is laconically summarized by Frank Kermode:

The Merchant of Venice is 'about' judgment, redemption and mercy; the supersession in human history of the grim four thousand years of unalleviated justice by the era of love and mercy. It begins with usury and corrupt love;

it ends with harmony and perfect love. And all the time it tells its audience that this is its subject; only by a determined effort to avoid the obvious can one mistake the theme of *The Merchant of Venice*.[12]

In this view, developed by John Russell Brown, C. L. Barber, John Palmer, Lawrence Danson, and others,[13] the wealth so mechanistically prized by Shylock is set against what Brown calls 'love's wealth,' possessiveness against prodigality, giving against taking. For Barber, 'the whole play dramatizes the conflict between the mechanisms of wealth and the masterful, social use of it'. Problems that stumped other critics have been resolved. The bond plot is related to the casket plot, for example, by the positing of a central theme. In Brown's words:

Shall we say it is a play about give and take? – about conundrums such as the more you give, the more you get, or, to him that hath shall be given, and from him that hath not, shall be taken away even that which he hath? The two parts of the play are linked by these problems: Portia is the golden fleece, the merchants venture and hazard as any lover; the caskets deal all in value, the bond and the rings are pledges of possession.[14]

One of the most comprehensive accounts to date is John R. Cooper's 'Shylock's Humanity', which argues that at the play's core is a theological distinction between the values of Christianity and those of a Pauline version of Old Testament Judaism.[15] This view, essentially shared by the group of critics I have been discussing, and carried to an extreme by the man who sees the play as a Shakespearean *Commedia*, sets the law, a rational principle according to which men should get exactly what they deserve, against Christian mercy, which gives freely to those who hazard all they possess. Cooper notes that not all the Christians in the play act like ideal Christians – a fact on which a number of schematic interpretations founder – and argues that

the fundamental opposition in the play is not between Jew and Christian but between two sets of values. On the one hand, there is the uncalculating generosity and forgiveness, the sense of one's own unworthiness and the infinite value of others, the attitude referred to by Portia as 'mercy'. On the other hand, there is the hard-headed attitude of those who have a high estimation of their own value and rights, and who demand just payment for themselves, whether in the form of money, or revenge, or a wife. (p. 123)

In this account as in others the opposition in the play is seen as symbolized by the inscriptions on the caskets: Morocco trusts appearances and puts his faith in gold as Shylock does; Arragon demands what he deserves, insisting like Shylock on a rational justice; both are beaten by Bassanio, who gives and hazards all. The opposition is seen by some as figured in the symbolic connotations of the metals of which the caskets are made, and by most as embodied geographically in Belmont, home of music and love, and the commercial Venice.

If I suggest that these critics are wrong, I shall have gravely misstated my argument. What they describe is there, and reflecting on our experience of the play we recognize the patterns identified. Their analysis integrates the techniques developed in the last half-century for literary study and, perhaps more important, arises from unmistakably personal experiences of the play. Thus they hear verbal nuances and know how to talk about them; they know the significance of motifs and echoes, of dramaturgic and metrical effect, of structure and symbol, character and genre. Yet even their own writing conveys a sense of uneasy tentativeness that speaks of more than simple modesty or rhetorical disclaimer. In the first passage I cited, for example, Kermode puts eloquent quotation marks around the word 'about' when he tells us what the play is 'about'. Palmer, less insistent than some critics that the theme really dominates the play, seems dubious even about as much theme as he asserts: 'Nothing is further from Shakespeare's mind than to convey a lesson. But the lesson is there, product of a perfectly balanced and sensitive mind intent upon the dramatic presentation of human realities'.[16] I quoted before Barber's capsule summary of the theme: 'The whole play dramatizes the conflict between the mechanism of wealth and the masterful, social use of it'. But listen to the reservations implied by the sentence that follows: 'The happy ending, which abstractly considered as an event is hard to credit, and the treatment of Shylock, which abstractly considered as justice is hard to justify, work as we actually watch or read the play because these events express relief and triumph in the achievement of a distinction'. And later, after his demonstration of the total efficiency with which the play communicates its complex set of interrelated judgments on character, wealth, and love so that the audience is clearly instructed by the end: 'I must add, after all this praise for the way the play makes its distinctions about the use of wealth, that *on reflection*, not when viewing or reading the play, but when thinking about it, I find the distinction, as others have, somewhat too easy'.[17] And he goes on, with characteristic sensitivity, to demonstrate how much of the play – Portia's facile generosity, Shylock's comeuppance, Antonio's fudging of the usury argument, Shylock's large place in our consciousness – fails to fit even so subtle a schematization as he had made. Brown, you will recall, presents his summary as a question: 'Shall we say it is a play about . . .?' and I suggest that his rhetorical choice reflects a tacit acknowledgment that in some sense the formulation is narrower than the play. Look at the sentences immediately preceding his question: 'So *The Merchant of Venice* dances to its conclusion, its many elements mingling together joyfully. Perhaps when the dance is in progress, it is undesirable to look too closely for a pattern. But the dance does satisfy, and it is worth while trying to find out why'. Or, in a passage from another essay on the play: 'Because such judgments are not made explicit in the play, we, as an audience in the theatre, may never become consciously aware of them; we would almost certainly fail in our response if, during performance, our whole attention was given to recognizing and elucidating such judgments'.[18]

Why, if as I have claimed the criticism of these men adds up to a synthesis that comes closer than anything before it to explaining the play, is their presentation so hedged? I suggest that they recognize that they have not in fact explained the very things that provoked them to the elucidation of meaning in the first place, the questions that the play like any good play raises in order to drive us to search for answers that are not forthcoming. Each critic in his own way suggests some conflict between the thematic pattern he identifies on reflection and his actual experience of the play. Barber, whose major contribution in *Shakespeare's Festive Comedy* consists, after all, in far more original, useful, and exhilarating modes of criticism than the thematic formulation I have excerpted here, addresses the problem himself:

No figure in the carpet is the carpet. There is in the pointing out of patterns something that is opposed to life and art, an ungraciousness which artists in particular feel and resent. Readers feel it too, even critics: for every new moment, every new line or touch, is a triumph of opportunism, something snatched in from life beyond expectation and made design beyond design. And yet the fact remains that it is as we see the design that we see design undone and brought alive.

(p. 4)

If on reflection, through the contemplation of thematic patterns, we manage to be satisfied by an understanding that seems to resolve the constant inner conflict which the process of *The Merchant of Venice* sets going in us, we do so by treating as accidental rather than substantive the doubts with which we are left by the end.

Consider some of the problems that remain unresolved in the versions of the comedy we have been discussing. Present in only five scenes, Shylock speaks fewer than four hundred lines yet dominates the play, haunting our memories during the suddenly etherealized and equally suddenly trivialized final episodes as we try to reach a simple position on the fairness of his treatment, or even on the truth of his response to it, funny, deflated, proud, inscrutable: 'I pray you give me leave to go from hence,/I am not well' (iv.i.390–91). The play, we are told, is about the opposition of mercy to legalism. Cooper, subtle enough to realize that the distinction must not be made by separating out Christian lambs and Jewish goats, must nonetheless belie our own experience of the play, as he admits, in order to judge the disposition of the villain: 'Though his forced conversion to Christianity seems to us to be cruel and insulting, we are meant, I think and as many critics have said, to see this as the altogether kindly conversion of Shylock to the new rule of mercy and thus his liberation from the dilemma of the old Law' (p. 121). Note how that 'we are meant', derived not from Cooper's response to something he sees as 'cruel and insulting' but from a thesis about what the play means, denies to Shakespeare's intention or the play's virtue what the comedy actually *does* to us. Abstractly considered, Shylock's enforced conversion might be judged benevolent, in that it is imposed upon him in order to assure his salvation. Not only is that salvation not mentioned, however, but the conversion is dictated as part of a settlement that is otherwise entirely fiscal, without any suggestion of kindness:

> So please my lord the Duke and all the court
> To quit the fine for one half of his goods;
> I am content, so he will let me have
> The other half in use, to render it
> Upon his death unto the gentleman
> That lately stole his daughter –
> Two things provided more: that, for this favour
> He presently become a Christian;
> The other, that he do record a gift,
> Here in the court, of all he dies possess'd

>   Unto his son Lorenzo and his daughter.
>   (IV.i.375–85)

If Antonio's plea for the mitigation of Shylock's sentence is a step back from the cruelty of the Duke's original plan, it nevertheless insists twice that all of the Jew's property must eventually fall into the hands of 'the gentleman/That lately stole his daughter'; and one doubts whether any actress could make Portia's demand that Shylock not only accept the judgement but profess satisfaction with it – 'Art thou contented, Jew? What dost thou say?' – sound 'altogether kindly'. The issue is not how Elizabethans felt about the relative advantages of dying in or outside the church, but how Shakespeare forces his audience to respond to this particular conversion in its context.

For Barber our response to Shylock is a problem, but, like some critics whose work his supplants, he suggests that in that respect the play failed because Shakespeare cared more about his villain than his purpose could afford. But Cooper has the superior technology, and his conclusion is cleaner: we must deny that we even care about Shylock's harsh dismissal and his forced conversion so that we may feel, in Brown's phrase, all the elements of the play 'mingling together joyfully'. How much more considerate both of art and of our response to it is Stanley Cavell's observation in an essay entitled 'A Matter of Meaning It':

> The artist is responsible for everything that happens in his work – and not just in the sense that it is done, but in the sense that it is *meant*. It is a terrible responsibility; very few men have the gift and the patience to shoulder it. But it is all the more terrible, when it *is* shouldered, not to appreciate it, to refuse to understand something meant so well.[19]

3

>   In Belmont is a lady richly left,
>   And she is fair and, fairer than that word,
>   Of wondrous virtues. Sometimes from her eyes
>   I did receive fair speechless messages.
>   Her name is Portia – nothing undervalu'd
>   To Cato's daughter, Brutus' Portia.
>   Nor is the wide world ignorant of her worth;
>   For the four winds blow in from every coast
>   Renowned suitors, and her sunny locks
>   Hang on her temples like a golden fleece,

Which makes her seat of Belmont Colchos' strond,
And many Jasons come in quest of her.
O my Antonio, had I but the means
To hold a rival place with one of them,
I have a mind presages me such thrift
That I should questionless be fortunate!

                                        (i.i.161–76)

If Quiller-Couch and, alas, too many modern directors can dismiss
Bassanio as a mere fortune hunter, we have been instructed to a
more complex judgment: though he is indeed interested in Portia's
money, Bassanio does not, as Shylock does, let money take the place
of values that matter more, and so as a social Christian he is allowed
to have it. Shylock loves only gold, material substance, we are told,
while Bassanio loves Portia as well as gold; after all, he compares
her with Brutus's Portia. Yet Bassanio's way of comparing his Portia
to Brutus's is to say that the one is 'nothing undervalu'd' to the
other; he praises her first for being rich and then for being fair; it is
the ambiguous quality of 'worth' that draws the world to her; his
game is thrift and his hope is to be fortunate; and he sees himself as
Jason stealing the golden fleece – a legend later reduced to its
crassest implications by Gratiano (iii.ii.241–3). And of course
Morocco's crazy apostrophe to the gold casket (ii.vii.36–60) will
reveal exactly the same confusion of values as Bassanio's speech,
echoing its images and language and even its word 'undervalued'
(l. 53) – and only moments before we hear of Shylock's similar
confusion between his daughter and his ducats. How is Morocco
really guilty when Bassanio is not? Portia's true gold may be
spiritual, but Bassanio gets himself out of trouble with his creditors
by her material wealth. Furthermore, if we are to believe that his
superiority consists in his ability to tell reality from appearance, we
are not allowed to forget that Portia of the beautiful soul is also a
beautiful woman, a romantic as well as a commercial prize. She
herself is delighted to be rid of Morocco because of his looks: 'Let
all of his complexion choose me so', she says as he leaves, and
insofar as the word points to temper as it does to appearance, inner
as well as outer, it suggests a correspondence between looks and
character that the casket plot seems to be denying.

   The thematic values identified by those who see the play as a
conflict between the Hebrew and Christian dispensations point to
rejection of the wealth returned in abundance to the Christian

company and to a demonstration of the virtue of impoverished love. That the comic resolution demands worldly success as well, a return of more than has in fact been hazarded, suggests a conflict between Christianity and comedy as deep as the one generally seen between it and tragedy.[20] If, as Brown says, the comic point is that those already rich spiritually are materially enriched by the happy outcome, my point is that constant signals in the play imply that it isn't all so simple and that they keep us from the single-minded joy Brown sees as our final state. Everything Brown says is there, and yet by the end we are not so sure that it resolves the tensions the play has aroused in us.

One might discuss at length other elements in the play that cause uneasiness in an audience and difficulties for a critic who wants to make a schematic analysis – the pointed contrast between a Belmont and a Venice not really so different from one another; the peculiar characterization of the melancholy Antonio, the link between his sadness and Portia's in their opening lines, and the fact that the play is named after him; the ring plot which, though it enables Portia to teach once again her lesson about bonds and love, reminds us of her trickery and her tendency to domineer, so inconsistent with the moving spontaneity of her emotions both as Bassanio chooses the lead casket and as she speaks of mercy. But I shall cite, and briefly, only two matters.

First, the characterization of Lorenzo and Jessica has been disputed often enough to suggest that their ambivalence is built into the play. The judgements of their best critics reflect difficulty with them. Harold C. Goddard sees their villainy as necessary to prod Shylock to revenge. Sigurd Burckhardt condemns them as an inversion of the true bonded love of the play's theme, lawless and mean-spirited, 'spendthrift rather than liberal, thoughtless squanderers of stolen substance', trading for a monkey 'the ring which ought to seal their love'.[21] Yet Brown sees them as exemplars of 'the central theme of love's wealth'. He too sees them as squanderers, but in 'joyful celebration'; he praises their '*unthrift* love' and argues that if Jessica's 'reckless prodigality is a fault, it is a generous one and an understandable excess after the restriction of her father's precept'.[22] Plainly Lorenzo and Jessica subvert any schematic reading of the play. If, for example, some signals suggest that the conversion forced on Shylock is an act of kindness, Lorenzo makes us resist that interpretation of Christian treatment of the Jew:

> she hath directed
> How I shall take her from her father's house;
> What gold and jewels she is furnish'd with;
> What page's suit she hath in readiness.
> If e'er the Jew her father come to heaven,
> It will be for his gentle daughter's sake;
> And never dare misfortune cross her foot,
> Unless she do it under this excuse,
> That she is issue to a faithless Jew.
>
> (II.iv.29–37)

If, as Burckhardt thinks, Lorenzo and Jessica help silhouette Portia's genuine value, their presence in Belmont and their common cause with her against Shylock complicate the play for interpretation, as does the strange excursus on music that Lorenzo delivers in the last act.

And that takes me to my second matter, the beads of language, imagery, and ideas threaded on the string of music. It is a commonplace that that music – the music of the heavenly choirs, the music that Portia has sounded as Bassanio makes his choice – accompanies the life of grace, sensibility, love, and play, the life won by those who triumph in the play, while Shylock hates 'the vile squealing of the wry-neck'd fife' (II.v.29ff.) and mocks those who 'cannot contain their urine' 'when the bagpipe sings i' th' nose' (IV.1.49–50). As Lorenzo puts it, the play seems to say:

> The man that hath no music in himself,
> Nor is not mov'd with concord of sweet sounds,
> Is fit for treasons, stratagems, and spoils;
>
> .   .   .   .   .   .
> Let no such man be trusted.
>
> (v.i.83–8)

But Lorenzo is a poor witness, since 'treasons, stratagems, and spoils' characterizes his exploits at least as accurately as it does those of Shylock, who has other personality problems. Furthermore, Lorenzo's dialogue with Jessica is sandwiched between the episodes of Portia's stratagem against Bassanio, the ring plot, and helps both to undercut the enormous emotional claim she has made on the audience in the trial scene and to call attention to the triviality at best of the game she plays with the ring. We might note also that the chief other entry of music into the play is the song that Portia has sung during Bassanio's ordeal with the caskets, and interestingly that song has occasioned a still unsettled debate as to whether it is simply a pretext to suggest 'lead' through rhymes with 'bred', 'head', and the like.

4

Once again, my point is not that critics who are demonstrably right about so much are to be dismissed, lightly or otherwise. But one may justifiably ask how so much brain power in the most sensitive and highly trained critical audiences has produced so little that can't be punctured simply by watching one's own responses to details of a play. One may ask furthermore why critical readings of similar methodology and equal brilliance by critics of different temperaments so often add up to radically opposed interpretations. My guess is that our troubles stem in good part from the value we have put on reductiveness. We have been betrayed by a bias toward what can be set out in rational argument. Before the full impact of the new romantic understanding of art hit the professional study of literature, that bias reflected itself in the decision of literary scholars to concentrate on matters now seen as less than central to the understanding of the work itself. But, under the delayed influence of Coleridge and his contemporaries in England and Germany, literary study began to realize how far it was from dealing with the experience of art and began to come closer to it by focusing on the interpretation of texts. To be responsible, however, the newer study had to produce conclusions which were derived as logically and argued as closely as demonstrations of source and influence had been. Attracted by the spectacular possibilities of a new technology – W. Empson of course wanted to irritate with his arbitrary precision [in *Seven Types of Ambiguity*, 1930], but was nonetheless pleased to be able to number the types of ambiguity – critics fell into an invisible trap, the fallacy of misplaced concreteness: what can be brought by self-contained argument to a satisfying conclusion is what is worth discussing, and responses that don't work into the argument must be discounted. Given a romantic inheritance, given a genuine sense of the integrity of a single poem or play or novel, given a puritanical bias which assumes that the value of literature is moral and familiarly expresses itself in the notion of the professor of literature as lay preacher, given a long history of assumption that art is valuable at least half because of what it teaches, and given an art which is verbal, so that virtually all the patterns, parallels, structural juxtapositions, image clusters, ironic repetitions, variations, and generic conventions a critic can find can be translated into other words, was it not inevitable that the bias toward a criticism that would produce discrete and rational arguments should culminate in the study of meaning?

There is nothing surprising about our bias towards rationality. It is perfectly consistent with our hopes for civilization, with our needs, both inner- and outer-directed, to write prose that is logical, coherent, defensible, documentable. And the critical paradigm that establishes meaning as the principle of unity in a work and our experience of it is consistent with patterns that *do* exist in the plays – otherwise I could not have distinguished among the kinds of criticisms I have discussed – and that need to be explicated. But it is time to recall that all intellection is reductive, and that the closer an intellectual system comes to full internal consistency and universality of application – as with Newtonian mechanics – the more obvious become the exclusiveness of its preoccupations and the limitations of its value. What our successful criticism of meaning has made clear – and I include not only naive reduction but also that much more sophisticated criticism which argued so cogently against the heresy of paraphrase while still being concerned with summary thematic statements[23] – is its consistent suppression of the nature of aesthetic experience.

Should it not have disturbed critics interested in hypostatizing meaning that no two critics of any play really agree with one another in their formulations, that no two performances reflect identical interpretations or produce uniform responses in their audiences, that all of us return to plays we know intimately to discover that we respond to them in entirely new ways? Is not the disagreement about works of art as significant a fact for the critic as the interpretation he favours? Might a fruitful criticism not begin and end there as validly as it does with reduction to thematic descriptions of unity?

Confidence in our methodology has enabled us over the years to sidestep the implications of what we know about the creative act. No reputable critic would attempt to validate his analysis by claiming that the meaning he extracts was in the author's conscious and explicit intention, and even poets now accept the thesis that what the critic reveals in their work, no matter how unfamiliar to them, may have been a dominant factor in preconscious activity during composition. Even E. D. Hirsch, the literary theorist who states most insistently that meaning is entirely a product of authorial control – a position with which, as will shortly become clear, I do not myself disagree – readily grants that 'it is very possible to mean what one is not conscious of meaning'.[24] Now if we validly appeal to pre- or subconscious layers of the artist's experience, we ought to be ready to do the same for the audience, whose experience of a theme may be just as remote from consciousness. And if we do so wholeheartedly, we are likely to find little reason why an abstract idea should have been the central factor either in creation or in audience experience, particularly when that idea must inevitably be stated as a 'meaning' on which no two experiences of the work can agree.

'One thematist's gestalt is not another's,' Richard Levin justly observes (p. 29), and he shrewdly demonstrates how critics attempting to make more inclusive and definitive thematic statements than their predecessors remain trapped in hermeneutic solipsism. . . . Acknowledging that even 'good' critics do the same thing as 'bad' ones, admitting that he cannot find any model to replace the pernicious critical mode he attacks, Levin nevertheless fails to recognize the dimensions of the problem he is dealing with. And, directing his scrutiny exclusively to the performance of critics, he fails equally to recognize the ultimate cause of our critical sins: the experience of literature. A play we care about provokes us to form a gestalt, and the powerful experience of doing so may tempt us to formulate it thematically. Our formulations differ widely enough to enable Levin's mockery, and they are inadequate enough to serve very poorly, as I have tried to show, what is communicated by the plays they describe. Nevertheless, even at their worst they speak for the conflicts, tensions, implications, and significant fields of force that contribute to our sense that a play is an autonomous, coherent, and meaningful whole. To repudiate that sense because critics have too often translated it into excessively narrow thematic formulations, as Levin does, or to argue that it is too subjective to allow for descriptions of the common experience of an audience, as Norman Holland does,[25] is to deny the possibility of authorial communication or communal aesthetic experience, to deny that at a certain level of experience a work of art controls the responses of audiences who

share its culture, even though each member of the audience
may interpret those responses differently. The eddying signals
communicated by a play arouse a total and complex involvement of
our intellect, our moral sensibility, our need to complete incomplete
patterns and answer questions, our longing to judge, and that
involvement is so incessantly in motion that to pin it down to a
'meaning' is to negate its very essence.

The essence of our experience is our haunting sense of what
doesn't fit the thesis we are tempted at every moment to derive. If
one hallmark of an authentic work of art and a central source of its
power is its ability to drive us to search out its central mystery,
another way may be its ultimate irreducibility to a schema. Both of
these qualities are present in Shakespeare's plays. They are there
because Shakespeare put them there. If we are going to call the
distillation of our experience of one of the plays its meaning, we
must acknowledge that it includes both the paradigm to which the
controlling patterns of the play tempt us to reduce our experience
and elements of that experience which resist or weaken or complicate
or contradict the paradigm. It is this whole, 'meant so well', to
which Stanley Cavell points when he claims that 'the artist is
responsible for everything that happens in his work – and not just
in the sense that it is done, but in the sense that it is *meant*'. Both
the evidence of the critical consensus and the evidence of rational
disagreement in the interpretation of a play like *The Merchant of
Venice* lead us back to a particularly powerful authorial control all
too susceptible of simplistic hypostatization. It is the critic's job,
considering the evidence of others' responses as well as his own, to
comprehend as much as possible of what is contained in the intention
of a work. 'All valid interpretation of every sort,' as E. D. Hirsch
puts it, 'is founded on the re-cognition of what an author meant.'[26]

Like many insights that have attained widespread acceptance,
Keats's definition of 'negative capability' has been allowed to lose
its cutting edge.[27] If Keats speaks as rightly as I think he does for
artists and for us as their audiences, then the critic must learn to
defer his 'irritable reaching after fact and reason' and learn to think
of 'uncertainties, mysteries, doubts' as the stuff of our experience of
art. To put it another way, he must treat experience as the subject
of discussions of art. That is the point of John Dewey's profound
and too little heeded *Art as Experience* [1934], which sees the creation
of art and the response to it as quintessentially like life, characterized

by process, tension, resistance, and an ineffable sense of integrity. Keats's insight is implicit in the criticism of Kenneth Burke, who has insisted on asking what the poem does for the poet and his readers rather than what it says, who sees a play by Shakespeare as 'a device for the arousing and fulfilling of expectations in an audience', and who has defined 'the symbolic act' as *'the dancing of an attitude'*.[28] For Dewey and Burke the job of the critic is to analyze in the work a set of highly complex interrelations among its elements which the audience, experiencing those elements as they are presented, perceives as a unity. And for Dewey and Burke form and content are inseparable because the experience of the work is one – hence 'the dancing of an attitude.'.

That phrase, strikingly similar to Brown's reading of *The Merchant of Venice* as a dance, tempts one to wonder how much of Burke's power derives from his having first been a music critic. René Wellek, developing a theory of literature, could, despite all his better intentions, validate the search for meaning by calling the work of art 'a system of norms of ideal *concepts* which are intersubjective'.[29] But the music critic cannot look for a conceptual content at the centre of a work's intention and power. The attraction of the word 'theme' for literary critics may be its musical implications, but its prime meaning as they use it is its older lexical meaning, the text of a sermon or the subject of a discourse. For the musicologist a theme is generally one among several, and it is never to be confused with meaning. If he wants to discuss meaning, the music critic has no choice but to study in minute particularity the ways in which at each point a composition arouses and fulfills, or fails to fulfill, an audience's expectations. A new criticism of Shakespeare might well begin with the music analysis of Leonard B. Meyer. Morally concerned with music as an art that communicates, Meyer has derived from gestalt theory instruments for the analysis of the artwork's complex and significant control of its audience's responses. Interestingly, he is concerned with devices very much like those that have attracted literary critics of recent generations: the use of one phrase to make us think of another, recurrence, variation, parallelism, the apparent emergence of pattern out of linked details. But he is not interested in the kind of reduction that such discovery generally elicits from literary critics.[30]

The good Shakespeare critic must point out the patterns of the dance. He must find terms in which the oppositions and conflicts and problems within a play can be stated while recognizing the reductiveness of those terms. He must fight the temptation to proclaim what it boils down to; he must fight against the urge to closure which, as a gifted audience, he feels with particular intensity. He must learn to point to the centres of energy and turbulence in a play without regarding them as coded elements of a thematic formula. And while rejecting narrow conclusions drawn by other critics, he must be able to learn from the perceptions that have led to those conclusions.

One need only describe such a hypothetical paragon to recognize that such critics already exist. Two of those to whose thematic statements I have objected, C. L. Barber and John Russell Brown, more characteristically employ enormously suggestive and nonreductionist methodologies; the latter has himself argued repeatedly for a theatrical recreation of Shakespeare that will not try to pin the plays down to interpretations that constrict the range of meanings in them. Other exemplars come readily to mind. Maynard Mack's already classic essay on 'The Jacobean Shakespeare' treats patterns with the imagination and respect generally accorded only to meanings (as if most critics were driven by their irritable reaching after fact and reason always to shout, like Amy Lowell, 'Christ, what are patterns for?'). Stephen Booth's goal is to contribute to 'an analytic criticism that does not sacrifice – or at least tries not to sacrifice – any of a work of literature to logical convenience or even to common sense', and he infuriatingly refuses to find a conclusion in the turbulence he demonstrates in Shakespeare. Marvin Rosenberg's historical criticism, based on the history of performance, demands that we build into our understanding of the greatest tragedies the full range of interpretations they have provoked. Susan Snyder demonstrates 'that tragedy's ground is the disputed border – or no-man's-land – between a just and orderly pattern for life on the one hand and an amoral patternlessness on the other', and studies the complexity produced by generic signals rather than thematic simplicity. E. A. J. Honigmann has made a strong case that we value Shakespeare as we do 'partly because forcing secret and contrary impressions upon us, [he] makes us work harder', and that though we share our experience with the rest of the spectators on a given occasion, our 'various responses mix', 'interpenetrate one another and may not be tidily unscrambled'. Michael Goldman has demonstrated how far-reaching, subtle, and lucid a criticism may be when it is based on attending to how the plays make our bodies feel. And an extraordinary group of new psychoanalytic critics, including Janet Adelman, C. L. Barber, Coppélia Kahn, Arthur C. Kirsch, Murry M. Schwartz, Meredith Skura, Richard Wheeler, and others – have succeeded brilliantly by rejecting the formulas and reductive tropes of the psychoanalytic criticism of earlier generations.[31] No one reading the great number of new books on Shakespeare being published every year can fail to notice – *pace* Levin – that surprisingly many of them are valuable and permanent contributions to our knowledge and understanding; no one attending annual meetings of the Shakespeare Association of America, or other gatherings where new ideas about Shakespeare are discussed, can fail to come away at least as excited by the sense that we are making communal progress in our understanding of Shakespeare and of the nature of art as he is dismayed by the prevalence of naive and self-aggrandizing critical reductiveness.

5

The challenge to criticism, I have been suggesting, is to embark on a self-conscious reconsideration of the phenomena that our technology has enabled us to explore, to consider the play as a dynamic interaction between artist and audience, to learn to talk about the process of our involvement rather than our considered view after the aesthetic event. We need to find concepts other than meaning to account for the end of a play, the sense of unverbalizable coherence, lucidity, and unity that makes us know we have been through a single, significant, and shared experience. We need to learn to distinguish between the art represented in its extreme form by the murder mystery, in which the end completes the gestalt figure that tells us unequivocally how we should have responded to every detail along the way, and Shakespeare's profounder art, an art no less powerful in drawing us to a final vantage point from which we may look back over the whole, but an art ultimately irreducible to an explanatory schema.

To get down to cases, what can we do with *The Merchant of Venice*? Two obvious places to begin are its genre and its history, both on stage and in the study, and in both places we come immediately to the same realization. *The Merchant of Venice* is a comedy, inviting us

to celebrate a happy resolution and the reassertion of the values of
a community that includes us. Shakespeare's comedy normally
involves the overthrow of a threat, often the ejection of a character
whose inability to participate in the communal resolution threatens
community itself. But *The Merchant of Venice* plays on that convention
by investing enough of our emotions in its outsider to make us at
least uneasy about his discomfiture; the play unsettles one's normal
reaction to the end of a comedy. So much is indicated by the centuries
of reaction to Shylock and concomitantly to other characters that
I indicated earlier. I hope I have made it clear that audience
responses to Shylock or Bassanio or Portia which are alternately or
exclusively hostile or sympathetic are the result of ambivalent signals
built into the play. The countless such signals in *The Merchant of
Venice* are part of an entire system. If for a moment, or an entire
production, we are led to respond sympathetically to Shylock, we
necessarily respond with less sympathy to Jessica or Portia, and vice
versa. The potential fullness of a reading in which one element or
another in the play can come to seem like the center of the play's
values and the focus of its allegiances is paradoxically the source of
both its inexhaustible complexity and its vulnerability to powerful
productions in which the play seems to belong completely to Shylock
or to Belmont. The best reading and the best production, one might
guess, would have to take account of the possibilities of both
readings.

As the critical consensus has repeatedly shown in recent years,
the terms in which the central conflicts of *The Merchant of Venice* can
be paraphrased or summarized are remarkably clear. As the entire
critical history of the play has made equally apparent, the play's
ultimate resolution of those conflicts is anything but clear or simple.
The deep polarities in the comedy are luminously evident long
before the end. The life-and-death struggle between them makes us
feel the need to take a stand on one side or the other. And yet the
same play that makes that demand refuses to permit an unequivocal
resolution in favour of one character or group of characters or one
term in a thematic debate. The way in which an unresolvably
problematic sense of human experience is built into the structure of
the play can be suggested by an attempt to list some of the
incompatible elements, provocative of inconsistent responses, that
must be included in an adequate description of each of the polarities
the play develops. On the one side, as we have seen, we find Shylock,

trickery, anality, precise definition, possessiveness, contempt for prodigality, legalism, the Old Testament, Jews, dislocated values, mechanistic ethics and psychology, a fondness for bonds, stinginess, a wronged father, a conventional comic butt, an outsider, a paradoxical honesty about intention, a repressive father, distrust of emotion and hatred of music, bad luck, and failure. On the other we find Portia, but also Antonio, Bassanio, Lorenzo, Jessica, and Gratiano; freedom, metaphorical richness in language, prodigality, transcendence of the law, intense commitment to legalism, stealing, the New Testament, Christians; values that sometimes seem simple and right, sometimes complex and right, sometimes complex and wrong; love, generosity, cruelty to a father, life within a charmed circle, self-deception about motivation, youth rebelling against conventional comic repressive fatherhood, love of emotion and music, supreme trickery, a fondness for bonds, good luck, success.

At every point at which we want simplicity we get complexity. Some signals point to coherence – thus the conflict between the ideas of prodigality and possessiveness, or between two definitions of prodigality. But just as many create discomfort, point to centrifugality – virtually every mention of a ring and every episode involving one, the grouping of characters, the links between scenes that constantly ask us to reassess what we've just seen and interpreted in terms of what we're now seeing. In terms of moral content that we can extract, we come away with precious little: by the end we know as we knew before we began that cruelty is bad and love better, just as we know in *King Lear* that love between fathers and daughters is a good thing. If *The Merchant of Venice* or any of Shakespeare's great plays were to be judged by what we can claim to have learned from it, or by its ability to lead critics to clear formulations that agree with each other, society would pay even less for English departments than it does now. Yet by the end we have been through a constantly turbulent experience which demands an incessant giving and taking back of allegiance, a counterpoint of evershifting response to phrase, speech, character, scene, action, a welter of emotions and ideas and perceptions and surprises and intuitions of underlying unity and coherence rivalled only by our experience in the real world so perplexingly suggested by the artifact to which we yield ourselves.

I have called this chapter 'Meaning and *The Merchant of Venice*'. I have voiced reservations about readings of *The Merchant of Venice* that have claimed to be able to make precise formulations of its meaning, and have tried to show that such attempts are inadequate to the experience of the play. At the same time I have argued against critical positions that, recognizing the shortcomings of such attempts to stipulate meaning, would assert that a play has no meaning, and I have suggested that, despite other inadequate paraphrases, *The Merchant of Venice* does have a meaning. The time would seem to have arrived for me to attempt my own statement of that meaning. I hope that it is clear by now, however, that I do not think that the meaning that is there can be stated as a thematic paradigm. The power of the play is its power to create the illusion of a life that is like our lives, a world like our world, in which as in our life and our world experience tempts us to believe itself to be reducible to fundamental terms but cannot be adequately analyzed in those terms. In *The Merchant of Venice* as in the life we live outside the theatre we are driven to formulate questions which – despite the fact that we manage to go on living our lives – we cannot begin to answer. The problem is the one with which Kant begins the *Critique of Pure Reason*:

Human reason has this peculiar fate that in one species of its knowledge it is burdened by questions which, as prescribed by the very nature of reason itself, it is not able to ignore, but which, as transcending all its powers, it is also not able to answer.[32]

We can neither ignore nor answer the questions with which our reason is burdened. It is this quality of our existence that is ultimately suggested by our being tempted to and frustrated by the search for meaning in *The Merchant of Venice*, this conviction that the world makes sense but that the sense once abstracted no longer fits it. The attempt to state the meaning of the play is therefore not much more likely to produce an accurate account than an attempt to state the meaning of life. But to say that we cannot profitably talk about the meaning of life is not to say that life is meaningless. *The Merchant of Venice* is a model of our experience, showing us that we need to live as if life has meaning and rules, yet insisting that the meaning is ultimately ineffable and the rules are provisional. The experience of the play, like the experience of a sonata – or of life itself – is one of process, and involves not just a final cadence or even the recapitulation of some main themes, but a whole sequence of contrasting but related developments. That is why Dewey's consideration of art as experience and of experience as process remains so important. Properly understood, the play as a whole is identical with its meaning.

To argue thus is perhaps to declare one's continuity with the New Critical tradition, as it has recently been described with brilliance and something less than admiration by Gerald Graff: to endow 'texts with the most complicated of meanings' while seeming 'to call into question the notion that a literary work could even possess anything so didactic as a meaning;' ' "denying," ' in words Graff quotes from Hazard Adams, ' "the adequacy of any critical statement and constantly urging us to look again" '.[33] Though I do not share the tendency sometimes ascribed to the New Critics to see literature as nonreferential, as having no connection with a world outside, I obviously do share their paradoxical interest in scrutinizing the ways in which a literary work means while insisting that the meaning cannot be adequately paraphrased. . . . But I do not want to argue . . . that the sort of ambiguity I have demonstrated in *The Merchant of Venice* is the ultimate meaning of all literature, even of all the plays of Shakespeare. . . . Certain kinds of critical reduction lead us to recognize the particular complexities of Shakespeare's plays. But the forms of complexity are not identical with one another, and they constitute not a celebration of 'ambiguity' as the meaning of life but a set of perceptions of demarcated aspects of existential complexity.

SOURCE: *Shakespeare and the Problem of Meaning* (Chicago and London, 1981) Chapter 1, pp. 1–32.

NOTES

Abbreviated and renumbered from original by editor.

1. [Editor's note: see, for example, Stanley Fish, *Self-Consuming Artifacts: the Experience of Seventeenth Century Literature* (Berkeley, Cal., 1978); Norman Holland, *The Dynamics of Literary Response* (New York, 1975); Jacques Derrida, *Writing and Difference*, tr. Alan Bass (Chicago, 1978); Harold Bloom, *A Map of Misreading* (Oxford, 1975).] For hostile accounts of these and other attacks on the old consensus, see M. H. Abrams, 'How to Do Things with Texts', *Partisan Review* 46 (1979), 566–588, and Gerald Graff, *Literature against Itself: Literary Ideas in Modern Society* (Chicago, 1979).

2. Richard Levin, *New Readings vs. Old Plays: Recent Trends in the Reinterpretation of English Renaissance Drama* (Chicago, 1979).

3. For a useful survey of the theatrical vicissitudes of Shylock, see Toby Lelyveld, *Shylock on the Stage* (Cleveland, 1961).

4. Paul N. Siegel, *Shakespeare in His Time and Ours* (Notre Dame, 1968), p. 245; John W. Draper, 'The Theme of *The Merchant of Venice*', *Stratford to Dogberry: Studies in Shakespeare's Earlier Plays* (Pittsburgh, 1961), p. 128; Harold C. Goddard, *The Meaning of Shakespeare* (Chicago, 1960 ed.), I, 85.

5. H. B. Charlton, *Shakespearian Comedy* (London, 1966 ed.), p. 159; Norman Nathan, 'Three Notes on *The Merchant of Venice*', *Shakespeare Association Bulletin* 23 (1948), p. 155; Goddard, *op.cit.*; John Palmer, *Comic Characters of Shakespeare* (London, 1946), pp. 64–65, and George W. Keeton, *Shakespeare and His Legal Problems* (London, 1930), pp. 10–21.

6. L. Teeter, 'Scholarship and the Art of Criticism', *ELH* 5 (1938), 187, accurately sums up the conflict: 'There is little doubt that Shakespeare, consciously at least, intended this passage to raise a laugh at the expense of Shylock. Yet to many cultured readers of today it is to a large extent a pathetic speech arousing a sympathetic pity for the mistreated father.' C. L. Barber, *Shakespeare's Festive Comedy* (Princetown, 1959), p. 184, argues that at the end of this scene 'there *is* pathos; but it is being fed into the comic mill and makes the laughter all the more hilarious.'

7. Lawrence W. Hyman, 'The Rival Lovers in *The Merchant of Venice*', *Shakespeare Quarterly* 21 (1970), 109; see also Peter G. Phialas, *Shakespeare's Romantic Comedies: The Development of Their Form and Meaning* (Chapel Hill, 1966), p. 135, where virtually the same statement is made.

8. Hyman, *op. cit.*, p. 110.

9. A few instances will suffice. Draper, *op. cit.*, p. 135: 'Shylock the Jew was merely Venetian local color; Shylock the usurer was a commentary on London life.' Bernard Grebanier, *The Truth about Shylock* (New York, 1962), p. x: 'Shylock is not only a Jew, he is also a prototype of the banker', and Shakespeare's real interest is in attacking the impersonality of banks. Siegel, *op. cit.*, p. 245, justifies audience hatred of Shylock on the grounds that Shakespeare was after Puritans rather than Jews. Thomas H. Fujimura, 'Mode and Structure in *The Merchant of Venice*', *PMLA* 81 (1966), 504, writes: 'The most serious obstacle to grasping the ironic mode in which he is presented is to regard Shylock primarily as a Jew. In adapting the bond story, Shakespeare stressed his Jewish traits, no doubt for the practical reason that the associations worked to communicate the theme with the greatest economy on the Elizabethan stage. But he is hateful not because he is a Jew but because he is Shylock . . . Jessica . . . is ashamed not of her father's Jewishness but of his "manners", that is, his character. Shylock's Jewishness is thus, in Aristotelian terms, an "accident", his substance is his spiritual deadness or leadenness.'

10. Fujimura, *op. cit.*, p. 501.

11. A notable example of this sort of reductiveness is the account by Phialas, *op. cit.*, where the literal meaning of the plot is traded in for a symbolic reading which, when it cannot be demonstrated fully to dominate the play, is patronized as a relatively primitive attempt by Shakespeare (though far advanced beyond the earlier plays) to dispose of some themes the dramatist had been working out. See especially pp. 153, 168–69.

12. Frank Kermode, 'The Mature Comedies', in John Russell Brown and Bernard Harris, eds., *Early Shakespeare*, Stratford-upon-Avon Studies, 3, (London: 1961), p. 224.

13. Brown, introduction to his New Arden edition of *The Merchant of Venice* (London, 1955); 'The Realization of Shylock: a Theatrical Criticism', in *Early Shakespeare*, pp. 187–210; 'Love's Wealth and the Judgement of *The Merchant of Venice*', *Shakespeare and His Comedies* (London, 1957), pp. 45–81; Barber, *op. cit.*, pp. 162–91; Palmer, *op. cit.*; Danson, *The Harmonies of The Merchant of Venice* (New Haven, 1978).

14. Brown, Introduction to Arden edition, p. lviii.

15. John R. Cooper, *Shakespeare Quarterly* 21 (1970), 117–24.

16. Palmer, *op. cit.*, p. 86.

17. Barber, *Shakespeare's Festive Comedy*, pp. 170, 189.

18. Brown, *Shakespeare and His Comedies*, p. 74.

19. Stanley Cavell, *Must We Mean What We Say?* (New York, 1969), pp. 236–37.

20. John S. Coolidge remarks: 'The question is often asked whether there can be such a thing as Christian tragedy; this play seems to ask whether there can be such a thing as Christian comedy. Shakespeare answers in the affirmative, relying on the great biblical principle by which the old creation both points toward and rejects the new, while the new both abolishes and fulfills the old' ('Law and Love in *The Merchant of Venice*', *Shakespeare Quarterly* 27 (1976), 260).

21. Sigurd Burckhardt, *Shakespearean Meanings* (Princeton, 1968), p. 224.

22. Brown, *Shakespeare and His Comedies*, p. 70.

23. Though I. A. Richards, Empson, et al., succeeded in establishing the invalidity of simple meanings consistent with one statement quoted from a literary context, and Richards in his *Philosophy of Rhetoric* (New York, 1936) argued for a 'context' theory of meaning, the fruit of their labor has been a more deft exploration of more complex and inclusive meanings which ultimately leads to paraphrase.

24. E. D. Hirsch, Jr., *Validity in Interpretation* (New Haven, 1967), p. 22.

25. *Poems in Persons: An Introduction to the Psychoanalysis of Literature* (New York, 1973) and *Five Readers Reading* (New Haven, 1975).

26. Hirsch, *op. cit.*, p. 126.

27. Hyder Rollins, ed., *The Letters of John Keats, 1814–1821* (Cambridge, 1958), I, 193.

28. Kenneth Burke, *The Philosophy of Literary Form* (New York, 1957), pp. viii, 9; italics his.

29. René Wellek, *Theory of Literature*, new rev. ed. (New York, 1956), p. 156.

30. See especially *Emotion and Meaning in Music* (Chicago, 1956) and *Music, the Arts, and Ideas: Patterns and Predictions in Twentieth-Century Culture* (Chicago, 1967).

31. Maynard Mack, 'The Jacobean Shakespeare: Some Observations on the Construction of the Tragedies', in John Russell Brown and Bernard Harris, eds., *Jacobean Theatre*, Stratford-upon-Avon Studies, I (London, 1960); Stephen Booth, 'On the Value of *Hamlet*', in Norman Rabkin, ed., *Reinterpretations of Elizabethan Drama* (New York, 1969), pp. 137–76; E. A. J. Honigmann, 'Shakespearian Tragedy and the Mixed Response', An

Inaugural Lecture (University of Newcastle upon Tyne, 1971), pp. 25, 24; Michael Goldman, *Shakespeare and the Energies of Drama* (Princeton, 1972); Marvin Rosenberg, *The Masks of Othello, The Masks of King Lear, The Masks of Macbeth* (Berkeley and Los Angeles, 1971, 1972, 1978); Susan Snyder, *The Comic Matrix of Shakespeare's Tragedies* (Princeton, 1979); for book-length studies by the psychoanalytic critics named, see Coppélia Kahn, *Man's Estate: Masculine Identity in Shakespeare* (Berkeley and Los Angeles, 1980), Meredith A. Skura, *The Critic and the Psychoanalyst: Literary Uses of the Psychoanalytic Process* (New Haven, 1980), and Richard P. Wheeler, *Shakespeare's Development and the Problem Comedies: Turn and Counterturn* (Berkeley and Los Angeles, 1980); see also Coppélia Kahn and Murray Schwartz, eds., *Representing Shakespeare: New Psychoanalytic Essays* (Baltimore, 1980).

32. Immanuel Kant, preface to the first edition, *Critique of Pure Reason*, tr. Norman Kemp Smith (London, 1934), p. 5.

33. *Literature against Itself*, pp. 143, 144.

Maynard Mack Rescuing Shakespeare (1979)

'Good people, bring a rescue or two'. *King Henry IV*, Pt. 2

I

The rescue of Shakespeare's plays, like Tennyson's brook, goes on for ever. They were rescued in the first instance, we may properly recall, by his colleagues Heminges and Condell from the casual depredations of time. Later on, they were rescued from the impertinence of neo-classical rules, the rationalism of the eighteenth-century textual editors, the *O altitudos* of Romantic criticism, and the sheer clutter of the Victorian proscenium stage. In our own day, owing probably to the fact that much of the Shakespeare industry is now situated in the hungry Academy, this process has accelerated. During a bare half-century we have seen the School of Character Analysis, very much in the ascendant when I went to university, ousted by the School of Imagery and New Criticism, and both of these, during especially the last decade, giving ground steadily to what I will call the School of Performance, since its chief tenet seems to be that Shakespeare's plays are only to be known aright in actual productions. Meantime, ever more visible in the wings, though perhaps not yet quite ready to seize centre-stage, the School of Psychoanalysis, with Tarquin's ravishing strides, comes on apace.

All this is doubtless as it should be, lest one good custom corrupt the world. Moreover, we do learn something from each vogue as it passes, if only that it is not the direct 'hot line' to the white radiance of eternity that it claims to be, but only a more or less cloudy prism that, if properly angled, may refract some shadow of it. We can profit greatly, for example, by accepting the notion that Shakespeare can be only or best known in performance if we recall simultaneously that, in *actual* performance, the plays have always reflected, and always will reflect, the theatre, the technology, the acting and managerial styles, and the tastes, prejudices, and expectations of the audiences of a particular epoch. This is to say nothing of the added personal particularities that divide, say, a Burbage from a Betterton from an Olivier. Successful production of Shakespeare, as every drama critic will be happy to remind us, has always depended on the effort 'to harness his power to the images and self-images of the times'.[1]

In one respect the current emphasis on the performed play resembles the New Critical and psychoanalytic approaches: all three in their pure forms eschew history. The New Critics, we all know, consciously scanted the historical dimensions of a literary work in order to establish more clearly its self-sufficiency as a work of art – on the whole, a worthwhile effort despite certain costs. The psychoanalysts also scant history, chiefly because it seems irrelevant to the world of timeless truth to which they believe their insights belong: the id, ego, and superego of the Freudians (not to mention the so-called Family Romance) and the anima/animus polarity of the Jungians (together with the collective unconscious) are presumed to stand outside or above history and to be unaffected by it, like the *primum mobile* in the old cosmology. As for the performance approach, though this is emphatically, sometimes even excruciatingly, historical in the sense that what emerges from it is the reflection of a specific time-bound epoch, it is likely on that account to become all the more distanced from Shakespeare's own epoch and to undercut his habits of thought to indulge others more congenial. The point is put forcibly for us who [saw] the plays at Stratford [in 1978] by a reviewer of . . . *The Taming of the Shrew*. A *Shrew* staged straight, he notes, might well seem 'annoyingly archaic and chauvinistic: Petruchio would be guillotined by today's sisters, and a tamed Kate

would deserve her own equal rights amendment'.[2] *Mutatis mutandis,*
a contemporary of Dryden's or Johnson's might have spoken in this
vein about Shakespeare's original *King Lear* after seeing Nahum
Tate's, which held audiences spellbound for a hundred and fifty
years. As the death of Cordelia seemed unacceptable then because
it jarred with conceptions of divine justice, so the submission of
Kate seems unacceptable now because it jars with conceptions of
sexual justice. In either case, Shakespeare is re-directed out of his
world into some other.

  Let me say at once that in the theatre I have no quarrel with this.
Quite the reverse. Though it may be that even in the theatre
a boundary line is usefully drawn between interpretation and
manipulation, the experience of several centuries testifies that a
living secular theatre cannot afford to pay overmuch attention to
history, and will fail if it does. The academic study of Shakespeare,
on the other hand, seems to me to have more complicated and
perhaps more confusing goals. If no one wants his students to view
the plays as historical tracts, and no one in his right mind does,
equally no one wants his students to suppose that Shakespeare's
greatness lies in his thinking like us. 'The past', writes L. P. Hartley,
in a sentence that I should like to see emblazoned on a good many
classroom doors, 'is a foreign country: they do things differently
there.'[3] Literary study, I cannot but think, has among its chief
rewards our encounter not simply with versions of ourselves but
with the historical not-ourselves, the Other, the foreign country;
where virginity, for instance, instead of being as with us a nuisance
to be jettisoned at the nearest motel, turns out to be a prized
possession; or where adultery, no longer regarded merely as a recipe
for getting through the boredom of a longish weekend in Hampstead,
can be described as an act

> That blurs the grace and blush of modesty;
> Calls virtue hypocrite; takes off the rose
> From the fair forehead of an innocent love;
> And sets a blister there.
>
> (*Hamlet,* iii.iv.41–5)

Poor Hamlet – of course he must be mad! – or have incestuous
thoughts about his mother: how else account for so much ado about
nothing? As for Othello, *he* comes to think his wife has been slept
with and makes such a dither about it you might think he'd lost his
ticket to the World Cup.

II

So I have elected . . . to make a journey of another kind. I want to attempt an exploration, even if in an hour's lecture it has to be shockingly superficial, of some of the relationships, or interfaces, as a geologist might call them, between the fictional worlds that Shakespeare gives us in his plays and the historical 'real' world of Elizabethan and early Jacobean England. The particular cluster of relationships I have in mind concerns the family: both as Shakespeare shapes it for his own structural and expressive purposes on stage and as it actually existed and functioned in the cities, towns, and villages of England, and in the manors and great houses of the squirearchy and aristocracy.[4] What, one wonders, were the vital interconnections of these two domesticities, historical and dramatic? At what points in which plays may one reasonably suppose that a contemporary spectator sensed cross-currents between the conflicts and configurations before him in the playhouse and those known from family life around him, or possibly from his own? Or to put these questions somewhat differently and in a form perhaps more manageable, what do we know about the family of history that might cast at least an oblique light on the Shakespearian family of art?

At first glance, the family of art looks to be entirely *sui generis*. If we imagine an English county populated only by the types represented in the plays, the purposeful artificiality of Shakespeare's family world becomes strikingly apparent. A huge pyramidal base of affluent households, each widening out from some centre of authority such as king, prince, duke, rich merchant, or wealthy heiress, rests upside-down on an awesomely narrow apex of what a sober-minded modern historian would call economic support services. Servants and kept fools seem to be in reasonable supply; friars and priests likewise when needed to confirm a marriage or justify a bed-trick, though rarely for devotions; soldiers abound. But there are scandalously few burghers for the county town; still fewer lawyers, doctors, schoolmasters; no field or farmhouse labourers whatever, at any rate none identified as such (unless we suppose that Audrey and her William from *As You Like It* qualify, or one or more of Falstaff's Gloucestershire draftees in *2 Henry IV*), and only a handful of artisans, rather oddly assorted: a butcher and a bellows-mender, for instance, but no baker, and the only cobbler in the county one who learned his trade in Julius Caesar's Rome!

Such discrepancies divide Shakespeare's domestic worlds sharply from the one discovered to us by twentieth-century Tudor demographers. Yet in some sense, of course, Aristotle's claim for the higher truth of poetry holds even here. It was in these affluent great halls, after all, that the moral authority of English civilization was sustained, at least through Queen Elizabeth's time, as Shakespeare could not be unaware. And if in his *dramatis personae* the lower ranks seem to be mostly satellites of this authority, fringe for the kite's tail, this is in fact a true reflection of their historical situation – though with his customary acumen the playwright remembers what a kite's tail is for and gives to several of these hangers-on some shrewdly corrective counterthrusts against the follies, snobberies, and affectations of their betters.

Even more remarkably artificial at first glance is the constitution of the individual Shakespearian family. Putting aside the history plays, where family constituencies are determined in considerable part by factors outside the playwright's control, one may say that if you had been born into one of Shakespeare's imaginary households in the tragedies or comedies, you would have grown up, in a statistically startling number of instances, even allowing for sixteenth- and seventeenth-century death rates, with only one parent and that parent your father. Two figures tell all. Among the seventy young people of assorted ages and backgrounds that we meet with in these plays, Shakespeare allots a single parent to fifty-eight, a full complement to only twelve; and for fifty of the fifty-eight the allotted parent is male. About the female parent, furthermore, an extraordinary conspiracy of silence reigns. Should your father refer to your mother at all, it would doubtless be only to confirm his own paternity – as when Prospero reassures Miranda on this score by telling her 'Thy mother was a piece of virtue, and She said thou wast my daughter' (*The Tempest*, I.ii.56–7) – and you, on your side, would show a corresponding disinclination to inquire further. There is, in truth, amazingly little interest in either mothers or mothering in most of Shakespeare, and the comparatively few mothers who are brought to our attention as mothers, though they include such exemplary figures as the Countess of Rossillion, Lady Macduff, Virgilia, and Hermione, include also Tamora, cruel Queen of the Goths in *Titus Andronicus*, Gertrude in *Hamlet*, Lady Macbeth (a mother at least by her own testimony), Volumnia in *Coriolanus*, and the poisoning queen in *Cymbeline*, mother of the clod Cloten.

Not – one may perhaps reasonably conclude – a puff for radiant Elizabethan motherhood. The fathers in these plays come off better.

If there is some personal bias underlying this treatment of mothers, we must leave it to be discovered by the psychobiographers; but the dramatic economies that Shakespeare achieves in this way are obvious enough, and one might argue, here again, that under these surface differences from historical reality there lurks a species of higher truth in the uncompromising image we are given of the actual disposition of power on the Elizabethan domestic scene. Fathers dominate Shakespeare's stage for the same reason and in the same ways that they dominate his society. The almost total authority granted them by law and custom meant that they inevitably became the initiators and prohibitors of action, the dispensers and withholders of wealth and privilege (including the privilege of marriage), and the meters-out of unappealable decrees both wise and unwise – all perquisites of power that in the real world as in fable precipitate drama. Mothers, lacking final authority altogether unless they were widows or queens, the playwright quite understandably shears away, either in the interest of dramatic clarity or possibly to convenience the boy-actors, who must always have found it less taxing to play Rosalind than Volumnia.

One other respect in which Shakespeare's families are statistically arbitrary is in the disposition of pairs of brothers into one good brother, one bad. Of the ten prominent brother-pairs in the comedies and tragedies, the two Antipholuses and the two Dromios in *The Comedy of Errors*, and the two sons of Duncan in *Macbeth*, constitute three. The other seven are Don John and Don Pedro in *Much Ado About Nothing*; Duke Ferdinand and Duke Senior, Oliver and Orlando in *As You Like It*; Claudius and Hamlet's father in *Hamlet*; Edmund and Edgar in *King Lear*; and Antonio and Prospero, Alonso and Sebastian in *The Tempest* – all seven divided in the same way as the archetypal brothers in Scripture, Cain and Abel. Clearly, Shakespeare's preoccupation with this archetype, returned to so often in so many forms, far exceeds its incidence in everyday experience, Elizabethan or our own. Yet as a way of dramatizing the mystery that this ancient story commemorates – registered, it tells us, in our very genes – the fiction of the good and evil brother can hardly be improved on. It had, moreover, some plausibilities for Shakespeare's audience that are now much attenuated. The primogenitural system, giving the estate to the eldest son and requiring no necessary (indeed, tending to discourage) provision for the other children, opened so many grounds for selfishness in the heir and resentment in the disinherited that fraternal jealousies and intrigues were as common as quills on the fretful porpentine. Younger brothers, comments one seventeenth-century observer, 'are often the most unnatural enemies of their own house, upon no stronger provocation than what nature and their own melancholy thoughts present them'.[5] This sounds almost like a real-life formula for a fictional Don John. Had the observer gone on to deplore the frequent indifference and sometimes active hostility of the elder brothers, as he might equally have done, he would have sketched the real-life formula from which the Oliver of the early scenes of *As You Like It* is drawn. For contemporary spectators, in other words, an Oliver/Orlando or Don John/Don Pedro situation, though not one likely to be met with seven times in every ten, could, and did, provide an arresting image of a serious contemporary issue, even when viewed through the highly tinted lenses of stage comedy and pastoral romance.

III

In the foregoing examples, resemblances between Shakespeare's stage-world and the world his audiences brought with them lie just beneath a surface of apparent difference. Often the relation is more direct. To return to our earlier case in point, if you had been born into one of Shakespeare's stage families, it is just short of certain that you would not have been nursed by your mother, but by a supposedly more vigorous woman of lower caste, in whose keeping you would have been placed, or who, alternatively, would have been brought into your household for the purpose. From the evidence of the plays this has been the fortune of (at the very least) Richard III (*Richard III*, ii.ii.30), Juliet (*Romeo and Juliet*, i.iii.68–9), Marina (*Pericles*, iii.iii.39–40), the two sons of Cymbeline (*Cymbeline*, iii.iii.103–4), Mamillius (*The Winter's Tale*, ii.i.56), and the putative father of Jack Cade, who bases his claim to the crown on the circumstance that his allegedly Plantagenet father, having been put out to a wet nurse, was thus stolen and so kept from his rightful inheritance (*2 Henry VI*, iv.ii.137–41). Here and there in the plays, it is true, a few characters speak as if mothers nursed their own children. Lavinia, in *Titus Andronicus*, for instance, chooses to assume that Tamora's sons have their cruelty direct from her breasts (II. iii. 144–5), and Aufidius tells the Volscians that Coriolanus has whined and roared away their victory 'at his nurse's [meaning his mother's] tears' (*Coriolanus*, v.v.97–8). Malvolio, too, getting in a thrust at women generally, says of the disguised Viola/Cesario waiting at Olivia's gate that 'he speaks very shrewishly. One would think his mother's milk were scarce out of him' (*Twelfth Night*, i.v.153–4). But these are put-downs, not facts. The only unmistakable testimonies in Shakespeare to a *well-born* woman's nursing her own child (the peasant Joan La Pucelle was of course nursed by hers: 1 *Henry VI*, v.iv.27–9) are Rosalind's witty warning to Orlando ('Oh, that woman that cannot make her fault her husband's occasion, let her never nurse her child herself, for she will breed it like a fool', *As You Like It*, iv.i.155–7); Lady Macbeth's much-debated assertion that she has known 'How tender 'tis to love the babe that milks me' (*Macbeth*, i.vii.55); Cleopatra's 'Dost thou not see my baby at my breast, That sucks the nurse asleep' (*Antony and Cleopatra*, v.ii.307–8), and Hermione's complaint, at her trial, that her newborn child 'is from my breast – The innocent milk in it most innocent mouth – Hal'd out to murder' (*The Winter's Tale*, iii.ii.97–9).

The conflicting evidence on this matter in the plays mirrors with some accuracy the confused situation in the times. For though the Humanists, especially More and Erasmus, had advocated breast-feeding by the mother since early in the century (the Reformers all following suit), and though occasionally an aristocratic mother would have it recorded on her tombstone that she had nursed her children herself, the advice fell on deaf ears so far as most of the rich were concerned, and indeed many middle- and lower-class families as well; and the practice of 'fostering out', as it was called, continued not much abated well into the eighteenth century – both Pope and Johnson, it is well known, having probably contracted their lifelong tubercular infections from this source.

After nursing, weaning. Shakespeare's evidence on this matter is somewhat surprising. Most Renaissance medical authorities favoured weaning between 18 and 24 months (Queen Elizabeth herself was weaned at a little over a year), but the only actual weaning referred to in the plays, Juliet's, comes at a full 3 years – a far higher upper limit than any recognized by the paediatric writers (with one Elizabethan exception) from Macrobius to Nicholas Culpepper in the eighteenth century.[6] What one suspects without being able to prove is that Shakespeare is in this matter a safer guide to actual practice than the doctors (whose aim is usually more normative than descriptive), and perhaps particularly to provincial practice in the countryside where he grew up. His age for first walking tallies better with the authorities. Juliet, you will recall, at the time of her weaning at age 3 'could stand high-lone', could in fact run and waddle all about, and the day before had taken a fall and broken her brow. The nurse's emphasis on these attainments suggests that they were quite recent, and if so, they are not such as we would today single out for comment; by our expectations, in fact, they seem rather backward. But a recent study of the ages of children at first walking in the past indicates that at least well into the seventeenth century these dates ran late, James VI of Scotland, later to be James I of England, having walked first at about 5 years and a child of Anne Clifford's a half-century later at 34 months.[7] Hence Juliet at or somewhat under 36 months may again conform to the experience of the time.

By this age, in Shakespeare's day, whether you were male or female, you had long been wearing a costume very like your mother's. For boys, therefore, it was a great day when they could throw this off and go 'breeched', like their fathers. Mamillius in *The Winter's Tale* appears to be on the brink of this *rite de passage* at the very moment when his father becomes mindlessly jealous:

> Looking on the lines
> Of my boy's face, methoughts I did recoil
> Twenty-three years; and saw myself unbreech'd,
> In my green velvet coat; my dagger muzzled. . .
>   (I.ii.153 ff.)

The historical interest of this passage is that it establishes the approximate age at which Leontes should be visualized by actor and director. The breeching of a boy child took place between 5 and 7 – never, so far as I can discover, later than 7 – which means that Mamillius cannot be 10 here, as the Arden editor assumes (by 10, in any case, he would no longer be in the care of women), but must be reckoned an unbreeched 5, 6, or 7, and Leontes, therefore, probably not more than 28 to 30. Thus at the time of Perdita's recovery, he may be imagined to be somewhere between 44 and 46, approximately Shakespeare's own age at the time of writing the play.

At any age from 7 on, if you were a child of well-bred or aristocratic parents, you would be sent off to school or to another household, preferably one sufficiently prestigious and influential to be advantageous to your parents and your own future, to learn the arts and manners of 'gentilesse'. The commonest age for this removal was around 10. Ten was also a common age for children of the lower ranks to be put out to domestic service and apprenticeships. The upshot of this displacement – which one present-day historian calls a scheme of 'institutionalized abandonment'[8] – was that about three-quarters of the adolescent girl population and about two-thirds of the equivalent boy population lived away from home during the growing years of maximum psychic change and instability, when sexual and other appetites were keenest, under no other authority than that which their patrons or employers could establish over them, often by the whip. This, surely, is what the old shepherd in *The Winter's Tale* is grumbling about when he wishes there were 'no age between ten and three-and-twenty, or that youth would sleep out the rest; for there is nothing in the between but getting wenches with child, wronging the ancientry, stealing, fighting' (III.iii.59–63). The old shepherd's upper limit appears to derive from contemporary work conditions as well. Twenty-three is the final year allotted to immaturity in a variety of Elizabethan regulatory statutes, including the Statute of Artificers (established in 1563, reaffirmed in 1573) which calls attention to 'the licentiouse libertye of youthe before thei come to xxiiii yeares of aige', complains that some before reaching that age 'have three or foure children, which often thei leave to the parish where thei dwelle to be kept', and then, still on the ground that till age 24 a man is for the most part 'wilde, withoute judgment, & not of sufficyent experience to governe himselfe', prohibits any craftsman under 24 from taking an apprentice.[9] The aim of such statutes was to deny the entry of the young worker as a full adult into the labour market, but its side effect was to postpone marriage and settling down till after the dangerous period of which the old shepherd complains.

IV

It may be apparent by this point that the historical family of
Shakespeare's day was in several respects very different from ours.
The 'nuclear family', as sociologists call it, where the primary
bonding is between father, mother, and children, had been shaking
free for a century or more from the extended kinship family of earlier
times, in which the first loyalty is to the clan. Not that this transition
was as clear to the people going through it as it seems to students
of family history today, or would have been viewed in the same
terms in which we view it. Nevertheless, important changes in the
character of family bonding were in the making, and new habits
and expectations rubbed elbows with older ones. Some interesting
testimony to this effect appears in *3 Henry VI*. There (II.v.55 ff.) we
are shown, in a famous allegorical moment much like the garden
scene in *Richard II*, a father who has killed his son and a son who
has killed his father, their political allegiances having differed, one
loyal to the house of Lancaster, the other to the house of York.
Under the older kinship family of the period of Wars of the Roses,
when this action is supposed to have taken place, such divisions
would not have been typical, as presented here, but exceptional,
and in fact almost unthinkable. Shakespeare has given his material
an anachronistic turn, consciously or otherwise, to stress the dread
disorders brought about by faction, ruinous even to the sacred
patrilinear relationship of father and son – disorders soon to be
repeated in the real world during the English Civil War, when one
aristocratic family in seven was divided 'father against child or
brother against brother'.[10] At the same time, however, whether or
not the playwright grasped it intellectually, this confrontation of
fathers and sons with opposing political loyalties illustrates the
intensifying individualism requiring personal moral choice that was
steadily eroding clan collectivism and replacing it with questions for
the individual conscience like those soon to be scrutinized in *Hamlet*.

This does not mean, of course, that the patterns of feeling by
which the extended kinship family had been supported became
extinct. Far from it. Shakespeare's evidence is again interesting. For
in the same play in which the autonomy of the individual conscience
is imaged, whether or not intentionally, in the divided loyalties of
fathers and sons who have killed each other, the boy Rutland pleads
for his life to an angry Clifford, whose father has been killed by

Rutland's father, only to hear his plea answered in the following terms:

> Had I thy brethren here, their lives and thine
> Were not revenge sufficient for me;
> No, if I digg'd up thy forefathers' graves
> And hung their rotten coffins up in chains,
> It could not slake mine ire nor ease my heart.
> The sight of any of the house of York
> Is as a Fury to torment my soul;
> And till I root out their accursed line
> And leave not one alive, I live in hell.
>
> (I.iii.25–33)

Senecan and rhetorical as this is, it expresses vividly the law of the vendetta by which clan and bloodline become responsible for the crime of any individual belonging to them – a law that had been observed as recently as the 1530s by Henry VIII himself in punishing the whole of the De la Pole family for the offence of a single member and was still being observed by a succession of heads of aristocratic houses during Shakespeare's lifetime, even to muggings and murders in the streets of London, to which, because of that city's attractions, lineage quarrels often got transferred from their country origins. The feud in *Romeo and Juliet* with its street-fighting, like the questionings about revenge later raised in Hamlet, had applications for contemporaries much closer home than Elsinore and Verona.

It will be apparent by now, too, that the early nuclear family was considerably less intimate and more austere than most of those we see today. It was bound together far more by external pressures from law, custom, tradition, and public opinion, combined with the immense interior pressure of patriarchal authority upheld by elaborate rituals of deference and respect. 'Laugh not' with thy son, writes Thomas Becon in his *Catechism* of 1560, echoing the author of Ecclesiasticus:[11]

lest thou weep with him also, and lest thy teeth be set on edge at the last. Give him no liberty in his youth and excuse not his folly. Bow down his neck while he is young: hit him on the sides while he is yet but a child, lest he wax stubborn and give no force of thee, and so thou shalt have heaviness of soul.

With minor changes of emphasis, this is approximately the burden of all domestic advice books down to Richard Baxter and beyond.

Keep your distance from your children, never make companions of
them, set them a good example. If you have to beat them, remind
them that they have sinned against God as well as against you so
that they will understand the beating to be for God's glory; and see
to it that after punishment they kneel down and pray Him to 'bless
and sanctify' their stripes to their spiritual improvement. For in His
infinite providence and wisdom – so one apologist insists in a
particularly inspired passage – God has uniquely framed the human
posteriors to support blows without risk of injury.[12]

Such nonsense is happily missing from Shakespeare's stage, but
we do, of course, hear sometimes of whips and cudgels, and the
rituals of obedience are well observed. 'For what I will, I will, and
there an end', says Proteus' father in *The Two Gentlemen of Verona*
(i.iii.65), referring to his intention to send his son to join Valentine
at the Emperor's court; and this is likewise the expectation of old
Capulet when he makes his 'desperate tender' (*Romeo and Juliet*,
iii.iv.12–14) of Juliet's love to Paris, and earlier, when he compels
Tybalt to simmer down with a rousing blow (i.v.75–86). Unlike
Tybalt, however, most Shakespearian children obey without the
need of violence, or else disobey by stealth, and when they know or
fear they have offended, kneel for pardon. They also kneel for
blessing, and out of this custom, as we all remember, Shakespeare
manufactures some wonderfully humorous scenes like that in which
old Gobbo blesses his upwardly mobile son in *The Merchant of Venice*
(ii.ii.28 ff.), along with some of the most touching incidents in
dramatic literature, as when Cordelia kneels to Lear (*King Lear*,
iv.vii.57–8), Marina to Thaisa (*Pericles*, v.iii.46), and Perdita to
Hermione (*The Winter's Tale*, v.iii.119). What one would like to know
is whether those yet more poignant moments in which parent kneels
to child, as happens with Volumnia (*Coriolanus*, v.iii.169) and Lear
(*King Lear*, iv.vii.59), were ever to be found in the actual lives of
Elizabethan families, or are creations of the imagination solely:
intimations of a world where the comic principle of misrule and
topsy-turvy becomes transformed to tragic splendour by the needs
and frailties we all share.

However this may be, the deference system as we find it in
Shakespeare's family of art derives directly from its counterparts in
history. Like the society around it, the Elizabethan family depended
for the attainment of its goals on a structure of strict obedience; and
this presupposed, in turn, as Henry Bolingbroke knew so well, the
maintenance of a certain ritual space around the patriarchal head,
be he king or father, to preserve his person 'fresh and new', his

presence 'like a robe pontifical, Ne'er seen but wond'red at', and his state 'Seldom, but sumptuous', like a feast (*1 Henry IV*, iii.ii.55–9).

What, then, *were* an Elizabethan family's goals? If propertied, as all of Shakespeare's families are, its chief goals, not surprisingly, were self-perpetuation together with self-advancement in either wealth or influence or both. For a deeply religious family, on the other hand, especially one with Puritan leanings, the pursuit of goals like these was complicated by the conviction that its members were pilgrims *en route* to a celestial destination and must therefore consistently support and edify each other in the struggle to avoid sin.[13] Some coloration from this aspect of contemporary Puritanism may just conceivably have been borrowed by Shakespeare for his portraiture of certain siblings. Isabella's behaviour with Claudio in *Measure for Measure* should probably be left out of account as a special case; but Luciana, to take a simpler example from *The Comedy of Errors*, has little to say to her sister Adriana during her troubles with her husband that is not morally admonitory: no expressions of sisterly tenderness break forth to comfort Adriana in her confusion and despair. A similar constraint, though touched with somewhat greater tenderness, seems to pervade the parting of Laertes and Ophelia (*Hamlet*, i.iii.5–51). Each lectures the other with a moralizing zeal reminiscent in tone, though not in language, of contemporary Puritan manuals, a tone that after another century of such influence will sour into the appalling self-complacencies of Richardson's model book of *Letters* and Defoe's *Religious Courtship*.

Still, even by a family with deep religious convictions, survival and advancement had to be kept firmly in mind, and the two main ways that the age left open for reaching these objectives were successful marriage and prudent transmission of family possessions at death. To these considerations let me now briefly turn.

V

Elizabethan marriages, as we all know and Shakespeare repeatedly tells us, were arranged marriages, unless they were elopements – the latter sometimes undertaken, as by Anne Page in *The Merry Wives of Windsor*, to avoid an undesirable partner. Marriage could be entered into easily, English custom and canon law demanding only espousals *de presenti* before witnesses, with no necessary mediation by the church till James I's time, and, once consummation had taken place, any contract became unbreachable. Shakespeare's marriages – rather interestingly, since so many of his plays were written before the requirement of clerical mediation by the canons of 1604 – are entered into without exception before a priest and in a church or friar's cell, and his opinion of marriages celebrated less formally *may* lurk in Jaques' counsel to Touchstone when the latter is about to let the ignorant Oliver Martext marry him to Audrey under the nearest tree.

And will you, being a man of your breeding, be married under a bush, like a beggar? Get you to church and have a good priest that can tell you what marriage is; this fellow will but join you together as they join wainscot; then one of you will prove a shrunk panel, and like green timber warp, warp.

(*As You Like It*, III.iii.72–7)

    Marriage being thus readily accessible, fathers had to look to their daughters or they would be snatched away from under their noses like the wench cited by Biondello in *The Taming of the Shrew*, who got herself 'married in an afternoon as she went to the garden to fetch parsley to stuff a rabbit'. The legal age of consent for girls was 12, for boys 14, and though we know that very youthful marriages like Juliet's were statistically the exception, not the rule, they did occur. Elizabeth Manners, for example, married the second Earl of Exeter in 1589, aged something more than 13, and bore him a child by the time she was $14\frac{1}{2}$ – very much the performance that Lady Capulet claims for herself.[14] True, this sort of thing was roundly disapproved of on the ground that parturition was dangerous for young mothers and would produce spindly offspring; nevertheless, as Touchstone was to put it, 'wedlock would be nibbling' (*As You Like It*, III.iii.71). Among the rich, six per cent of the children of peers married at 15 or under in the later sixteenth century, twenty-one per cent at 17 or under; and while these proportions are statistically negligible, they represent nearly forty individual unions. Among the middling and poor, likewise, despite the control exercised on some groups by the Statute of Artificers, early marriages remained common enough to impel Stubbes in his *Anatomie of Abuses* (1583) to complain that 'every sawcie boy' can 'catch up a woman and marie her' (Shakespeare himself, of course, fits into *this* category), and then, says Stubbes, fill the land 'with such store of poore people that in short time . . . it is like to growe to great povertie. . . .'.[15] Nor, apparently, was the problem confined to saucy boys. 'The forward Virgins of *our Age*', says the author of a marriage manual of 1615, addressing, it would appear, chiefly the middle classes, 'are of Opinion' that, for marrying, '*Fourteen* is the best Time of their Age, if *Thirteen* be not *better* than that; and they have for the most Part the Example of their Mothers before them, to confirm and approve their Ability.'[16]

If, then, Shakespeare's disposition of the nuptial age question seems ambiguous or inconsistent, it may be all the truer as a reflection of the varying usage of the day. In the comedies, with the possible exception of Hermia and her friend Helena, who are evidently quite young (Hermia's wooing, we notice, has been with bracelets of hair and sweetmeats), and also Anne Page, who is not yet 17, he parades before us an unexceptionable series of young women who give the distinct impression of being comparatively adult: Kate, Bianca, Sylvia, Julia, Portia, Rosalind, Celia, Beatrice, Hero, Viola, Olivia, and more. Yet in Juliet's case he has gone out of his way to lower to 14 the 16 years she is allotted in his source, and in the romances shows us a 16-year-old Perdita, a 15-year-old Miranda, and a 14-year-old Marina, all married or about to be at the end of the play.[17]

For the kinds of well-placed family that Shakespeare portrays, the pressure to marry young came, as in old Capulet's case, from the opportunity to make a good match.[18] This meant, apart from the rough equivalencies of blood and breeding that all Shakespeare's matches presuppose, a suitable jointure in the form of an annual income to be settled on the bride by the groom's father, to take effect at the time of the groom's death, and a suitable bridal portion to be paid outright in cash by the bride's father. We do not know what immediate portion Juliet would have brought Paris (in the long run she is heir to all that Capulet has) but we are told that the shrew Kate is to bring immediately, to the man who marries her, twenty thousand crowns, the equivalent approximately of £5,000. As this is an extraordinary figure in the 1590s, about two and a half times the going portion even among the highest peerage,[19] it seems clear that Baptista's announcement of this figure is part of the joke about Kate and may very possibly in the playwright's time have brought down the house.

Similar laughter no doubt attended the bidding between Tranio (playing Lucentio) and Gremio for the other daughter Bianca; but the cream of the jest in the original is not that Baptista's computer blows up, as [in the 1978 production] at Stratford, but much more probably, it seems to me, that the enormous traffic in heiresses in the 1590s is being spoofed. This was a traffic highly competitive in two directions. On the man's side, marriage with an heiress was reckoned – throughout this whole period – to be the one widely available road to riches, and to travel it successfully seems to have had clinging to it, at any rate in Shakespeare's mind, the same romantic aura of high risks and fabulous rewards as hung about the great merchant-venturers with their argosies abroad. One may note the imaginative pairing of the two activities in Bassanio's quest for Portia as the Golden Fleece (*The Merchant of Venice*, i.i.168–72) juxtaposed with Antonio's investments in similar expeditions elsewhere; or in Romeo's breathless exclamation at Juliet's beauty:

> I am no pilot; yet, wert thou as far
> As that vast shore wash'd with the farthest sea,
> I should adventure for such merchandise;
> (*Romeo and Juliet*, ii.ii.82–4)

or in Troilus's imagination of Cressida as a fabulous Indian pearl, in pursuit of which he is the merchant-venturer and Pandarus his 'bark' (i.i.99–103). Possibly a tinge of these associations lingers here in *The Taming of the Shrew* when Gremio bids for Bianca with an argosy and Tranio/Lucentio replies with a whole merchant fleet plus its escort: 'three great argosies, besides two galliasses And twelve tight galleys'. But whether this is the case or not, an electricity from beyond the playhouse crackled about such bidding in Shakespeare's time that one wants one's students to be aware of.

What one also wants them to be aware of is the electricity in the lines themselves. . . . The device of the exploding computer seemed to me quite brilliant as a way of conveying the element of absurdity in the Bianca contest, but it misses altogether – in fact it tends to dissipate in farce – the great swell and billowing of the Renaissance imagination to which the playwright gives free play in Gremio's inventory:

> Basins and ewers to lave her dainty hands;
> My hangings all of Tyrian tapestry;
> In ivory coffers I have stuff'd my crowns;
> In cypress chests my arras counterpoints,
> Costly apparel, tents, and canopies,
> Fine linen, Turkey cushions boss'd with pearl,
> Valance of Venice gold in needle work;
> Pewter and brass. . . .
> (*The Taming of the Shrew*, ii.i.340–51)

This is a kind of riches that computers do not compute.

The other side of this competitive traffic was the woman's. For her, too, if she were a gentlewoman, the occasion was momentous, for the age offered no alternative career. The nunneries – 'convenient stowage for . . . wither'd daughters', as Milton would later put it with a Protestant contempt – were gone.[20] Gone too was the confessional, which in the older time could offer an oppressed wife both an outlet for her woes and the support of another authority figure against her husband's tyranny – and sometimes it offered yet more, as we know from the fabliaux. Equally gone were the theology and cult-practices that gave a virgin life its social and moral status. Meditations on the art not of keeping but of losing one's virginity now become the fashion, as in Parolles's conversation with Helena in *All's Well that Ends Well*, and fall in snugly with Reformation propaganda against celibacy – for 'your virginity, your old virginity, is like one of our French wither'd pears: it looks ill, it eats drily'. By an accompanying transvaluation, the dedicated virgin now becomes the 'old maid', a drag upon her family[21] and hence condemned to lead apes in hell, as the adage had it, and as Kate and Beatrice remind themselves. And the figure of the shrew, who often enough in the real world was simply a woman cruelly trapped into an unpalatable arranged marriage (or else, like Beatrice, and possibly Kate, one whose apprehension of such a fate impelled her to keep up an ostensibly invincible front), legally under her husband's thumb and denied all those freedoms sexual and other that the double standard allowed her husband to claim – this figure edges forward into the limelight as an interesting type, worthy now of more sympathetic examination, like Paulina in *The Winter's Tale*, or even, as in Beatrice's case, of becoming the true heroine of the play.

In short, the competition not simply for a husband but for a husband one could live with was on, intensified and complicated on the one hand by the emergent individualism we have seen elsewhere, which set a high value on personal choice, and on the other by an increase in population that enlarged the number of daughters in the race but not the fixed number of male heirs to estates – so that bridal portions had dramatically to increase. From 1530 to 1570 the average bridal portion among the well-to-do more than doubled, from about £400 to about £1,000. In the 1580s and 1590s it doubled again to about £2,000, the new figures being forced by the competition of the richer squirearchy. As a result the relation between the size of the portion (the cash-down settlement by the bride's father) and the size of the jointure (the annual income guaranteed the wife by the groom's father if the groom died) took a major shift from about five to one in the mid sixteenth century, to about six and two-thirds to one in the mid seventeenth.[22]

The interest of these figures for us is that in one case we seem to be able to compare information that Shakespeare lets slip with these historical norms. Anne Page in *The Merry Wives of Windsor* will have £700 from her grandfather's will at age 17 – so Hugh Evans informs Shallow and Slender – plus a substantial addition we are told her father is to make (i.i.46–7). The jointure that Shallow offers her on Slender's behalf is £150 a year (iii.iv.49). This is near enough to five to one, even without the expected paternal increment, to make us at least wonder whether Shakespeare's figures may not be fairly sophisticated. Certainly, at any rate, the £150 jointure would be bound to register on a contemporary audience in some degree and would provoke either a laugh for being too outrageously high or low, or else simply a flicker of recognition. Here again, it seems to me, the gap between the academic study of Shakespeare's text and Shakespeare on stage shows clearly. There is no way that the significance of this £150 figure can be conveyed, artistically, to a twentieth-century theatre audience, nor for that audience does it greatly matter. Yet for a student of the text, a little attention to history can help shape the response that the playwright expected. Shallow's offer is evidently a sound one, and Anne's father is right to be attracted by it – except for the one circumstance that his wife has spotted, but he has not, or is willing to overlook. 'That Slender', she says, in a passage which sketches more clearly than any other in Shakespeare the material context in which Elizabethan marriages were made: 'That Slender, though well landed, is an idiot; And he my husband best of all affects. The Doctor' – and now she turns to Caius, an idiot yet more egregious, though in this case she is the one oblivious – 'is well money'd, and his friends Potent at court; he, none but he, shall have her.'

In the upshot, you will recall, neither has her. Master Fenton, who has blood and breeding but no money, wins her because he has her love, and the words with which at the play's end he excuses what he has done sum up a position whose validity was oftener and oftener being recognized by the marital advice-books as the century turned:

                         Hear the truth of it.
You would have married her most shamefully,
Where there was no proportion held in love.
The truth is, she and I, long since contracted,
Are now so sure that nothing can dissolve us.
Th'offence is holy that she hath committed;
And this deceit loses the name of craft,
Of disobedience, or unduteous title,
Since therein she doth evitate and shun
A thousand irreligious cursed hours
Which forced marriage would have brought upon her.
                    (*The Merry Wives of Windsor*, v.v.207 ff.)

VI

Shakespeare's role in these anatomies of mating was, one supposes, like the role of art for the Renaissance generally, *dulce et utile*, both entertaining and doctrinal. Viewed in one light, what he brought his audiences was escape into a golden world, where colliding aims could be adjusted amiably with respect for personal choice, as by Theseus in *A Midsummer Night's Dream*; or where the stratagems of youth triumphed and were accepted by parents with a certain grace, as in *The Taming of the Shrew* and *The Merry Wives of Windsor*; or where the father's will, quite literally in this case a will, bears the magical attribute of yielding only to the suitor who is also loved, as in *The Merchant of Venice*. Cheek by jowl with this, however, he brought a pervasive sanity of outlook and a humorous acceptance of human limitations such as intelligent participation in the personal relations of the *real* world also required. It would have been hard, surely, for a spectator to leave a performance of any of his comedies, even the earliest, without an exhilaratingly renewed consciousness of the illusions and enchantments of falling in love, the obscurity and complexity of the motives involved in giving oneself or being given to another, and the enormous risks and rewards of that commitment.

   As much may be said of the tragedies, though in them the subject-matter shifts to husbands and wives, or parents and children, and the action darkens to include adultery, suicide, and murder. In both forms he holds up before his patrons some of their most cherished stereotypes and invites them, if they have eyes to see, to see. Women, urges the popular preacher Henry Smith in his *A Preparative to Marriage* of 1591, speaking for the vast majority of contemporary moralists non-Puritan as well as Puritan, should be silent and obedient, and should stay at home.[23] Consciously or not, Shakespeare appears to be laughing this kind of stereotype out of court in *The Merry Wives of Windsor*. Mistress Page – with the full approval of her husband, says Mistress Quickly admiringly – is free to 'Do what she will, say what she will, take all, pay all, go to bed when she list, rise when she list, all is as she will; and truly she deserves it; for if there be a kind woman in Windsor, she is one.' Mistress Ford has not the same degree of confidence from her husband, but goes her merry ways nonetheless, as great a talker and gadabout as her friend Mistress Page, and as great an offence to contemporary notions of what a good wife should be. In Coriolanus' wife Virgilia, on the other hand, we meet with a woman who is almost a paradigm of Elizabethan middle-class canons of wifely behaviour, presented with great sympathy and obviously in somewhat favourable contrast to her witty but brittle and gossipy friend Valeria, in whose mouth 'housekeepers' and 'stitchery' seem to be primarily terms of disdain. In Shakespeare's book there are plainly as many ways of being a woman as there are women – an attitude that must have seemed to those who stopped to think about it a social revolution in itself.

Doctrinal, too, I am inclined to think, is the circumstance that the plays contain so few disloyal wives – the fear of cuckoldry being the great bogeyman that it was – and so many loyal ones. Loyal, moreover, like Mistress Ford, Desdemona, Hermione, and Imogen, in the most trying circumstances. The misguided outbursts of their husbands echo rather closely in substance, it is true, traditional indictments found in misogynistic literature from the Church Fathers down; and possibly, as one recent commentator argues, Shakespeare as a master showman was not above providing this kind of gratification for some parts of his audience. But the important point, of course, is precisely that the outbursts are misguided; the husbands are wrong. Moreover, they are responding with what is essentially a stereotypical passion, however brilliantly expressed, to the most stereotypical of the anxieties to which the double standard gave rise. 'Chastitie', Vives had urged in his *Instruction of a Christian Woman* (1524), 'is the principall vertue of a woman, and counterpeyseth with al the reste: if shee have that, no man wyll loke for anie other: and if she lacke that, no man wyll regarde other.'[24] Though Shakespeare knows this attitude well enough and sets as much store by sexual fidelity as he does by all the other loyalties, civilities, and restraints that differentiate men and women from animals, the form of fidelity he values most obviously transcends the physical and applies equally to men and women. What Portia expects from Brutus, by reason of 'that great vow Which did incorporate and make us one' is his companionship and total trust, as if she were his second self:

> Am I your self
> But, as it were, in sort or limitation?
> To keep with you at meals, comfort your bed,
> And talk to you sometimes? Dwell I but in the suburbs
> Of your good pleasure? If it be no more,
> Portia is Brutus' harlot, not his wife.
> (*Julius Caesar*, ii.i.282–7)

That this same ideal should appear in Shakespeare's earliest play, *The Comedy of Errors*, gives it, I think, an added significance. If you play me false, Adriana says to Antipholus of Syracuse, thinking him her husband, I shall be as stained by your adultery as if I had committed the act myself:

> How comes it now, my husband, O, how comes it,
> That thou art then estranged from thyself?
> Thyself I call it, being strange to me,
> That, undividable, incorporate,
> Am better than thy dear self's better part.
> Ah, do not tear away thyself from me. . .
> For if we two be one, and thou play false,
> I do digest the poison of thy flesh,
> Being strumpeted by thy contagion.
> (ii.ii.118–23, 141–3)

Yet this is also the playwright who could create in Cleopatra the *ultima Thule* of the strumpet and enchantress type, transforming it from a man-destroying Radigund or Circe figure to a vulnerable woman – 'commanded By such poor passion as the maid that milks And does the meanest chares' (iv.xv.73–5) – and allowing it, up to a point, to declare and vindicate itself against the cool Octavia and the prurient gossips and the unforgiving self-righteousness of Puritan Rome. Whatever Shakespeare may have intended by this virtuoso performance, it could only have been achieved by a mind sceptical everywhere of cultural stereotypes and sensitive to, though not necessarily abstractly conscious of, the changes in outlook in his

own time that would gradually make it possible for a play to be
written called *All for Love: or, The World Well Lost*, and for an epic
poem to be written about a 'Paradise within thee, happier far'.

VI

In *The Taming of the Shrew*, after he has been outbid by Tranio
impersonating Lucentio, Gremio turns to face him and expresses
doubt that Lucentio's father will make good on the lavish promises
just made to Baptista in his name.

> Sirrah young gamester, your father were a fool
> To give thee all, and in his waning age
> Set foot under thy table. Tut, a toy!
> An old Italian fox is not so kind, my boy.
>   (II.i.392–5)

Though Shakespeare cannot have been aware of it at the time,
Gremio's 'Your father were a fool To give thee all' points forward
to another 'old kind father, whose frank heart gave all'. It also points
outward. For if marriage was the next to commonest means by
which property changed hands in Shakespeare's time, inheritance
was the most common and the question of how best to pass on what
one had, and when, was a live issue for all classes except the poorest,
and those among the rich whose estates were strictly entailed on the
male heir. Then as now many a man longed like Lear to shake all
cares and business from his age, conferring them on younger
strengths, but for a variety of reasons found it impolitic to do so.
Contemporary attitudes, as Keith Thomas has pointed out, show
'an underlying hostility toward those who opted out of the economic
process and a reluctance to devote much of society's limited resources
to their maintenance':[25] a hostility that seems certain to reappear in
the industrialized countries of our own day as ageing populations
on Social Security or other forms of national support become an
increasing burden to the lessening populations still at work.
  In Shakespeare's time, resentment against the old could spring
from other causes as well. The work system was rigged, as we have
seen already, to delay full participation in it by the young, and other
age requirements advanced as the century wore on. The age of first
communion rose from infancy to between 12 and 14. The legal age

of majority moved upward from 12 and 14 towards 21. Even 21 came under strain from the civil lawyers who favoured the Roman law majority of 25. Moreover, it was the elderly – men in their forties, fifties, sixties – who were visibly entrenched in the seats of power, no less in the villages than in Parliament, the Courts, or Privy Council. To a youth looking about him with appraising eyes in the first decade of the new century, oppression by the elderly – who made up a very much smaller part of the total population then than now – must have seemed very real, a case of the tail wagging the dog, and the grumblings he had just heard in the new play at the Globe could easily have elicited a warm degree of understanding even if not approval.

> This policy and reverence of age makes the world bitter to the best of our times; keeps our fortunes from us till our oldness cannot relish them. I begin to find an idle and fond bondage in the oppression of aged tyranny, who sways, not as it hath power, but as it is suffer'd.
>
> (*King Lear*, i.ii.45–9)

There were other stresses of course too. Many that exist always between youth and crabbed age were aggravated under Elizabeth by social and religious change. The natural scorn that vigour often feels for decay, particularly for the old 'fuddy-duddy' . . . was sharpened during this period by wider dissemination and improvement of schooling to the point at which it was easy for a successful child on the make, like Launcelot Gobbo, to look down patronizingly on the ignorance of his parent and, as he says, 'try confusions with him' (*The Merchant of Venice*, ii.ii.33). It was evidently this sort of role-reversal that decided a schoolmaster of Henry Peacham's never to 'teach any Scholler he had, further than his Father had learned before him', lest the sons should prove 'saucy rogues' and 'controule' their fathers.[26] On similar intellectual grounds the early offspring of the English Reformation felt privileged to mock their parents: 'My father', said one, 'is an old doting foole and will fast upon the fryday, and my mother goeth alwayes mumbling on her beades. But you shall se me of another sorte, I warraunt you'.[27] This catches the tone and almost the substance of Edmund's sneer at Gloucester's belief in 'These late eclipses'. As the dissenting sects multiplied, such attitudes multiplied with them: 'If there were any good to be done in these days,' Henry Smith assured his congregation, 'it is the young men that must do it; for the old men are out of date, their

courage stoops like their shoulders, their zeal is withered like their
brows, their faith staggereth like their feet, and their religion is dead
before them.'[28]

As for some of the other defects that overtake the ancientry, these
were found as disgusting, or at least as off-putting, as they have
been in every period. 'Their eyes purging thick amber and plumtree
gum', complains Hamlet, out of Juvenal (*Hamlet*, II.ii.196–7). 'Their
spittings, coffings, froward dispositions, So irksome are', adds a
poem of 1639.[29] 'Has any man', asks a preacher in 1613,

ever seene a poore aged man live at curtesie, in the house of his sonne with
his daughter in law? doth not the good father in a short time, either by his
coughing or spitting or teastiness or some sooneseene untowardnesse or
other, become troublesome, either to his owne sonne or to his nice daughter
in law with continuing so long chargeable & so much waited on, or to the
children, with taking up their roome at the fire, or at the table, or to the
servants, while his slow eating doth scant their reversions.[30]

The moral of such anecdotes, naturally enough, was: Be careful
how you give away your property before death. The formal transfer
of material resources by parents, advises a current sociological
handbook, 'weakens their control over the junior generation, with
the possible result of neglect or non-support';[31] or, as in the
Renaissance any fool knew, 'fathers that bear bags Shall see their
children kind' (*King Lear*, II.iv.49–50). Any fool, but not necessarily
every wise man. Sir Robert Plumpton, for instance, drew up in 1516
an indenture with his son and heir William Plumpton by which
Will was to have 'ordering and charge of all the household and
goods therto longing, and his said father, and my lady his wife, to
take their ease and rest at the proper costs and charges of the said
Will'. In addition, Will was to retain 'al such servants as he thinks
necessary or profitable for the wele of the said house except that the
said Sir Robert his fader shall have three at his own pleasure, such
as he will apointe.'[32]

How the Plumpton experiment worked out we do not know, but
it is recorded that Sir William Lisle in the mid seventeenth century
met his end in a single 'nasty chamber, being all his son would
allow him for his men, horses, dogs, provisions, and for the cooking
of them'.[33] Two stories, two centuries apart, will indicate how deeply
ingrained in popular thought the apprehension of such an end at
the hands of one's heir had become. One is an *exemplum* from a

Middle English sermon, probably late fourteenth century, which
tells of a rich man who married off his daughter and gave with her
to his son-in-law his goods, his house, and all his land to provide
for his support in future. The first year, his son-in-law

sett hym at is owne dische, and clothed hym in ys owne clothinge. And the
second yere he sett hym at the ende of is borde, and suffred hym to fare
sumwhat wers than he dud hym-selfe, both of mete and of clothe. And the
thrid yere he sett hym with is children in the flore at the harthes ende; and
the chambur that he leye in he seid that he muste nedes owt ther-of, for is
wiff moste lie ther-in to that she were delyvered of hure child. And undur
this coulour he put the old man owte of is chambur and in a lytill hows at
the utmaste gate, ther he made hym for to lie.[34]

The other story is from *Pasquil's Jests*, published in 1604, only a
year or two before *King Lear* was composed. This time it is to his
own son that the old man gives all he has:

After the deed of gift was made, awhile the olde man sat at the upper end
of the table; afterwards, they set him lower, about the middle of the table;
next, at the tables end; and then, among the servants; and, last of all, they
made him a couch behind the doore and covered him with olde sackcloth,
where, with grief and sorrow, the olde man dyed. When the olde man was
buried, the young man's eldest child sayd unto him: 'I pray you, father,
give me this olde sackcloth.' 'What wouldst thou doe with it?' sayd his
father. 'Forsooth', sayd the boy, 'it shall serve to cover you, as it did my
old graundfather.'[35]

My point is not, of course, that Shakespeare had all or any of
these episodes in mind when writing *King Lear*, though the gradualism
of the old man's humiliation in the two stories just recounted perhaps
indicates the existence of a formula that may have been influential
in the framing of Acts I and II. My point is simply that for an
audience of contemporaries, much in the experience of the play was
certain to come home with the pang of familiar and homely truth,
even though raised to the grandeur of a tragic parable. Thus what
evidence we have suggests that, beneath the elaborate rituals of
respect, many of the young in Elizabeth's and James's time were
capable of entertaining such feelings of resentment as Edmund voices,
even if not ordinarily accompanied by his homicidal intentions; and
that many of the old, for whatever psychological reasons, behaved
as tyrannically as Lear does – or Egeus in *A Midsummer Night's
Dream*, for that matter – when at last set free by seniority or status

from the yoke that they themselves had worn. Thus, too, it need not have been impossible for a Jacobean spectator to view the literal love-test from the source-play with which the tragedy begins as a piece of dramatic shorthand, standing for all those efforts by which, in his own family or in others, he had seen the very old seek assurances of affection, longed for all the more, no doubt, when least deserved. Perhaps he could also recognize in the old king's intuitions of a world coming apart at the seams a similar fusion of the homely and grand: on the one hand, an ancient father's querulous response to losses of authority and power, including his own physical and mental power, enlarged by vanity and terror to cosmic scope; on the other, a probing at the profoundest level of those family and human-family bonds which, while they hold, prevent humanity from preying on itself, like monsters of the deep. I have often wondered, indeed, considering the prominence in this play of actions of ignoble obedience and servility set over against actions of noble disobedience and independence, whether it may not have seemed to a particularly thoughtful spectator that he was watching a critique of the entire contemporary structure of authority from the monarch to the patriarch – and moreover, as we see probably much more clearly than Shakespeare's audience could, of all authority as such: a tragic critique because the playwright knows that authority is not dispensable even in a world where parent has learned to kneel to child. There must always be someone who can 'Rule in this realm, and the gor'd state sustain'.

But these are speculations, nothing more. All that I would claim for certain is that here, as in his other plays, Shakespeare keeps up an elusive but fascinating traffic between the world of history and the world of art, and that our chances of learning more about his achievement in the latter depend in large part on our learning more about the former. 'The very principle of myth', writes Roland Barthes, 'is that it transforms history into nature.'[36] I believe that this is true in a deeper sense than M. Barthes intends; and, accordingly, when in company with Dryden and a long line of later critics we admire Shakespeare as the poet of 'Nature', we must not forget the history he has transformed.

SOURCE: *Rescuing Shakespeare* (Oxford, 1979). International Shakespeare Association Occasional Paper No. 1.

NOTES

1. Richard Elder, 'Can We Rethink Shakespeare without Submerging Him?' *NY Times*, 16 July 1978: Section D, p. 3.

2. Mel Gussow, 'An Auspicious Year at Britain's Stratford', *Ibid*. p. 4.

3. *The Go-between* (London, 1953), p. 9.

4. I am particularly indebted in what follows to the brilliant work done during the last two decades in Tudor history, social history, and demography by Joel Hurstfield (*The Queen's Wards: Wardship and Marriage under Elizabeth I*; London, 1958), Peter Laslett (*The World We Have Lost*, London, 1965; *Family Life and Illicit Love in Earlier Generations*, Cambridge, 1977); Lawrence Stone (*The Crisis of the Aristocracy, 1558–1641*, Oxford, 1965); *The Family, Sex, and Marriage in England, 1500–1800*, New York, 1977), and Keith Thomas ('The Double Standard', *Journal of the History of Ideas*, xx, 1959, 195–216; 'Age and Authority in Early Modern England', *Proceedings of the British Academy*, lxii, 1976, 205–48).

5. G. Davies, ed., *Autobiography of Thomas Raymond and Memoirs of the Family of Guise* (London; Camden Society, 3rd ser., xxviii, 1917), 114.

6. Lloyd De Mause, 'The Evolution of Childhood', *The History of Childhood*, ed. Lloyd De Mause (New York, 1974), p. 36. The Elizabethan exception is John Jones whose *The Arte and Science of Preserving Bodie and Soule, in Healthe, Wisedome, and Catholike Religion* (1579), pp. 42–5, sets the weaning period between 7 and 36 months.

7. De Mause, p. 50.

8. De Mause, p. 32.

9. *Tudor Economic Documents*, ed. R. H. Tawney and Eileen Power (3 vols., London, 1924), i. 358, 356, 354.

10. Stone, *The Family*, p. 127.

11. *The Catechism of Thomas Becon*, ed. John Ayre (Cambridge, 1844), p. 354; Ecclus., 30: 10–12. Compare the experience of Lady Jane Grey, confided to Roger Ascham when she was fifteen: 'When I am in the presence either of father or mother, whether I speake, kepe silence, sit, stand, or go, eate, drinke, be merie or sad, be sowying, plaiying, dauncing, or doing anie thing els, I must do it, as it were, in such weight, mesure, and number, even so perfitelie, as God made the world, or els I am so sharplie taunted, so cruellie threatened yea presentlie some tymes, with pinches, nippes, and bobbes, and other waies which I will not name, for the honor I beare them, so without measure misordered, that I thinke my selfe in hell. . .' *The Scholemaster* (1570), *English Works*, ed. W. A. Wright (1904), pp. 201–2.

12. Bartholomaeus Battus, *The Christian Man's Closet* (tr. William Lowth, 1581), p. 26.

13. L. L. Schücking, *The Puritan Family: A Social Study from the Literary Sources* (London, 1969), p. 91. Though it may or may not be significant, it is interesting that the childhood attachments Shakespeare describes so winningly never occur within the family. See *A Midsummer Night's Dream*, I. i. 214 ff.; III. ii, 198 ff.; *As You Like It*, I. iii. 68 ff.; *The Winter's Tale*, I. ii. 67 ff.

14. For an illuminating discussion of Juliet's age at marriage in the light of Elizabethan social history, see Laslett, *World*, pp. 81–9.

15. Leaf H₅, recto.

16. *A Discourse on Marriage and Wiving and of the Mystery Contained Therein* (1615), *Harleian Miscellany* (1744), ii. 147–8.

17. Antigonus in *The Winter's Tale* (II. i. 144 ff.) sets the female breeding age at 14.

18. Additional pressures sometimes came from a father's determination to arrange his children's marriages himself; for if he died before they were of an age to inherit, they became wards of the crown, their guardianship purchaseable for a fee, and with it the privilege of choosing their marriage-partners.

19. Stone, *Crisis*, p. 638.

20. Milton, *Animadversions upon the Remonstrant's Defense against Smectymnuus, Complete Prose Works*, ed. D. M. Wolfe, i (1953), 718.

21. Partly owing to the necessity of supporting her, but partly also to the loss of family advantage from marrying her well. See the comment of the Marquis of Argyle in 1661, quoted by Stone (*Crisis*, p. 646): 'in great and noble families . . . interest forbids perpetual virginity'.

22. Stone, *Crisis*, pp. 643–5.

23. *Works* (Edingburgh, 1866–7), i. 29–30.

24. Tr. Richard Herde (1557), leaf J₄, verso.

25. 'Age and Authority', p. 237. I am indebted to this essay for referring me to several of the works cited below.

26. *The Compleat Gentleman* (1622), p. 27.

27. John Christopherson, *An Exhortation to all menne to take hede and beware of rebellion* (1554), leaf T₂, verso.

28. 'The Young Man's Task', *Works*, i. 228.

29. H[umphrey] M[ill], *Poems* (1639), leaf M8, recto.

30. Foulke Robartes, *The Revenue of the Gospel Is Tythes* (Cambridge, 1613), pp. 114–15.

31. Jack Goody, 'Aging in Nonindustrial Societies', *Handbook of Aging and the Social Sciences*, ed. R. H. Binstock and E. Shanas (New York, 1976), p. 119.

32. *Plumpton Correspondence*, ed. T. Stapleton (Camden Society, 1839), pp. cxxii–xxv.

33. *A Royalist's Notebook*, ed. Francis Bamford (London: Constable, 1936), p. 124.

34. *Middle English Sermons*, ed. W. O. Ross (Oxford, 1940), pp. 89–90.

35. *Pasquils Jests, mixed with Mother Bunches Merriments* (1604). W. C. Hazlitt, ed., *Shakespeare Jest-Books* (3 vols. 1864), i. 61.

36. *Mythologies* (Paris: Éditions du Seuil, 1957), p. 237: 'Nous sommes ici au principe même du mythe: il transforme l'histoire en nature.'

Jonathan Dollimore   King Lear and Essentialist Humanism   (1984)

When he is on the heath King Lear is moved to pity. As unaccommodated man he feels what wretches feel. For the humanist the tragic paradox arises here: debasement gives rise to dignity and at the moment when Lear might be expected to be most brutalised he becomes most human. Through kind-ness and shared vulnerability human kind redeems itself in a universe where the gods are at best callously just, at worst sadistically vindictive.

In recent years the humanist view of Jacobean tragedies like *Lear* has been dominant, having more or less displaced the explicitly Christian alternative. Perhaps the most important distinction between the two is this: the Christian view locates man centrally in a providential universe;[1] the humanist view likewise centralises man but now he is in a condition of tragic dislocation: instead of integrating (ultimately) with a teleological design created and sustained by God, man grows to consciousness in a universe which thwarts his deepest needs. If he is to be redeemed at all he must redeem himself. The humanist also contests the Christian claim that the suffering of Lear and Cordelia is part of a providential and redemptive design. If that suffering is to be justified at all it is because of what it reveals about man's intrinsic nature – his courage and integrity. By heroically enduring a fate he is powerless to alter, by insisting, moreover, upon *knowing* it, man grows in stature even as he is being destroyed. Thus Clifford Leech, an opponent of the Christian view, tells us that tragic protagonists 'have a quality of mind that somehow atones for the nature of the world in which they and we live. They have, in a greater or lesser degree, the power to endure and the power to apprehend' (*Shakespeare's Tragedies*, London, 1950, p. 15). Wilbur Sanders in an influential study argues for an ultimately optimistic Shakespeare who had no truck with Christian doctrine or conventional Christian conceptions of the absolute but nevertheless affirmed that 'the principle of health – grace – is not in heaven, but in nature, and especially in human nature, and it cannot finally be rooted out'. Ultimately this faith in nature and human nature involves and entails 'a faith in a universal moral order which cannot finally be defeated' (*The Dramatist and the Received Idea* (Cambridge, 1968), pp. 336–7).

Here as so often with the humanist view there is a strong residue of the more explicit Christian metaphysic and language which it seeks to eschew; comparable with Sanders' use of 'grace' is Leech's use of 'atone'. Moreover both indicate the humanist preoccupation with the universal counterpart of essentialist subjectivity – either ultimately affirmed (Sanders) or recognised as an ultimate tragic absence (Leech).[2] The humanist reading of *Lear* has been authoritatively summarised by G. K. Hunter (he calls it the 'modern' view of the play):

[it] is seen as the greatest of tragedies because it not only strips and reduces and assaults human dignity, but because it also shows with the greatest force and detail the process of restoration by which humanity can recover from degradation . . . [Lear's] retreat into the isolated darkness of his own mind is also a descent into the seed-bed of a new life; for *the individual mind is seen here as the place from which a man's most important qualities and relationships draw the whole of their potential*' (*Dramatic Identities and Cultural Tradition* (Liverpool, 1978), pp. 251–2, my italics).

What follows is an exploration of the political dimension of *Lear*. It argues that the humanist view of that play is as inappropriate as the Christian alternative which it has generally displaced – inappropriate not least because it shares the essentialism of the latter. I do not mean to argue again the case against the Christian view since, even though it is still sometimes advanced, it has been effectively discredited by writers as diverse as Barbara Everett, William R. Elton and Cedric Watts.[3] The principal reason why the humanist view seems equally misguided, and not dissimilar, is this: it mystifies suffering and invests man with a quasi-transcendent identity whereas the play does neither of these things. In fact, the play repudiates the essentialism which the humanist reading of it presupposes. However, I do not intend to replace the humanist reading with one which rehearses yet again all the critical clichés about the nihilistic and chaotic 'vision' of Jacobean tragedy. In *Lear*, as in *Troilus*, man is decentred not through misanthropy but in order to make visible social process and its forms of ideological misrecognition.

Redemption and Endurance:
Two Sides of Essentialist Humanism

'Pity' is a recurring word in *Lear*. Philip Brockbank, in a recent and
sensitive humanist reading of the play, says: 'Lear dies "with pity"
(iv.vii.53) and that access of pity, which in the play attends the
dissolution of the senses and of the self, is a condition for the renewal
of human life' [*Proceedings of the British Academy*, 62 (1976), 109–34].
Lear, at least when he is on the heath, is indeed moved to pity, but
what does it mean to say that such pity is 'a condition for the
renewal of human life?' Exactly whose life is renewed? In this
connection there is one remark of Lear's which begs our attention;
it is made when he first witnesses 'You houseless poverty' (iii.iv.26):
'O, I have ta'en/Too little care of this!'. Too little: Lear bitterly
reproaches himself because hitherto he has been aware of yet ignored
the suffering of his deprived subjects. (The distracted use of the
abstract – 'You houseless poverty' – subtly suggests that Lear's
disregard has been of a general rather than a local poverty.) He has
ignored it not through callous indifference but simply *because he has
not experienced it.*

King Lear suggests here a simple yet profound truth. Far from
endorsing the idea that man can redeem himself in and through an
access of pity, we might be moved to recognise that, on the contrary,
in a world where pity is the prerequisite for compassionate action,
where a king has to share the suffering of his subjects in order to
'care', the majority will remain poor, naked and wretched. The
point of course is that princes only see the hovels of wretches during
progresses (walkabouts?), in flight or in fairy tale. Even in fiction
the wheel of fortune rarely brings them that low. Here, as so often
in Jacobean drama, the fictiveness of the genre or scene intrudes;
by acknowledging its status as fiction it abdicates the authority of
idealist mimesis and indicates the better the reality it signifies;
resembling in this Brecht's alienation effect, it stresses artifice not
in the service of formalism but of realism. So, far from transcending
in the name of an essential humanity the gulf which separates the
privileged from the deprived, the play insists on it. And what clinches
this is the exchange between Poor Tom (Edgar) and Gloucester.
The latter has just arrived at the hovel; given the circumstances,
his concern over the company kept by the king is faintly ludicrous
but very telling: 'What, hath your Grace no better company?'
(iii.iv.138; cf. Cordelia at iv.vii.38–9). Tom tells Gloucester that he

is cold. Gloucester, *uncomprehending rather than callous*, tells him he will keep warm if he goes back into the hovel (true of course, relatively speaking). That this comes from one of the 'kindest' people in the play prevents us from dismissing the remark as individual unkindness: judging is less important than seeing how unkindness is built into social consciousness. That Gloucester is unknowingly talking to his son in this exchange simply underscores the arbitrariness, the woeful inadequacy of what passes for kindness; it is, relatively, a very precious thing but as a basis for human kind's self-redemption it is a non-starter. Insofar as Lear identifies with suffering it is at the point when he is powerless to do anything about it. This is not accidental: the society of *Lear* is structured in such a way that to wait for shared experience to generate justice is to leave it too late. Justice, we might say, is too important to be trusted to empathy.

Like Lear, Gloucester has to undergo intense suffering before he can identify with the deprived. When he does so he expresses more than compassion. He perceives, crucially, the limitation of a society that depends on empathy alone for its justice. Thus he equates his earlier self with the 'lust-dieted man . . . *that will not see Because he does not feel*' (iv.i.68–70, my italics). Moreover he is led to a conception of social justice (albeit dubiously administered by the 'Heavens', 1.67) whereby 'distribution should undo excess, And each man have enough' (iv.i.71–2).

By contrast, Lear experiences pity mainly as an inseparable aspect of his own grief: 'I am mightily abus'd. I should e'en die with pity. To see another thus' (iv.vii.53–4). His compassion emerges from grief only to be obliterated by grief. He is angered, horrified, confused and, above all dislocated. Understandably then he does not empathise with Tom so much as assimilate him to his own derangement. Indeed, Lear hardly communicates with anyone, especially on the heath; most of his utterances are demented mumblings interspersed with brief insight. Moreover, his preoccupation with vengeance ultimately displaces his transitory pity; reverting from the charitable reconcilation of V. iii to vengeance once again, we see him, minutes before his death, boasting of having killed the 'slave' that was hanging Cordelia.

But what of Cordelia herself? She more than anyone else has been seen to embody and symbolise pity. But is it a pity which significantly alters anything? To see her death as *intrinsically* redemptive is simply to mystify both her and death.[4] Pity, like kindness, seems in *Lear* to be precious yet ineffectual. Far from being redemptive it is the authentic but residual expression of a scheme of values all but obliterated by a catastrophic upheaval in the power structure of this society. Moreover the failure of those values is in part due to the fact that they are (or were) an ideological ratification of the very power structure which eventually destroys them.

In *Lear*, as we shall see in the next section, there is a repudiation of stoicism similar to that found in Marston's *Antonio's Revenge* [1600]. Yet repeatedly the sceptical treatment, sometimes the outright rejection, of stoicism in these plays is overlooked; often in fact it is used to validate another kind of humanism. For convenience I call the kind outlined so far ethical humanism and this other one existential humanism. The two involve different emphases rather than different ideologies. That of the latter is on essential heroism and existential integrity, that of the former on essential humanity, the universal human condition. Thus, according to Barbara Everett (in another explicitly anti-Christian analysis):

> In the storm scene Lear is at his most powerful and, despite moral considerations, at his noblest; the image of man hopelessly confronting a hostile universe and withstanding it only by his inherent powers of rage, endurance and perpetual questioning, is perhaps the most purely 'tragic' in Shakespeare. ('The New *King Lear*', *Critical Quarterly*, 2 (1960), 333)

Significantly, existential humanism forms the basis even of J. W. Lever's *The Tragedy of State* (London, 1971), one of the most astute studies of Jacobean tragedy to date. On the one hand Lever is surely right in insisting that these plays 'are not primarily treatments of characters with a so-called "fatal flaw", whose downfall is brought about by the decree of just if inscrutable powers . . . the fundamental flaw is not in them but in the world they inhabit: in the political state, the social order it upholds, and likewise, by projection, in the cosmic state of shifting arbitrary phenomena called "Fortune"' (p. 10). By the same criteria it is surely wrong to assert (on the same page) that: 'What really matters is the quality of [the heroes'] response to intolerable situations. This is a drama of adversity and stance . . . The rational man who remains master of himself is by the same token the ultimate master of his fate.' In Lever's analysis Seneca is the ultimate influence on a drama (including *King Lear*) which celebrates man's capacity inwardly to transcend oppression (p. 9).

If the Christian mystifies suffering by presenting it as intrinsic to God's redemptive and providential design for man, the humanist does likewise by representing suffering as the mysterious ground for man's *self*-redemption; both in effect mystify suffering by having as their common focus an essentialist conception of what it is to be human: in virtue of his spiritual essence (Christian), essential humanity (ethical humanist), or essential self (existential humanist), man is seen to achieve a paradoxical transcendence: in individual extinction is his apothesis. Alternatively we might say that in a mystifying closure of the historical real the categories of idealist culture are recuperated. This suggests why both ethical and existential humanism are in fact quasi-religious: both reject the providential and 'dogmatic' elements of Christianity while retaining its fundamental relation between suffering, affirmation and regeneration. Moreover they, like Christianity, tend to fatalise social dislocation; its causes are displaced from the realm of the human; questions about them are raised but only rhetorically, thus confirming man's impotence to alleviate the human condition. This clears the stage for what really matters: man's responsive suffering and what it reveals in the process about his essential nature. Recognisable here is the fate of existentialism when merged with literary criticism as a surrogate or displaced theology; when, specifically, it was co-opted to the task most symptomatic of that displacement, namely the obsession with defining tragedy. It will be recalled that for the existentialist existence precedes essence, or so said Sartre [1905–1980] who later tried to develop this philosophy in the context of Marxism. In literary criticism the social implications of existentialism, such as they were, were easily ignored, the emphasis being instead on a modernist angst and man's thwarted spiritual potential. This is another sense in which existential humanism is merely a mutation of Christianity and not at all a radical alternative; although it might reluctantly have to acknowledge that neither Absolute nor Essence exist, it still relates man to them on a principle of Augustinian privation: man understands his world only through the grid of their absence.

King Lear: A Materialist Reading

More important than Lear's pity is his 'madness' – less divine furor
than a process of collapse which reminds us just how precarious is
the psychological equilibrium which we call sanity, and just how
dependent upon an identity which is social rather than essential.
What makes Lear the person he is – or rather was – is not kingly
essence (divine right), but, among other things, his authority and
his family. On the heath he represents the process whereby man
has been stripped of his stoic and (Christian) humanist conceptions
of self. Consider what Seneca [*d.* A.D. 65] has to say of affliction
and philosophy:

Whether we are caught in the grasp of an inexorable law of fate, whether it
is God who as lord of the universe has ordered all things, or whether the
affairs of mankind are tossed and buffeted haphazardly by chance, it is
philosophy that has the duty of protecting us.[5]

Lear, in his affliction, attempts to philosophise with Tom whom he
is convinced is a 'Noble philosopher', a 'good Athenian' (III.iv.168
and 176). It adds up to nothing more than the incoherent ramblings
of one half-crazed by just that suffering which philosophy, according
to the stoic, guards against. It is an ironic subversion of neo-
stoic essentialism, one which recalls [Francis] Bacon's essay 'Of
Adversity,' where he quotes Seneca: '*It is true greatness to have in one
the frailty of a man, and the security of a god*' only to add, dryly: 'This
would have done better in poesy, where transcendences are more
allowed'. . . . Bacon [1561–1626] believed that poesy implies idealist
mimesis – that is, an illusionist evasion of those historical and
empirical realities which, says Bacon, 'buckle and bow the mind
unto the nature of things'.[6] He seems to have remained unaware
that Jacobean drama was just as subversive of poesy (in this sense)
as he was, not only with regard to providentialism but now its
corollary, essentialism. Plays like *Lear* precisely disallow 'transcendences': in this at least they confirm Edmund's contention that 'men
Are as the time is' (v.iii.31–2). Montaigne [1533–92] made a similar
point with admirable terseness: 'I am no philosopher: Evils oppresse
me according as they waigh'.[7] The Fool tells Lear that he is 'an O
without a figure' (I.iv.192); both here and seconds later he anticipates
his master's eventual radical decentredness, the consequence of
having separated 'The name, and all th' addition' of a king from

his real 'power' (I.i.135, 129): 'Who is it that can tell me who I am?'
cries Lear; 'Lear's shadow' replies the Fool.

After he has seen Lear go mad, Gloucester offers this inversion of
stoicism:

> Better I were distract
> So should my thoughts be sever'd from my griefs,
> And woes by wrong imagination lose
> The knowledge of themselves.
>   (IV.vi.281–4)

For Lear dispossession and displacement entail not redemptive
suffering but a kind of suffering recognition – implicated perhaps
with confession, depending on how culpable we take this king to
have been with regard to 'the great *image* of authority' which he
now briefly demystifies: 'a dog's obey'd in office' (IV.vi.159, my
italics). Lear does acknowledge blame, though deludedly believing
the power which made him blameworthy is still his: 'Take that of
me, my friend, who have the power To seal th' accuser's lips'
(IV.vi.169–70). His admission that authority is a function of 'office'
and 'power', not intrinsic worth, has its corollary: power itself is in
control of 'justice' (l. 166) rather than vice versa:

> The usurer hangs the cozener.
> Through tatter'd clothes small vices do appear;
> Robes and furr'd gowns hide all. Plate sin with gold
> And the strong lance of justice hurtless breaks;
> Arm it in rags, a pigmy's straw doth pierce it.
>   (IV.vi.163–7)

Scenes like this one remind us that *King Lear* is, above all, a play
about power, property and inheritance. Referring to Goneril, the
distraught Lear cries: 'Ingratitude, thou marble-hearted fiend, More
hideous when they show'st thee in a child Than the sea-monster'
(I.iv.259–61). Here, as throughout the play, we see the cherished
norms of human kind-ness shown to have no 'natural' sanction at
all. A catastrophic redistribution of power and property – and,
eventually, a civil war – disclose the awful truth that these two
things are somehow prior to the laws of human kindness rather than
vice-versa (likewise, as we have just seen, with power in relation to
justice). Human values are not antecedent to these material realities
but are, on the contrary, in-formed by them.[8]

Even allowing for his conservative tendency to perceive all change as a change for the worse, Gloucester's account of widespread social discord must surely be taken as at least based on fact: 'These late eclipses in the sun and moon portend no good to us . . . Love cools, friendship falls off, brothers divide; in cities, mutinies; in countries, discord; in palaces, treason . . . there's son against father; the King falls from bias of nature: there's father against child' (I.ii.99–111). ' 'Tis strange', concludes the troubled Gloucester and exits, leaving Edmund to make things somewhat less so. Significantly, Edmund does not deny the extent of the discord, only Gloucester's mystified sense of its cause. In an earlier soliloquy Edmund has already repudiated 'the plague of custom . . . The curiosity of nations' which label him bastard (I.ii.3–4). Like Montaigne he insists that universal law is merely municipal law. . . . Here he goes further, repudiating the ideological process whereby the latter is misrecognised as the former; he rejects, that is, a way of thinking which represents the contingent as the necessary and thereby further represents human identity and the social order as metaphysically determined (and therefore unalterable): 'When we are sick in fortune, often the surfeits of our own behaviour, we make guilty of our disasters the sun, the moon, and stars; as if we were villains on necessity; fools by heavenly compulsion . . . by a divine thrusting on' (I.ii.122–31). Closely related to this refusal of the classical ideological effect is the way Edmund also denaturalises the theatrical effect: 'Pat! He comes like the catastrophe of the old comedy. My cue is villainous melancholy' (I.ii.128–9). Yet this revolutionary scepticism is discredited by the purpose to which it is put. How are we to take this? Are we to assume that Edmund is simply evil and therefore so is his philosophy? I want to argue that we need not. To begin with we have to bear in mind a crucial fact: Edmund's scepticism is made to serve an *existing* system of values; although he falls prey to, he does not introduce his society to its obsession with power, property and inheritance; it is already the material and ideological basis of that society. As such it in-forms the consciousness of Lear and Gloucester as much as Cornwall and Regan; consider Lear first, then Gloucester.

Lear's behaviour in the opening scene presupposes first, his absolute power, second, the knowledge that his being king constitutes that power, third, his refusal to tolerate what he perceives as a contradiction of that power. Therefore what Lear demands of

Cordelia — authentic familial kind-ness — is precluded by the very
terms of the demand; that is, by the extent to which the occasion as
well as his relationship to her is saturated with the ideological
imperatives of power. For her part Cordelia's real transgression is
not unkindness as such, but speaking in a way which threatens to
show too clearly how the laws of human kindness operate in the
service of property, contractual, and power relations:

> I love your Majesty
> According to my bond . . .

> I
> Return those duties back as are right fit . . .
> Why have my sisters husbands, if they say
> They love you [i.e. Lear] all?
> (i.i.91–2; 95–6; 98–9)

Presumably Cordelia does not intend it to be so, but this is
the patriarchal order in danger of being shorn of its ideological
legitimation — here, specifically, a legitimation taking ceremonial
form. (Ironically yet predictably, the 'untender' (l. 105) dimension
of that order is displaced on to Cordelia). Likewise with the whole
issue of dowries. Prior to Lear's disowning of Cordelia, the realities
of property marriage are more or less transmuted by the language
of love and generosity, the ceremony of good government. But in
the act of renouncing her, Lear brutally foregrounds the imperatives
of power and property relations: 'Here I disclaim all my paternal
care, Propinquity and property of blood' (i.i.112–13; cf. ll. 196–7).
Kenneth Muir glosses 'property' as 'closest blood relation' (Arden
ed. *King Lear* (1964), p. 11). Given the context of this scene it must
also mean 'ownership' — father owning daughter — with brutal
connotations of the master/slave relationship as in the following
passage from *King John*: 'I am too high-born to be *propertied*, To be
a . . . serving-man' (v.ii.79–81). Even kinship then — indeed *especially*
kinship — is in-formed by the ideology of property relations, the
contentious issue of primogeniture being, in this play, only its most
obvious manifestation. Later we witness Lear's correlation between
the quantity of retainers Goneril will allow him and the quality of
her love: Regan offers twenty-five retainers, upon which Lear tells
Goneril: 'I'll go with thee. Thy fifty yet doth double five-and-twenty,
And thou art twice her love' (ii.iv.257–9).

Gloucester's unconscious acceptance of this underlying ideology is conveyed at several points but nowhere more effectively than in Act II scene i; even as he is coming to terms with Edgar's supposed treachery he is installing Edmund in his place, offering in *exchange* for Edmund's 'natural' behaviour – property:

> of my land
> Loyal and natural boy, I'll work the means
> To make thee capable.
>   (II.i.83–5)

Thus the one thing which the kind Gloucester and the vicious Cornwall have in common is that each offers to reward Edmund's 'loyalty' in exactly the same way (cf. III.v.16–18). All this would be ludicrous if it were not so painful: as their world disintegrates Lear and Gloucester cling even more tenaciously to the only values they know, which are precisely the values which precipitated the disintegration. Hence even as society is being torn apart by conflict, the ideological structure which has generated that conflict is being reinforced by it.

When Edmund in the forged letter represents Edgar complaining of 'the oppression of aged tyranny' which commands 'not as it hath power, but as it is suffered' (I.ii.47–8), he exploits the same personal anxiety in Gloucester which Cordelia unintentionally triggers in Lear. Both fathers represent a challenge to their patriarchal authority by offspring as unnatural behaviour, an abdication of familial duty. The trouble is they do this in a society where 'nature' as ideological concept is fast losing its power to police disruptive elements – for example: 'That nature which contemns its origin Cannot be border'd certain in itself' (IV.ii.32–3). No longer are origin, identity and action a 'natural' ideological unity, and the disintegration of that unity reveals something of fundamental importance: when, as here (also, e.g. at I.ii.1–22) nature is represented as socially disruptive, yet elsewhere as the source of social stability (e.g. at II.iv.176–80), we see an ideological construct beginning to incorporate and thereby render visible the very conflicts and contradictions in the social order which it hitherto effaced. In this respect the play activates a contradiction intrinsic to any 'naturalised' version of the Christian metaphysic; to abandon or blur the distinction between matter and spirit while retaining the basic premises of that metaphysic is to eventually construe evil as at once utterly alien to the human condition (unnatural) yet disturbingly and mysteriously inherent within it (natural) and to be purged accordingly. If deep personal anxiety is thus symptomatic of more general social dislocation it is also what guarantees the general reaction formation to that dislocation: those in power react to crisis by entrenching themselves the deeper within the ideology and social organisation responsible for it.

At strategic points in the play we see how the minor characters have also internalised the dominant ideology. Two instances must suffice. The first occurs in Act II scene ii where Kent insults Oswald. He does so almost entirely in terms of the latter's lack of material wealth, his mean estate and consequent dependence upon service. Oswald is, says Kent, a 'beggarly, three-suited, hundred-pound, filthy, worsted-stocking . . . superserviceable . . . one-trunk-inheriting slave' (II.ii.15 ff; as Muir points out [in the Arden edition], servants were apparently given three suits a year, while gentlemen wore silk as opposed to worsted stockings). The second example involves the way that for the Gentleman attending Cordelia even pity (or more accurately 'Sorrow') is conceived as a kind of passive female commodity (IV.iii.16–23).[9]

We can now see the significance of Edmund's scepticism and its eventual relationship to this dominant ideology of property and power. Edmund's sceptical independence is itself constituted by a contradiction: his illegitimate exclusion from society gives him an insight into the ideological basis of that society even as it renders him vulnerable to and dependent upon it. In this respect Edmund resembles [other] malcontents [in Jacobean plays and literature]: exclusion from society gives rise both to the malcontent's sense of its worthlessness and his awareness that identity itself is dependent upon it. Similarly, Edmund, in liberating himself from the myth of innate inferiority, does not thereby liberate himself from his society's obsession with power, property and inheritance; if anything that obsession becomes the more urgent: 'Legitimate Edgar, I *must* have your land' (I.ii.16, my italics). He sees through one level of ideological legitimation only to remain the more thoroughly enmeshed with it at a deeper level.

Edmund embodies the process whereby, because of the contradictory conditions of its inception, a revolutionary (emergent) insight is folded back into a dominant ideology. Witnessing his fate we are reminded of how, historically, the misuse of revolutionary insight has tended to be in proportion to its truthfulness, and of how, as this very fact is obscured, the insight becomes entirely identified with (or as) its misappropriation. Machiavellianism, Gramsci has reminded us, is just one case in point (*Selections from Prison Notebooks* (London, tr., 1971), p. 136).

The Refusal of Closure

Lionel Trilling has remarked that 'the captains and kings and lovers and clowns of Shakespeare are alive and complete before they die' (*The Opposing Self* (New York, 1955), p. 38). Few remarks could be less true of *King Lear*. The notion of man as tragic victim somehow alive and complete in death is precisely the kind of essentialist mystification which the play refuses. It offers instead a decentring of the tragic subject which in turn becomes the focus of a more general exploration of human consciousness in relation to social being – one which discloses human values to be not antecedent to, but rather in-formed by, material conditions. *Lear* actually refuses then that autonomy of value which humanist critics so often insist that it ultimately affirms. Nicholas Brooke, for example, in one of the best close analyses of the play that we have, concludes by declaring; 'all moral structures, whether of natural order or Christian redemption, are invalidated by the naked fact of experience', yet manages in the concluding sentence of the study to resurrect from this unaccommodated 'naked experience' a redemptive autonomy of value, one almost mystically inviolable: 'Large orders collapse; but values remain, and are independent of them' (*Shakespeare: King Lear* (London, 1963), pp. 59–60). But surely in *Lear*, as in most of human history, 'values' are shown to be terrifyingly dependent upon whatever 'large orders' actually exist; in civil war especially – which after all is what *Lear* is about – the two collapse together.

   In the closing moments of *Lear* those who have survived the catastrophe actually attempt to recuperate their society in just those terms which the play has subjected to sceptical interrogation. There is invoked, first, a concept of innate nobility in contradistinction to innate evil and, second, its corollary: a metaphysically ordained justice. Thus Edgar's defeat of Edmund is interpreted as a defeat of an evil nature by a noble one. Also nobility is seen to be like truth – it will out: 'Methought thy very gait did prophesy A royal nobleness' (v.iii.175–6). Goneril is 'reduced' to her treachery ('read thine own evil', l. 156), while Edmund not only acknowledges defeat but also repents, submitting to Edgar's nobility (ll. 165–6) and acknowledging his own contrary nature (ll. 243–4). Next, Edgar invokes a notion of divine justice which holds out the possibility of rendering their world intelligible once more; speaking to Edmund of Gloucester, he says:

> The gods are just, and of our pleasant vices
> Make instruments to plague us:
> The dark and vicious place where thee he got
> Cost him his eyes.
>   (v.iii.170–3)

Thus is responsibility displaced; but perhaps Edgar is meant to wince as he says it since the problem of course is that he is making his society supernaturally intelligible at the cost of rendering the concept of divine justice so punitive and 'poetic' as to be, humanly speaking, almost unintelligible. Nevertheless Albany persists with the same process of recuperation by glossing thus the deaths of Goneril and Regan: 'This judgement of the heavens, that makes us tremble, Touches us not with pity' (v.iii.230–1). But when he cries 'The Gods defend her!' – i.e. Cordelia – instead of the process being finally consolidated we witness, even before he has finished speaking, Lear re-entering with Cordelia dead in his arms. Albany has one last desperate bid for recuperation, still within the old punitive/poetic terms:

> All friends shall taste
> The wages of their virtue, and all foes
> The cup of their deservings.
>   (v.iii.302–4)

Seconds later Lear dies. The timing of these two deaths must surely be seen as cruelly, precisely, subversive: instead of complying with the demands of formal closure – the convention which would confirm the attempt at recuperation – the play concludes with two events which sabotage the prospect of both closure and recuperation.

SOURCE: Chapter 12, *Radical Tragedy: Religion, Ideology and Power in the Drama of Shakespeare and his Contemporaries* (Brighton, 1984).

NOTES

Rearranged and renumbered from the original by editor.

1. Thus Irving Ribner (for example) argues that the play 'affirms justice in the world, which it sees as a harmonious system ruled by a benevolent God' *Patterns in Shakespearean Tragedy* (London, 1960), p. 117.

2. Other critics who embrace, invoke or imply the categories of essentialist humanism include the following: A. C. Bradley, *Shakespearean Tragedy* (London, 2nd ed., 1905), lectures 7 and 8; Israel Knox, *The Aesthetic Theories of Kant, Hegel and Schopenhauer* (New York, 1958), p. 117; Robert Ornstein, *The Moral Vision of Jacobean Tragedy* (Madison, Wisc., 1960), p. 264; Kenneth Muir, ed., *King Lear* (London, 1964), especially p. lv; Grigori Kozintsev, *King Lear: The Space of Tragedy*, tr. Mary Mackintosh (London, 1977), pp. 250–51. For the essentialist view with a pseudo-Nietzschean twist, see Michael Long, *The Unnatural Scene* (London, 1976), pp. 191–93.

Jan Kott suggests the way that the absurdist view exists in the shadow of a failed Christianity and a failed humanism – a sense of paralysis in the face of that failure (*Shakespeare Our Contemporary* (London, 1976), pp. 104, 108, 116–17).

3. Barbara Everett, 'The New *King Lear*', *Critical Quarterly*, 2(1960); William R. Elton, *King Lear and the Gods* (San Marino, Cal., 1968); Cedric Watts, 'Shakespearean Themes: The Dying God and the Universal Wolf', *Critical Dimensions*, ed. M. Curreli and A. Martino (Cuneo, 1978).

4. For John Danby, Cordelia is redemption incarnate; but can she really be seen as 'allegorically the root of individual and social sanity; tropologically Charity "that suffereth long and is kind"; analogically the redemptive principle itself'? (*Shakespeare's Doctrine of Nature* (London, 1949), p. 125; cf. p. 133).

5. Seneca, *Letters from a Stoic*, tr. Roy Campbell (Harmondsworth, 1969), p. 64.

6. Francis Bacon, *The Advancement of Learning*, in *Philosophical Works*, ed. John M. Robertson (London, 1905), p. 83.

7. Michel Montaigne, *Essays*, trans. John Florio (London, ed. 1965), III, 189.

8. In-form rather than determine: in this play material factors do not determine values in a crude sense; rather, the latter are shown to be dependent upon the former in a way which radically disqualifies the idealist contention that the reverse is true, namely, that these values not only survive the 'evil' but do so in a way which indicates their ultimate independence of it.

9. By contrast, compare Derek Traversi who finds in the imagery of this passage a 'sense of value, of richness and fertility ... an indication of redemption ... the poetical transformation of natural emotion into its spiritual distillation' (*An Approach to Shakespeare* (London, 3rd ed, 1969), II, 164).

Rosalie L. Colie   Studying
Shakespeare's Use of Genres   (1974)

I think it extremely important to locate a work within its genre, simply because genre offers a set of fairly fixed expectations by which to organize one's reaction to a work of literature. Though Croce[1] and new-critical theorists have marshaled strong arguments against a predestinating concept of extrinsic genres, Renaissance students have gradually gained sufficient confidence to insist upon the importance of genre at least for their fields. [E. D.] Hirsch has offered a concept of a work's 'intrinsic genre,' by which he seems to mean something very like the formal particularity attributed to any piece of work by linguistic structuralists. There can be, I suppose, as many intrinsic genres as there are works in existence – but even if that be so, our way of identifying intrinsic genres is by way of received extrinsic genres. I cannot, for instance, identify the genre, intrinsic or extrinsic, of *Troilus and Cressida*, and I remain puzzled by my own puzzlement in this case. I doubt if *Troilus and Cressida* is any more mixed in genre than *Cymbeline*, that comical-tragical-historical-pastoral play in the romance mode, or than *King Lear*; but *Troilus and Cressida*'s generic components are in such suspension that I cannot assign weight to them. I can identify them (I think), which makes it all the odder that I cannot really discuss the play in generic terms, as it certainly *should* be discussed. All this suggests that Mr. Hirsch is right: until we can assign a work within its genre, interpretation and criticism will not be directed to the play's fundamental problems.[2]

However important we find genres in literary interpretation and criticism, we cannot limit ourselves to *identifying* these genres. To read Julius Caesar Scaliger, or any of the great genre-critics of the Renaissance, one might get the notion that genre was viewed by literary men much as Michelangelo is said to have viewed the marble in which he worked, each piece of stone containing its own essential form, which it was the sculptor's job to liberate from its surrounding mass. Marble-hard, genre seems to resist the inferior technician (as the block that became the David resisted Bandinelli's hand), to submit only to the man who can discover its hidden form, clean and flawless. By such a critical theory, both theory and work of art disdain criticism and interpretation, confident of existing in a near-perfect world indifferent to audience, beholder, or reader.

Shakespeare offers a major argument against such a simplistic view of genre: his interest in the traditional aspects of his art lay precisely in their problematic nature, not in their stereotypical force. As I argue in [other] chapters [of this book] I think he worked from the hypothesis that the problematical in literary theory and practice has to do with the problematical in human life – that the letter exists to point the way to the spirit. No literary dictate can be allowed more importance than the specific demands of the imagination working on a specific problem – but also, an imagination cannot work on its problems *without* recourse to its intellectual and artistic environment, to its literary and moral correlatives. Shakespeare's work relies upon his means of expression for its 'meaning,' and in turn those means of expression are not neutral or empty forms. They too have their context of ideas, so that literary meanings, in this period at the very least, reach out to involve moral and social situations larger than the containments of a single play or poem. Dependent also practically and aesthetically upon what [E. H.] Gombrich has called 'the beholder's share',[3] Shakespeare could not have allowed himself the luxury, even if his temperament had permitted such self-indulgence, of attempting perfection in a world of platonic forms. Like Spenser, though very differently, Shakespeare accepted the mixed nature of living, the varieties of becoming, as the matter of literary works. For him, literary materials were not Michelangelo's marble.[4] He worked them as if they were clay, to be shaped into the likeness of life – or shaped, like Adam, into life itself. And like the sculptor's clay, Shakespere's materials came out of different crocks and were formed of different earths – that is, they came from different categorical and schematic sources, to be combined and recombined as imaginative and technical needs found practical.

On the whole, though Shakespeare's plays are notoriously and gloriously mixed in genre, their dramatic generic associations are usually clearly marked. In *The Winter's Tale* we cannot miss what is 'tragic', what 'comic', nor can we miss noticing how these two are conjoined under a pastoral umbrella. The non-dramatic genres are usually less clearly visible: in *Romeo and Juliet* the nondramatic generic contribution of sonneteering *is* manifest; far less so, although there it is far more important, in *Othello*. In *Love's Labour's Lost, inter alia*, we can recognize the generic shadow cast by the Renaissance dialogue both in the topics and in the interaction of characters in the play. In a later comedy, *Much Ado About Nothing*, debate has been animated, much as the convention of sonnet-criticism was in Shakespeare's *Sonnets*, into personality, so that debate- and dialogue-points are worked out in the dramatic action between Beatrice and Benedick, not argued pro and contra as in *Love's Labour's Lost*. Finally, in *Hamlet* we see and hear the debate reduced to a *device*, albeit an extremely important one, as Hamlet, that studious princeling, formulates his great soliloquy in scholastic terms. But the terms of his soliloquy on life and death, on living and dying, on action and retirement, are not such as to indicate his studious temperament only, though they surely do that; they are Hamlet's casuistic maneuvre to objectify and distance, for a while at least, an overwhelming and immediate life-problem.

In *Love's Labour's Lost*, the dialogue informs much of the play's structure, as the characters work out their comical destinies in a parody of the orthodox form. By no stretch of the imagination, for all its dialectics, could we call *Hamlet* generically a debate, of body and soul, of action and contemplation, important and problematical though those questions are in the play. On the other hand, *The Winter's Tale is* unmistakably a tragicomedy – more obviously so, for instance, than *Cymbeline*, a play which it resembles, and differently so from the terms laid down for the form by Guarini [1537 – 1612], the inventor of the genre. How free Shakespeare was in his generic experiments and manipulations we can read from Bernard Weinberg's important study of *Cinquecento* literary criticism:[5] genre-theory governed thinking about literature, so much so that it had to be altered, with enormous polemic, every time a major work failed to fit generic categories (the *Commedia*, *Orlando Furioso*, *Il Pastor Fido*). Although the contours of the theory of genres changed under the impact of new forms, in fact its ideology did not – Mazzoni's defence of Dante, Guarini's of pastoral drama, Pigna's of romance all insisted on an enlarged canon of acceptable generic categories, never questioning the rightness of genre-threory. In subsequent arguments about the precise nature of tragicomedy and its difference from comitragedy,[6] the clear assumption is present that each genre is somehow unique, and that distinctions between genres can be spelled out. But no such assumption governs Shakespeare's mixtures: though *The Winter's Tale* is tragicomic, neither Guarini nor Pontanus would have allowed it as exemplary, so idiosyncratic is it. Shakespeare's generic mixtures are remarkably independent of rule; however clearly we can see their practical connections with theoretical problems consciously raised by others, their freedom from orthodoxy and academicism remains their most engaging quality. Literary *dicta* were in the air, certainly, called up by the literary problems they were formulated to solve, but they seem never to have dictated to our playwright, who conspicuously flaunts his freedom and originality, even in the way he *interprets* literary problems, to say nothing of the solutions he found.

In [my] book, I am not sure whether I am offering 'interpretation' or 'criticism', recently wedged so far apart by theorists, though I hope to provide both; I am trying, in a sense slightly different from the ordinary one, to offer by example *explications de texte*, a way of explaining why a text is as it is and has taken the particular form it has. Although this requires recognizing literary forms as they appear in given works – requires, then, some sense of literary history – I do not in the least mean to imply that the naming of parts is sufficient tribute to any significant literary work. Rather, I think that what the parts *do* for and in the literary work is what counts, both as interpretation and as criticism. It matters that, just before taking her potion, Juliet utters a systematic meditation on death such as Louis Martz has taught us to recognize;[7] it matters that both Ophelia and Perdita, in very different styles and in very different contexts, imaginatively invoke a catalogue of flowers to 'match' the characters from a stranger world who intrude upon their private celebrations.

To develop a familiar example along these lines, Shakespeare offers us in the *Henry IV* plays a splendid creation, Sir John Falstaff, very different from the real and legendary Sir John Oldcastle, sometime companion to Prince Henry. *Why* this Falstaff? Some of the answer lies in the sources of the narrative. In the chronicles and onstage young Henry V had been fixed into a certain shape – a knobby, irregular, inconsistent shape, to be sure, but a shape firm enough to demand fairly strict *mimesis*. His madcap youth, his subservience to his father before and after the deathbed episode with the crown, his exemplary conduct as healer of national breaches and victor over foreign dangers were all fully established: Henry V was 'this star of England', the fulfilment of Respublica's long-thwarted hopes. It was difficult to find in the sources the resources to give this English princeling depth of character; some other means had to be found – so Falstaff was evolved as foil to a prince for whom there were insufficient conventional guidelines.

The prince was very 'given', in the factual ways of the literary *milieux* in which Shakespeare found him, the chronicles, chronicle-poems (*Mirror for Magistrates* and Daniel's *Civill Wars*), and a morality chronicle-play (*The Famous Victories*). For Falstaff the opposite is the case: brilliant studies have identified some of the many literary streams which conjoined to feed his substantial shape. We recognize in him the braggart soldier, the parasite, and the *buffone* of Latin comedy, *commedia erudita*, and *commedia dell' arte*;[8] we recognize in him (as does the English Hal) the Vice of the morality play,[9] *Mundus* with his *Infans*, Gluttony, Appetite, Riot, and the rest of the temptations besetting this important prodigal son; we recognize in him the Lord of Misrule and Carnival of folkish and medieval festivals;[10] we recognize in him, too, the *Roi des sots* of medieval *sottie*, the court-jester accompanying a ruler,[11] and the complex, critical, paradoxical ways of the Renaissance fool.[12] We recognize in this *puer senex* who insists on the privileges, both of youth and of age, in a particular person: Falstaff. Paradoxically, then, this remarkable mixture of generic characters and stereotypes, this man made of whole cloth (buckram) who seems to be, literarily at least, 'all the world', is far more mimetically 'real' than the actual young man of history whose companion he is.

And what an extraordinary, exceptional exemplar he is of all these types! – a *miles gloriosus* whose brags are transparent, even arranged to suit the prince's expectation, who, when faced with a 'real' braggart soldier from the repertory, Pistol, fearlessly drives him offstage; a parasite not just upon a powerful status-figure but also, *literally*, upon a hostel-keeper and a bawd; a Riot, a Master of the Revels, whose chief reveler knows throughout the game that it must one day end for good; a fool whose folly mocks himself as surely as it mocks king and royal justice; a devil whose temptations to this heir-apparent turn out to be as unavailing with that chill and distanced young man as Satan's importuning of Christ in the wilderness. Like Erasmus' Folly, Falstaff keeps us all off-balance – all save the prince, who knows even before the play begins that the revels must be ended and their master turned out of the game. In a final turning, perhaps owing something to the traditions of the morality-play, this *chevalier sans cheval*,[13] this riotous glutton, this fool is shown to be off-balance too, surprised by the forms of worldliness his tender lambkin now displays.

By both the morality reading and the Machiavellian reading, the *Henry IV* plays are a mirror of princes, a study in rulers' regimen, where we watch a young man learning to rule his nation, growing into his kingship, building his character into its ultimate calling. But much of this character-building is Shakespeare's, who shows us an increasingly able Hal simply by putting him in relation to various symbolic characters in the play; from these arrangements we see where Hal starts. He is characteristically 'between':[14] between Falstaff, the festive mock-king, and grim, lamenting, businesslike Henry IV; between Falstaff, a braggart soldier forced into the field, and another glorious soldier, the over-heroic Hotspur, who throws his cause away for the 'honour' Falstaff has the good sense to reject; between Falstaff, careless of his master's cause and of human life ('tush, man, mortal men, mortal men'), and Prince John of Lancaster, so careful of polity that he cares not for his pledged word or for human life; between Falstaff, openly flaunting his cheating, and that intransigent servant of the king, the Lord Chief Justice. These pairings serve to identify for us a prince who, though he does not really develop in the play, is seen responding to more and more situations; even more important are those situations in which Hal is, as it were, bounced off Falstaff himself. From these we learn, unexpectedly, how like the two are. They share real distaste for responsibility. Though Hal bites the biter Falstaff in the Gadshill episode, they are alike in the pleasure they take in deviancy, alike in their different parodies of the highborn robberies in the kingdom at large. Their joint misrule speaks to England's condition: the jests at Eastcheap (for all their underworld character), furthermore, have an innocence which the king and the plotters have long since forfeited. Both Hal and Falstaff are Machiavellian, manipulating others (Mistress Quickly, Francis, Poins) and each other, enigmatically in the buckram exchange after Gadshill, tolerantly in the judgment-scene and in Hal's permitting Falstaff to steal his honour in Hotspur's death. Though the plays make quite clear that Hal once crowned has no intention of condoning Falstaff, from Hal's first soliloquy, *via* Falstaff's impressment of men and dealings with Justice Shallow and Mistress Quickly, to the morality harshness of 'I know thee not, old man,' they also unequivocally show Hal's enjoyment of Falstaff and, before the prince's final departure to labour in his vocation, his *need* for a figure of diversion, to take the sting out of his own rebellion against rank, to provide outlet for his dissatisfactions with the quality of life at his father's court. What Falstaff offers Prince Hal is not only the symbolic freedoms of youth, but also a chance to practice at being human.

Shifting the level of discussion from the play itself to the making of the play, we can see how Shakespeare found refuge from a ticklish literary problem in the acomplishments of his profession. From his models, those static chronicles and poems from which he took his story, he had little to go on to make of his prince a credible personality, as he had so brilliantly managed with Richard II; neither had he in Hal's life a steady progression toward ever-greater success, a dramatic paradigm such as that offered by Richard's magnificient fall from fortune. The *schemata* to hand were simply insufficient to make this real king into a dramatic character; so the playwright had to turn elsewhere, to other dramatic contexts, and to make from the jumble of *schemata* available to him a figure (out of whole cloth, wholly out of cloth) allied with and foil to the Lusty Juventus who will, like his medieval forebear, ultimately redeem the time he spent in alehouse anarchy, as well as the time wasted in a misgoverned nation.

To think of Falstaff in connection with these denatured types is in part to denature him of his earthy reality, so convincing is the illusion that this particular character is a real individual. Not for nothing did Prince Hal want to pass the time till Falstaff should arrive, nor Queen Elizabeth want him back (at least, on the stage) after his banishment. This unmetaphored figure for the world ('all the world'), the flesh ('Ribs', 'Tallow', belly), and the devil ('old white-bearded Satan'), this voluntary anti-courtly fool forcing the problematics of public life upon us as upon the prince, gives form, in his very bulk and anarchic denial of all forms, to the dialectic which propels Hal out of Eastcheap to Shrewsbury and, finally, to Westminster and the responsibilities of Respublica. Quite simply, as we can see, though nature influences art, art influences art more: Shakespeare's success in making a 'realer' person out of the art-generated Falstaff than of the actual Henry Plantagenet is a primary example of the Aristotelian notion that poetry is more powerful than history.

The 'comical-tragical-historical method' of this play,[15] to say nothing of its satirical component too, will not have escaped notice. As Falstaff is compounded of character-types from different decorums, and brings something of all those decorums into the play with him, so is this a 'mungrell' play, the mingling of kings and clowns that Sidney so deplored. Of what is it made, after all? – a usurping King; Falstaff as burlesque player-king; chivalric Hotspur out of professional epic; the political magician Glendower and his lyrical daughter, out of romance; the tavern-frequenters out of city-pamphlets of city-roguery, with Hal moving enigmatically among them to claim a place and voice, after testing his own voice against under-skinker's and Hotspur's, as his own. As [W.] Empson long ago observed,[16] the superhistorical effect of this is to give the impression that all England is somehow involved in the play as Hal progresses to his exemplary rule: the literary decorums drawn on for the play imply a national culture of great complexity and offer a symbolic texture we may take as the thing itself.

* * *

Let the prince and Falstaff in their prodigality stand for a moment as metaphor for the poet's own prodigality: Shakespeare throws away more than most poets manage to put in, so that the student of his works and of Renaissance culture often feels (as [A. N.] Whitehead said of Plato) that wherever he goes, he meets Shakespeare coming back. But because the concealments of his art are very great, it is not always obvious beneath the more-than-sufficient play itself that there are literary and literary-theoretical problems just under the surface. Sometimes the problems seem submerged because we can recognize them only after long study; sometimes because Shakespeare took them for granted as we cannot, and therefore had no need to stress them; sometimes because critical concepts and their basic materials are so entirely transformed and digested into new forms (as in *Henry IV*) that they are not readily identifiable.

Most important of all, we often miss the literary-critical component of Shakespeare's work because he was doing so much else in his plays which has, as it ought to have, prior claim on our attention. At all ranges, he was prodigal, and we cannot take in everything at once. His illusionism, for instance, forces us to attend to different, often more naturalistic, aspects of his work from those more closely formal and conventional. Shakespeare's prodigality is balanced by his economies: sometimes he took incredible risks with materials and forms, forcing them far beyond their normal limits (the pastoral

pattern in *King Lear*; the sonnets to the lady); sometimes he altered
a 'source' or form minimally and nonetheless set his mark on it
(e.g., Rosalind's behaviour in the forest; Perdita's language at the
sheep-shearing; Parolles' virginity-speech). Read against the works
of most of his contemporaries, Shakespeare's plays show great
powers of naturalistic illusionism; his generosity in this respect is
manifest over and over again. The Nurse's great speech on Juliet's
broken brow calls up the whole domestic and psychological life of
the Nurse a decade before the play takes place – material, we realize
abruptly, with no particular relevance to the play; until we come to
understand what the Nurse's realistic, affectionate, lifelong picture
of Juliet does to modify Romeo's extraordinary language of idealiz-
ation. In the Queen Mab speech, Mercutio's wit and invention are
displayed in a set-piece, an aria, on a theme irrelevant to the plot's
action – after all, Romeo and Juliet never have time to be properly
visited by Queen Mab, which is part of the sadness of their situation.
But the speech is all the same fundamental to the theme of brilliant
youthfulness and to the sociological setting of these glittering,
imaginative, under-employed young men. From that speech we get
something else, too, aslant of the main action but supportive to the
play's theme: that is, a different sense of the wastefulness of the
foolish feud. As much as the deaths of Juliet and her Romeo, so
young and so alive, the waste of a man like Mercutio cries out for
civil settlement of the old men's vendetta. In this case, what seems
to be the overflow of prodigal invention turns out to have its own
economies: that contradictory double gift of prodigality and economy
Shakespeare displayed over and over again. The evidently tedious
Polonius is a good example of the way in which the playwright
communicates the ethos of an entire family, so that the behaviour
and fates of Laertes and Ophelia become more realistically intelligible
to us, once we know the father's expressions of value and modes of
behaviour.

In language, Shakespeare is as prodigal and as economical,
throwing away lines, speeches, even whole scenes. Whenever we
pause over language, we can see the ways in which apparently
careless lines and speeches support character, further plot, and stress
theme. Imagery tends to work on behalf of the play, as studies from
Miss Spurgeon's to Heilman's, Foakes', Clemen's, and Charney's
bear out.[17] But in addition, Shakespeare can, with the utmost
economy, make his language do two very different things at the

same time: he can write, for instance, an exchange between two characters which perfectly matches both characters' assigned roles and in which also one speaker (Hal, Hamlet, Edgar, Lear, in Zitner's examples),[18] without abandoning his own role or losing his sense of his interlocutor's, speaks through and beyond mere role to appeal to the responsible humanity of his hearer. Lear's press-money speech is, at one manifest level, the disjunctive utterance of an insane old man, an insane old king. It is also highly rational and organized, with classical references – but it takes a bit of distancing to see how that is so.[19] Hamlet's recorder speech, at first hearing so casual, so chancy, so whirling, focuses to comment on the human instrumentalism and manipulation that is a particular theme as well as a major plot-element of this play.

As his language is multiple, so is his use of conventional device. When Lear says to Cordelia, 'And fire us hence like foxes', a great deal is called up in that short phrase – farmers putting fire down foxholes to destroy the predators; Samson's trick with the foxes and the corn; the little destroyers of Canticles; the conventional morality which sent the doomed and damned to hellfire. To take an example different in kind, much like the Falstaff example, Iago is a masterpiece of mysterious psychological analysis, but he is also a stage machiavel, as such related to another Old Nick, the morality devil, characteristically a presenter of plots and playlets. We know this from [Bernard] Spivack's book,[20] but we must not forget that Iago is also a parasite, a malcontent, a Brighella,[21] and a braggart soldier as well. Further, as Falstaff also persuades us of a real past, involving Clement's Inn and the revels of Mile-end Green as well as the difficulties of the flea-bitten, down-at-heels, out-at-elbows gentry, so Iago has his correlatives in real life, a new man, a technician making his fortune in a world of changing opportunities by his practical skills and his sense of empirical adaptation. Hamlet is forced to cry revenge, like many another son stuck with a vendetta, but he is also – *why?* – marked with Montaigne's tendency to consideration and doubt. Unlike Montaigne [1533–92], though, he has the malcontent's sharp vision and sharp tongue. In Falstaff, Iago, and Hamlet many different traditions are gathered up, dramatic and nondramatic, to make highly successful theatrical figures. By combining traditions, sometimes in very simple ways, Shakespeare demonstrates his prodigality and the economy that results from that generosity: he had, evidently, no fear of running out of creativity, could pour out his invention like wine, the wine of Cana at that, multiplying to need. *Multum in parvo*: and in something already large, like a play, how much more!

Critically speaking, this compressed, allusive, suggestive pluralism can be seductive and misleading. Because Shakespeare said so much, and this 'much' all at once, it has been easy for readers of his works to assume that, in criticizing or commenting upon them, anything goes: works so inclusive *must* be hospitable, the justification seems to run, to *any* interpretation. So the wildest personal associations with the text can be considered to make some sense; indeed, in extreme instances, the critic can be enjoined to misunderstand the text to create a new insight of his own.

Well, anything did not go into the plays, so it does not make sense to assume that they send random messages out. With a little care and a little learning (small Latin helps here!), one can see what went in and, from that recognition, can even begin to see *why* certain things went in. Further, because of his peculiar openness to the mysteries of his craft and to his audience, Shakespeare played fair, providing us every time with directions to the literary or extraliterary context from which he drew – not, like [Ben] Jonson [1572–1637], as our schoolmaster, but simply as our playwright, communicating and sharing his insights into his (and our) culture. Shakespeare was neither pedant nor obscurantist nor monopolist: what he took from his culture he gave back with both hands, enriched, transvalued, transfigured.

To take forms – devices, stereotypes, genres, etc. – seriously is both to honour and to criticize them, to involve one's self in the very morality of one's craft. Shakespeare mocked, for instance, conventional forms of expression: in *Love's Labour's Lost*, figurative languages; in *Henry V*, bombast; in *Hamlet*, both stiff and pliable languages of courts. A master of stylistic alternatives, he could parody, could imitate, could write in counterpointed styles, could even 'invent' languages; but, excellent as he was at this aspect of his art, he did not do it for *epideixis* alone. In his work, linguistic habits always relate to ways of life, style to morality;[22] by his literary comments, Shakespeare offers, in entirely *literary* terms, moral commentary as well. So with ideas and themes, conventions, genres, modes: he looked 'through' them in more than one sense, as in *King Lear* he saw through the most ordinary rhetorical-moral paradoxes to far deeper moral meanings. The forms were transparent for him –

in Donne's word, 'throughshine' – and in turn become transparent for us. By seeing to the center of his professional artifices, he could present a familiar scheme without losing either its artificiality or its 'truth', so that literature itself can be experienced as at once a 'new' aesthetic experience and a critical experience. We see it anew, renewed, so that, for instance, the familiar triad of the world, the flesh, and the devil is forever unmetaphored and incorporated in Falstaff, and we know from Falstaff's very particularity how common, even commonplace, 'temptation' can be. It would be false to *moralize* Falstaff simply – false to the complex aesthetic experience, false to the sense of layered, interlocking life which the *Henry IV* plays communicate; but the moral *situation*, in all its problematic complexity, is precisely what is conveyed.

With all this to work on, offered in such fascinatingly literary terms, the literary critic has his hands full: a pluralism offering so many ways to understand art is itself the best argument against the proliferation of private visions, unregulated by textual respect, to which we are nowadays so often tempted.

SOURCE: Sections II and III òf the Introduction, *Shakespeare's Living Art* (Princeton, 1974), pp. 14–27.

NOTES

1. [Editor's note: See G. N. G. Orsini, *Benedetto Croce, Philosopher of Art and Literary Critic* (Carbondale, Ill., 1961).]

2. For 'intrinisic genres,' see E. D. Hirsch, *Validity in Interpretation* (New Haven, 1966), pp. 78–89; see also pp. 89–126, on genre; and pp. 127–207, on interpretation and criticism. [Editor's note: Sherman Hawkins gives a fine argument for considering Shakespeare's genres in 'The Two Worlds of Shakespearean Comedy', *Shakespeare Studies*, III (1967), 62–80.]

3. *Art and Illusion* (London, 1962), pp. 181–290. Important applications and extensions of this principle to literature are provided in the recent work of Stanley Fish, Paul Alpers, and Stephen Booth.

4. Nor, really, was Michelangelo so platonic as is usually supposed: I am indebted for help on this point to D. D. Ettlinger, Sears R. Jayne, and Gavriel Moses.

5. *A History of Italian Literary Criticism in the Renaissance* (Chicago, 1960).

6. See Colie, *Shakespeare's Living Art*, pp. 261–65.

7. *The Poetry of Meditation* (New Haven, 1954).

8. J. W. Draper, 'Falstaff and the Plautine Parasite', *Classical Journal*, XXXIII (1938), 390–401; D. C. Boughner, 'Traditional Elements in Falstaff',

JEGP, xliii (1944), 417–28; and 'Vice, Braggart, and Falstaff', *Anglia*, lxxii (1954), 35–61; D. B. Landt, 'The Ancestry of Sir John Falstaff', *Shakespeare Quarterly*, xvii (1966), 69–76; E. E. Stoll, *Shakespeare Studies* (New York, 1942); Northrop Frye, 'The Argument of Comedy', *English Institute Essays* (New York, 1949).

9. J. Dover Wilson, *The Fortunes of Falstaff* (Cambridge, 1943). See also James Monaghan, 'Falstaff and his Forebears', *Studies in Philology*, xviii (1921), 353–61.

10. C. L. Barber, *Shakespeare's Festive Comedy* (Princeton, 1959).

11. Enid Welsford, *The Fool* (London, 1935); J. W. Draper, 'Falstaff as Fool and Jester', *Modern Language Quarterly*, vii (1946), 453–62.

12. Walter Kaiser, *Praisers of Folly* (Cambridge, Mass., 1963), pp. 195–275.

13. Harry Levin, 'Falstaff Uncolted', *Modern Language Notes*, lxi (1946), 305–10.

14. Kaiser's discussions of Falstaff are particularly helpful on this point.

15. See Gareth Lloyd Evans' article in *Early Shakespeare*, ed. John Russell Brown and Bernard Harris (London, 1961), pp. 154–63.

16. *Some Versions of Pastoral* (reprinted New York, 1960).

17. Caroline Spurgeon, *Shakespeare's Imagery and What It Tells Us* (Cambridge, 1935); Robert B. Heilman, *This Great Stage* (Baton Rouge, 1948); and *Magic in the Web* (Lexington, 1956); R. A. Foakes, 'Suggestions for a New Approach to Shakespeare's Imagery', *Shakespeare Survey*, v (1952); Wolfgang Clemen, *The Development of Shakespeare's Imagery* (London, 1951); Maurice Charney, *Shakespeare's Roman Plays* (Cambridge, Mass., 1961); and *Style* in *Hamlet* (Princeton, 1969).

18. S. P. Zitner, [unpublished] 'Shakespeare's Secret Language', develops this point.

19. See Edmund Blunden, 'Shakespeare's Significances', in *Shakespeare Criticism, 1915–1935*, ed. Anne Ridler (London, 1962), pp. 326–42, and Zitner, '*King Lear* and its Language', in *Some Facets of King Lear*, ed. R. L. Colie and F. T. Flahiff (Toronto and London, 1974), pp. 3–22.

20. Bernard Spivack, *Shakespeare and the Allegory of Evil* (New York, 1958).

21. For this, I am indebted to June Fellows.

22. See Colie, *Shakespeare's Living Art*, chapters 1 and 4, for fuller discussion.

E. A. J. Honigmann   Impressions of
'Character'   (1976)

[Study of an audience's response to Shakespeare's plays] takes us beyond character. But [such studies] refer back to character, directly or indirectly, since a play's every word is channelled through a dramatic speaker. We must therefore consider the mode of existence of a dramatic character, and ask how an audience engages with a Hamlet or Lear. In this chapter I shall argue that in creating his tragic heroes Shakespeare often used impressionistic devices that leave the spectator in uncertainties. Just as Troilus exclaims 'this is, and is not, Cressid' (v.ii.144), we are bewildered by the Hamlet or Lear that we think we know: I propose to examine our relationship with the characters, our special ways of 'knowing' them, after which we shall be ready to ask more searchingly how we respond. It will be assumed that the reader is familiar with recent work on dramatic character – with historical criticism and with the replies it provoked.[1] And, now that the historical dust has settled, I shall also assume that we may guardedly speak of Shakespeare's character as life-like.

Whilst no self-respecting critic will henceforth wish to place Shakespeare's stage-persons on a psychiatrist's couch, to fish in imagined minds for a past that never was, a psychological or 'natural' bias still remains appropriate when we discuss a play's insistently life-like characters. If Shakespeare invites us to attend to the motives and inner self of a stage Hamlet it behoves us so to attend, and, as generations of theatre-goers have found, we can do this without getting into philosophical difficulties. When the play begins we don't ask awkward either/or questions about the stage-person's ontological status ('Is it Hamlet?', 'Is it Burbage?'), we settle instinctively for a compromise ('It's Burbage-as-Hamlet'), and we willingly allow the unique stage-person to have as many gestures, speeches and motives as the dramatist chooses. In saying this I am not arguing that we think of Shakespeare's characters as 'real persons' but only that when so directed we may evaluate a Hamlet's behaviour very much as we do a next-door neighbour's, with certain obvious reservations.

Shakespeare's plays, and especially his tragedies, require us to take an interest in motive, and often say so.

                              I do not know
          Why yet I live to say 'This thing's to do'
                                         (*Hamlet* iv.iv.43–4)

          Will you, I pray, demand that demi-devil
          Why he hath thus ensnar'd my soul and body?
                                         (*Othello* v.ii.304–5)

          Is there any cause in nature that makes these hard hearts?
                                         (*King Lear* iii.vi.76–8)

Even when the question 'Why?' is not so pointedly raised, an
audience cannot fail to grasp that the most casual remark may
illuminate a speaker's motives, since the dialogue never goes on for
long without signalling some kind of self-betrayal. Shakespeare's
language, whilst usually far from life-like, compels the audience to
look beneath the verbal surface and suggests a life-like inwardness
in the dramatic speaker.

This inwardness has caused a great deal of trouble.[2] May we
reasonably ascribe an 'inner self' to Hamlet and contend, say, that
conscientious scruples of which he himself remains unaware prevent
him from killing Claudius? To look for such unconscious or secret
motives, we are sometimes told, is to misunderstand a dramatic
character's mode of being. 'We persist in digging for them', it has
been said, 'but what happens usually is that our spade goes through
the other side of the drama'.[3] In other words, in pursuing secret
motives we go outside the play, and therefore waste everyone's time;
we are guilty of critical loitering with intent. Yet we might argue
that the merest hints that Othello suffers from a sense of social
insecurity, or Iago from a grudge against upper-class privilege,[4]
function as impressions, just as barely audible noises function as
noises; and in dramatic composition 'the impression is the fact'.
Even if Othello or Iago remains unaware of his own motive, and
the other characters fail to detect it, a dramatist can still reveal it to
the audience: and should this sound like a brazen assertion, one
that cannot be proved or disproved, secret motives being too slippery
to get hold of or to squeeze till they pop, let us remember that many
motives in drama are kept secret *for a time* and yet the audience
knows all about them.[5] Long before any of the *dramatis personae* say
so, we know that Orsino loves 'Cesario', that Cassio admires Othello
as his 'dear general', that Macbeth will not grieve when Lady
Macbeth dies. Secret motives are a standard feature of Shakespeare's

plays. Though they work more deviously in tragedy than in comedy, the fact that some are more secret than others need not mean that in digging for them 'our spade goes through the other side of the drama' but only that those who tunnel in dark places will occasionally lose their way.

The argument about secret motives resembles another one which also bears on our way of 'knowing' a dramatic character. The action of the play is the only reality, we are sometimes warned, and to try to go behind it is futile. What were the relations of Hamlet and Ophelia before Act I? 'The answer is, there were none. Outside of the play, previous to the opening of its action, Hamlet and Ophelia do not exist'.[6] Like secret motives, the previous relations of Hamlet and Ophelia are said to lie outside the play. How, then, do we define a play's *inside*? If the action of a play is the only reality, what precisely do we mean by *action*? Ophelia describes a visit from Hamlet which might be sited outside the play: 'My lord, as I was sewing in my closet . . .' (ii.ii.77ff.) Yes, the visit supposedly took place off-stage. But we hear Ophelia speak of it inside the play, and that makes a difference. The outside can be brought inside; or, more accurately, those inside may look outside and their statements about off-stage events will nevertheless remain securely within the play. (Such statements, moreover, could fairly count as part of the play's *action*, like all the other dialogue, since speech is one kind of action, arguably the most important kind in Shakespeare's tragedies.) Having heard that Hamlet importuned Ophelia with love, gave her remembrances and so on, spectators need not, after all, apologise if they catch themselves wondering about the couple's previous relations, as Shakespeare himself directs attention to the past *inside the play*. Unlicensed speculation would be futile, but, on the other hand, to refuse to take account of what is inside the play seems no less irresponsible.

As will have become clear, it is prudent to think of all outside events reported in a play as *reports* rather than as off-stage *events*, irrespective of their timing before the opening or between the acts or scenes. The reports 'exist', exactly like the other dialogue, and audiences respond to these reports as to other stage-impressions, evaluating them in the light of all the available evidence. Ophelia tells of Hamlet's frightening visit (ii.i.75ff.); there are no reasons to disbelieve the details (the doublet unbraced, stockings fouled, piteous look) but, having heard less than a hundred lines earlier that Hamlet might 'put an antic disposition on', we cannot help wondering whether she misunderstood an antic happening. Claudius describes recent political upheavals (i.ii.1ff.), Hamlet laments his mother's marriage (i.ii.129ff.), the Ghost discloses a murder most foul (i.v.9ff.); in these and many other reports we sense the speaker's special interest in an off-stage event and only partly believe him; and when different reporters express very different attitudes to the same events, as in the three instances just mentioned, we evaluate even more cautiously. Listening to reports we don't dispute their validity within the imaginative structure, though we may still refuse to believe what we hear.

Shakespeare's characters are also life-like in being presented to us from many points of view, which we have to piece together. When we compare another great dramatist interested in 'natural' effects, say Ibsen, we observe that Shakespeare's secondary persons distort the image of the hero much more, that the hero sees himself in more variously distorted ways, and that consequently, having to work harder to synthesise our impressions, our reward is a more genuinely complex understanding of character. Take Ibsen's Halvard Solness and Shakespeare's Lear, two autocrats challenged and destroyed by the younger generation. Some of the master-builder's closest associates think him a self-willed tyrant (his wife, his employees Knut and Ragnar Brovik), whilst two young girls who know him less well worship him as a hero (Kaja Fosli and Hilde Wangel); he himself, aware of both views, believes the former to be correct, at least as far as his recent career is concerned, but, infected by Hilde's enthusiasm, tries to live up to his heroic image by climbing the new tower built by his men, and falls to his death. Though things are complicated by Solness' conviction that his wife thinks him mad, more or less all the images of Ibsen's hero belong to one of two kinds, each of which seems fixed and static until quite near the end, when Solness himself attempts to bring the two closer together. As seen by other characters, Lear also presents two kinds of image, favourable and unfavourable, but both change, and sometimes we switch from one to another at bewildering speed. Goneril and Regan describe him publicly as 'dearer than eyesight', then privately as rash, unruly, unconstant (i.i); Goneril next complains that every hour 'he flashes into one gross crime or other' (i.iii). Progressive antagonism cannot go much farther, and the sisters thereafter talk of Lear from a 'fixed' point of view, as old and foolish. The more interesting prismatic effects come from those who are loosely considered Lear's friends, and from Lear himself. Cordelia claims that she loves him according to her bond (which her asides prove an understatement) (I.i), and later thinks him her 'poor father', treated worse than 'mine enemy's dog', yet addresses him as 'my royal lord' (IV.vii). The split between her private image of Lear and the one she publicly subscribes to thus creates a double exposure similar to Goneril and Regan's at the beginning, a not uncommon fragmentation in Shakespeare. Kent, himself a double image as Kent-Caius, clings to his vision of 'royal Lear' in two important scenes (III.ii, III.iv 1–108) where no one else present sees Lear steadily as he once was, and thus superimposes majesty on the stage-image of the frantic, dishevelled old man. But if Cordelia's private view of her 'dear father' and Kent's of his 'master' shed light from two different directions that are not too far apart, the Fool, scrambling together the oddest assortment of attitudes, views him from another angle entirely. He refers to the king as one who put down his own breeches, a pretty fellow, an O without a figure, a sheal'd peascod, a hedge-sparrow, an obedient father (I.iv), and so on: all derisive images, certainly, but each one presents a startlingly original perception that we have to relate to Cordelia's dear father, Kent's master and all other verbal and stage impressions. And as well as these sharply individualised images of Lear seen from the outside we must take into account the uncertainties of his inner vision. 'Who is it that can tell me who I am?' he asks, and soon projects himself in various mutually incompatible ways – as loving father and irate king (II.iv.99–100) or as one who kneels and curses (II.iv.150–66).

Others might wish to speak more positively for Ibsen; and Lear, I readily admit, looks like a special case, in so far as he suffers from more radical confusions than, for instance, Brutus or Macbeth. Nevertheless, though Shakespeare exploits his prismatic technique in special ways in *King Lear*, all his tragic heroes experience 'identity problems' and all are presented in richly diversified images. The spectator therefore constructs his own image of a Shakespearean character much as he comes to know flesh-and-blood beings, forever working at it as the play continues and as new impressions pour in. Secret motives and outside events reported in the play have a technical function in contributing to this impressionistic knowledge of character: precisely because we do not translate secret motives and reports into certainties they enable us to know Hamlet in a medium of doubts, inferences, likes and dislikes, knowledge and half-knowledge, the normal medium when one mind makes contact with another. From this intricate criss-cross of impressions we come to know Hamlet more intimately than we could from an authorised biography or from the smell of his underclothes – or from any critical explication, however inspired.

Arguing that Shakespeare's characters appear to be life-like and that we feel we know them so well because he used impressionistic devices, I can say with Dr Johnson, when he had mildly and modestly defended the poet of nature for disregarding the unities, that 'I am almost frighted at my own temerity'. I have gone as far as I dare, and the time has come to express reservations. First of all, let us admit that whereas we know other human beings from outside and ourselves from inside,[7] we combine these two very different modes of perception in our relationship with most of Shakespeare's tragic heroes. Strictly speaking, our knowledge of dramatic character will be *sui generis*, and comparisons with our intimate knowledge of human beings must not be pressed too hard.

Next it would be as well to give up all pretence of knowing 'the whole character' or 'the true character' of a dramatic creature, even though good critics have thought that this was possible. We must remember that however lightly a dramatist skips from Sicily to Bohemia, no matter how cleverly he juggles with the law of re-entry or double-time schemes, he still has to cram all he wants to say about character into the two or three hours' traffic of the stage. He proceeds selectively, using only what will be relevant to his plot, and so silently passes over facts that an Appointment Board would wish to hear about when assessing a whole character: Hamlet's age, his qualifications and previous experience as a revenger, and the three referees' letters from Wittenberg. It could be countered, of course, that a tragedy provides more insightful information, but not that it presents a complete character (if that can be done at all and isn't a fallacy of definition, a point that I find so abstruse that I prefer to leave it to our O-level examiners). Rather than claim too much we should therefore frankly admit that we possess no more than fleeting impressions of Shakespeare's characters. They all move through time and 'develop' in mysterious ways (*Othello* is by no means the only tragedy with a double-time scheme), from which it follows that even though a tragic character hangs together in our imagination, we should not presume to explain it except in tentative, impressionistic terms.

Another life-like feature that has encouraged misplaced confidence is the tragic hero's 'role-playing'. In the last two hundred years Morgann and others have remarked on this, but only after the new sociology had arrived could 'character and role' storm effectively into dramatic criticism, trailing clouds of jargon and also some useful distinctions. The shift to the more modern attitude becomes clear when we compare [Andrew] Bradley [1851–1935] and [F.R.] Leavis [1895–1979] on *Othello*. Bradley, it will be recalled, admired Othello's noble and trusting nature and thought him 'a changed man' once Iago's poison had begun to work; Leavis, on the contrary, thought Othello an 'obtuse and brutal egotist' who projects an idealised image of himself in the play's opening scenes, but, put to the test, reveals himself to be very different.[8] Both Bradley and Leavis thus recognised two Othellos in the play, the real Othello and another; Bradley assumed that we meet the real Othello first, at the beginning of the play, and Leavis that the essential man emerges in Act III. And who is right? Othello's role-playing, or 'idealised conception of himself', figures much more prominently in Leavis's essay, as might have been expected from one who was free to benefit from modern sociology. ('No amount of it', he darkly acknowledged, 'can forward our knowledge or understanding of anything' – but that was of sociology in another country and besides, *mutatis mutandis*, the wench is dead.) Leavis had all the advantages, and certainly deepened our understanding of Othello; but it remains to be asked whether *either* of the two Othellos, the noble Moor or the brutal egotist, necessarily represents the 'true' character. Could there not be an element of 'role-playing' in both? I am reluctant to accept that the real Othello only finds himself under stress, in Act III, in so far as he then adopts a way of thinking (in animal images and so on) already powerfully established as Iago's; it seems at least a possibility that, instead of casting off a role and discovering his character, Othello merely takes on a new role in Act III, one that reflects Iago's character as much as his own.

Notice that as soon as we begin to speak about role-playing in drama, the character or 'ghost in the machine' becomes more ghost-like, and is in danger of disappearing altogether. In the end all behaviour may seem to be role-playing of one kind or another: the more role-conscious we grow the more difficult is it to locate that

poor, bare, forked animal, 'unaccommodated man'. Recognising this
difficulty we have to admit that if the older character-criticism of
Shakespeare confused character with role and mood, and no doubt
with other ill-assorted inner processes, our modern role-theories can
also mislead. If we feel tempted to conclude, with [Ibsen's] Peer
Gynt, that after shedding our roles we shall find no self underneath,
that the 'Emperor of Self' could be an onion, without a heart, the
time has come to pause and to ask what we mean by character.

Different experts give different answers. The one that would
interest us most would be Shakespeare's – and, not surprisingly,
there are Big-Endians and Little-Endians who claim to have got
inside the dome-like head, and to know his thoughts. The historical
critics advise that Shakespeare must have pondered character in
Elizabethan terms to which, after all, he often alluded. Their
opponents see Shakespeare as 'not of an age but for all time', a
thinker so far ahead of his contemporaries that only the most modern
psychology can hope to explain character as he understood it. But
some compromise is surely possible when we recall that the wit and
wisdom of many centuries still circulated in Shakespeare's day,
together with the psychology of humours, and often anticipated our
most advanced discoveries. We investigate unified personality and
'self-consistency'; the Jacobeans read in their Bible that 'the good
that I would, I do not; but the evil which I would not, that I do'
(*Romans* vii.19), and might have considered this a helpful gloss on
Macbeth. We talk glibly about character and role; in the sixteenth
century the fashionable equivalent was 'all the world's a stage': 'All
the world doth practise stage-playing. Wee must play our parts
duly, but as the part of a borrowed personage. Of a visard and
apparence, wee should not make a real essence. . . . Wee cannot
distinguish the skinne from the shirt.'[9]

Though Elizabethan and modern psychological textbooks look
very different, general thinking about character need not have been
quite so far apart. Readers of Shakespeare, however, will not expect
to find his 'idea of character' in a textbook or in general thinking,
Elizabethan or modern, trusting their overriding impression that
his psychology was intuitive, exploratory and highly original. If, as
I think, this is correct, how can we hope to unravel his idea of
character?

One way might be to look into the future, from the sixteenth
century, not at this theorist or that but at the general movement of

ideas, on the assumption that Shakespeare helped to *create* the future. So many thinkers (including Freud) drew inspiration from the plays or had their theories tested in studies of the plays (by Morgann, Whiter, Ernest Jones and others) that later psychology may well throw light on Shakespeare's darker purposes. What general development, then, can we discern? We may safely say: a steady move away from the notion that character is fixed, defined, an object, a formula, an ascertainable humour, a ruling passion. Few, perhaps, would now go as far as [David] Hume [1711–76], an earlier Peer Gynt, who ridiculed the very idea of personal identity: 'I never can catch *myself* at any time without a perception, and never can observe anything but the perception.' According to Hume we are 'nothing but a bundle or collection of different perceptions, which succeed each other with an inconceivable rapidity'.[10] An alternative to Hume's scepticism was a pluralistic view of character, which may be illustrated from writers as far apart as Diderot (in *Le Neveu de Rameau*, [1761]) or Walt Whitman [1819–92]:

> Of every hue and caste am I, of every rank and religion . . .
> I resist any thing better than my own diversity.[11]

[August] Strindberg [1849–1912], in the Preface to *Miss Julie*, where he seems to have seen himself as an innovator, must therefore be regarded as the spokesman of a familiar idea, when he repudiated the 'bourgeois notion of the fixed state of the soul.'

My souls are conglomerates of a past stage of civilisation and our present one, scraps from books and newspapers, pieces of humanity, torn-off tatters of holiday clothes that have disintegrated and become rags – exactly as the soul is patched together.

Whitman and Strindberg are not names likely to figure in heavy type in a *History of Psychology*. I have cited them to illustrate a general trend, away from a 'fixed' view of character, in which literature supported theory. By no means all of those who adopt the more modern alternative of a divided self would agree that theirs is a pluralistic view, nor do I seriously suggest that Shakespeare's was (though after reading Bradley and Leavis on *Othello* we may despairingly clutch at such straws). Shakespeare, it would be safer to say, anticipated the trend and indeed helped to bring it about by *stretching* character, so that Othello encompasses the roles of noble

Moor and brutal egotist, not necessarily with the same commitment, and 'royal Lear' coexists from first to last with 'a very foolish fond old man', different scenes stressing different features of the same person. 'We know what we are, but know not what we may be.' Ophelia speaks for the tragic heroes (except that they only think they know what they are), each one being placed in a situation that activates unsuspected inner forces, each one being therefore stretched till we wonder whether he remains one person or has become another.

> Was't Hamlet wrong'd Laertes? Never Hamlet.
> (v.ii.225)

> That's he that was Othello – here I am.
> (v.ii.287)

It is not hard to understand why Shakespeare grew interested in this new way of looking at character: the more he stretched the hero, the more powerful the tragic effect. In his greatest tragedies the hero is invaded or possessed by an alien personality, and, challenged in his inmost being, appears to be 'taken over', sometimes briefly (Hamlet), sometimes for longer spells (Othello). The formula worked well, and it may be that Shakespeare actually thought of it as a kind of 'stretching' (in which case I need not apologise for this unpleasing word).[12]

> Avaunt? be gone! Thou hast set me on the rack.
> (*Othello* iii.iii.339)

> I am bound
> Upon a wheel of fire . . .
> (*King Lear* iv.vii.46–7)

Placing his tragic hero upon the rack, and thus making him act against his nature (as it was previously exhibited), Shakespeare achieved an effect that we may observe in his other plays as well. All the complex comic characters behave incongruously, from Petruchio's Kate to Caliban, as do the tragic heroes; arriving on the literary scene just as English drama advanced from Everyman to Faustus, from type to individual, Shakespeare stretched character by exploring its inexhaustible diversity, and so prepared the way for later pluralistic theories. But, despite superficial resemblances, the tragic heroes differ from all but a very small number of Shakespeare's other characters in so far as their diversity and incongruity is taken to quite extraordinary lengths, far beyond that of 'people we know'.

I have said that the tragic heroes affect us as life-like. It remains to be emphasised that though we see them from inside and from outside, and though they are presented in such a variety of character-revealing situations, they also affect us as infinitely more mysterious than Ibsen's life-like characters or Chekhov's. Our impressions become contradictory and cloudy: one might almost argue that we know too much about the tragic heroes, what with the emotional precision of their speech and the sheer turn-over of significant detail, to be able to penetrate beyond the verbal surface to the inner man. Hamlet plainly tells Guildenstern that he will not 'pluck out the heart of my mystery', and after nearly four hundred years of defeated criticism we must concede the point. Why then insist on his individuality, on a 'life-like' character, if it cannot be plucked out and analysed in detail? Because tragedy, affirming man's indomitable spirit in a hostile universe, particularly concerns itself with self-discovery, with the search for identity, with the uniqueness of the individual. As heat applied to metals burns away impurities, so the intensity of the tragic experience (to adapt Keats) 'makes all disagreeables evaporate' and reveals the quintessential man. Driven in upon himself and threatened in the very centre of his being, the hero, in tragedies of very different periods, asserts an inviolable sense of selfhood: 'I am Duchess of Malfi still!'; 'Ahab is for ever Ahab, man!'; 'I am not a dime a dozen! I am Willy Loman!' No tragedies make more of this sense of self than Shakespeare's, where the hero, looking 'in my heart's core, ay, in my heart of heart', sometimes seems to discover a 'deep self', the very life-principle of the individual.

> But there, where I have garner'd up my heart,
> Where either I must live or bear no life,
> The fountain from the which my current runs,
> Or else dries up – to be discarded thence![13]

We also believe in Shakespeare's tragic characters as 'individuals' because there are moments when we think we glimpse the ghost in the machine: though unable to drag it to the light of day and explain it, we react with the conviction that we have encountered the ghost,

that beneath all the roles there lurks an identifiable self. Granville-
Barker called them moments of *spontaneous revelation*. 'We learn much
about a man when we learn what qualities in other men or women
he unaffectedly admires', he explained, and as an example he cited
Hamlet's words to Horatio, which 'ring out like a true confession of
faith':[14] 'Since my dear soul was mistress of her choice . . .' But this
is not the best example. Hamlet has his reasons for making a
confession of faith, and creates the situation by calling for Horatio.
A more genuinely spontaneous revelation occurs when the situation
overwhelms the speaker and wrings from him a confession of feeling –
when Macbeth returns from murdering Duncan, when Lear kneels
to Cordelia, or when Othello, discovering Desdemona, discovers
himself:

> It gives me wonder great as my content
> To see you here before me. O my soul's joy!
> If after every tempest come such calms . . .
>   (ii.i.181–3)

In such passages of wonder we see beyond the noble posture and
its rhetoric 'into the life of things': as Othello responds spontaneously
to moral beauty we feel that he shares this beauty, that deep
answers unto deep.

Yet, it should be added, even when revealed spontaneously the
inward self only reaches us in refracted glimpses, inferred from the
emotion that bodies it forth. And when the tragic hero unpacks his
heart, turned inside out by that special instrument, the Shakespearian soliloquy, we again fail to see the inward self directly but
only glimpse it through a haze of self-scolding and self-deception.
This, therefore, is the paradox of character in Shakespeare: whereas
we think we know Hamlet perfectly, our knowledge is also oddly
restricted. We think we enjoy a god-like insight, and in a sense this
is true: we have special access to his inwardness, at times we share
his feelings and almost 'become Hamlet'. And yet Shakespeare also
went to unusual lengths to make his tragic hero inaccessible: he
gave him secret motives, he included reports of strange behaviour,
he shrouded the inner man in all the life-like trappings (roles,
relationships, self-deceptions, a misty personal past), he racked him
and made him act against his nature, he surrounded him with
plausible commentators who distort his image. A tragic hero thus
exists in the spectator's mind in a swirl of conflicting impressions –

which ... the dramatist conjured forth and controlled with the utmost care.

SOURCE: Chapter 2, *Shakespeare: Seven Tragedies. The Dramatist's Manipulation of Response* (London, 1976), pp. 4–15.

NOTES

1. Compare J. I. M. Stewart, *Character and Motive in Shakespeare* (London, 1949); S. L. Goldberg, *An Essay on "King Lear"* (Cambridge, 1974) ch. 2; Michael Black, 'Character in Shakespeare', *The Critical Review*, XVII (Melbourne, 1974), 110–19.
2. Una Ellis-Fermor explained the 'inwardness' of Shakespeare's characters in *Shakespeare the Dramatist* (London, 1961), pp. 21–59. See also Michael Goldman on the 'unsounded self', *Shakespeare and the Energies of Drama* (Princeton, N.J., 1972) and Lionel Trilling, *Sincerity and Authenticity* (London, 1972).
3. A. J. A. Waldock, *Hamlet: A Study in Critical Method* (Cambridge, 1931), p. 98.
4. Compare Honigmann, *Shakespeare: Seven Tragedies*, Chapter 6.
5. See also Una Ellis-Fermor, 'The Revelation of Unspoken Thought in Drama' in *The Frontiers of Drama* (London, 1945).
6. J. W. Mackail, *The Approach to Shakespeare* (Oxford, 1933 ed.), p. 25.
7. Compare Gilbert Ryle, *The Concept of Mind* (London, 1949), 'Self-knowledge'; Sydney Shoemaker, *Self-Knowledge and Self-Identity* (Ithaca, N.Y., 1963).
8. [See A. C. Bradley, *Shakespearean Tragedy* (London, 1904), Lectures 5 and 6; F. R. Leavis, 'Diabolic Intellect and the Noble Hero', reprinted in *The Common Pursuit* (London, 1952).] Compare Peter Ure, 'Shakespeare and the Inward Self of the Tragic Hero', 'Character and Role from *Richard III* to *Hamlet*', in *Elizabethan and Jacobean Drama* (Liverpool, 1974).
9. Montaigne, *Essayes*, trans. J. Florio, 3 vols (Everyman ed., 1910), III, ch. x.
10. David Hume, 'Of Personal Identity', in *A Treatise of Human Nature* [1739–40], I.
11. *Song of Myself*, XVI.
12. Compare Panofsky's view that the typical *figura serpentinata* of Mannerist art 'seems to consist of a soft substance which can be *stretched* to any length and *twisted* in any direction': *Studies in Iconology* (London, 1962 ed.), p. 176; my italics.
13. See *Hamlet* III. 2. 71, *Othello* IV. 2. 58ff.; also *Hamlet* V. 1. 251: 'This is I, Hamlet the Dane', *Antony and Cleopatra* III. 13. 92–93: 'I am Antony yet'. In Greek drama the hero sometimes asserts his 'sense of self' by naming his ancestors: 'Agamemnon's son am I, the son of one Held worthy to rule Greece' (*The Tragedies of Euripides*, trans. A. S. Way, 3 vols (1898), III, 158).
14. Harley Granville-Barker, *Prefaces to Shakespeare*, 4 vols (1927–45), III, 307–312.

John Russell Brown   Shakespeare's Text (1981)

The task of re-creating the plays, either in a reader's imagination or on the stage, raises searching questions about a text which lead on to careful dissection and enquiry. Absolutely everything counts: what is there in the text, what is missing, and what may be suggested.

The nature of the evidence, as it was first printed and as we read it today, must be considered very carefully. First we should face the question of authenticity: is this what Shakespeare himself wrote? Sometimes we have to answer that we do not know. For example, Hamlet arrives at his last dangerous and revealing moments through a series of less pressured encounters and his preparation is completed in talk with Horatio:

> If it be now, 'tis not to come; if it be not to come, it will be now; if it be not now, yet it will come – the readiness is all. Since no man owes of aught he leaves, what is't to leave betimes? Let be.
>
> (v.ii.207–10)

Most of these words could hardly be simpler, but the phrase 'Since no man owes of aught he leaves' raises obvious questions. It is here that Hamlet's thought takes a new line, after the conclusive 'the readiness is all'. With the new idea and new rhythm, Hamlet considers himself alongside other men and then goes back to the notion that a moment of decision, and probably of death, is about to occur 'betimes' or almost 'now'. So he comes to think of his own possessions and loss.

Or has he? At this point the printed evidence is very uncertain. The *second* single-volume, paperbound edition, which was probably printed from Shakespeare's own manuscript and is known now as the 'Good Quarto', reads:

> since no man of ought he leaves, knows what ist to leave betimes, let be.

Peter Alexander's edition (whose text is quoted in this book, and reproduced in the first version of the passage given here) dismisses this Good Quarto reading and borrows something from the different reading of the first collected, or 'Folio', edition of 1623, viz.:

since no man ha's ought of what he leaves. What is't to leave betimes?

But notice that Professor Alexander has retained the Good Quarto's 'let be' and modified the punctuation. Professor Kittredge attempted to make sense of the Quarto in another way:

Since no man knows aught of what he leaves, what is't to leave betimes? Let be.

Professor Sisson opted for:

Since no man of aught he leaves knows, what is't to leave betimes? Let be.

My own preference would be close to the Folio:

Since no man has aught of what he leaves, what is't to leave betimes? Let be.

In this reading 'has', rather than 'knows', accentuates the new idea of dispossession.

Almost every editor, no matter how closely he adheres to the better sense of the Folio, keeps the 'Let be' from the Quarto. But even here we should be wary. The Good Quarto has a comma and not a full stop before this phrase. Did Shakespeare punctuate as a talker not as a grammarian, so that his manuscript omitted the question mark? This could imply that, in Shakespeare's creating mind, Hamlet's involvement in questions ebbs slowly, even as he is phrasing one? Or is the comma in the Quarto text the error of a compositor working in the printing-house? This is the most likely supposition and implies that 'Let be', for all its brevity, is the representation of another entirely new thought. Then difficulty centres on how the words should be spoken. There is no stage-direction to help. Hamlet could speak to Horatio or to himself. The two words might be spoken quite sharply or, possibly, humorously in self-defence or self-disparagement. Try saying 'Let be' quietly and then loudly, slowly and then quickly, with a rising inflection and then a falling, after a long pause or immediately after the previous words. The very short sentence, varied by these mechanical means, can suggest very different reactions. Is the phrase part of Shakespeare's text or should we follow the Folio and omit it? Did

Shakespeare's manuscript indicate a quick and light delivery, following the previous words with almost no pause? Or is the actor free to make the new thought register according to his own enactment of the role?

In all these uncertainties, one thing is clear: that at a moment of crucial importance for the action, characters and argument of *Hamlet*, we cannot be sure of the evidence, neither of the text nor of what it implies when the text is put into action in performance. The life of the play in the minds of audiences or readers is still more unsure.

Even among the simple words of this passage, actual meanings and implications must be watched. *Owes*, in the sense of 'possesses', is obsolete today; and a reader will find himself consulting editorial annotations or a glossary to learn that the modern meaning of 'being indebted for' was no more common than the earlier sense that seems to be implied here. Attention to the authenticity of a text is inextricably involved with questions of meaning.

Common usage of the time is perhaps the greatest unknown of all when encountering Shakespeare's text for the first time. His written language was influenced by everyday talk, public pronouncements, literary traditions, and class, age and regional distinctions, as well as by the hugely complicated history of his own developing use of language, in both his personal and his literary lives. The words we read have lost some resonances and gained others; they have changed meanings, lost meanings and gained new ones. Their sound has altered, too. In studying Shakespeare we need great patience if we are to assess each word as carefully as we should.

Another crucial passage from *Hamlet* illustrates this:

> And enterprises of great pitch and moment,
> With this regard, their currents turn awry
> And lose the name of action. – Soft you now!
> The fair Ophelia. – Nymph, in thy orisons
> Be all my sins rememb'red.
>   (*Hamlet*, iii.i.86–90)

Considered objectively, as 'dead' evidence on the page, some of the simplest words should puzzle us. In Shakespeare's day, *Soft you* was used as an exclamation to enjoin silence and to prevent hasty action; the second sense, which is less familiar to us, is clear in *Twelfth Night*

(I.v.277), *The Comedy of Errors* (III.ii.69) and elsewhere in the plays. The phrase could also enjoin secrecy and concealment. So Hamlet's first thought on seeing Ophelia may be to delay or actually to prevent a meeting, and not, as we might judge from modern usage, to give expression to an instinctive surge of gentle feelings.

But then, in proverbial usage, *soft* was linked with *fair*, in the phrase *soft and fair*, meaning 'gently, peaceably'; there is a clear instance of this in *Much Ado About Nothing* (v.iv.72). So we must consider that the words *fair Ophelia* might come to Hamlet's mind as a quibble on 'Soft you', and this, together with alliteration, could imply a quickening sense of wonder and delight which overcomes the first defensive reaction. On the other hand, both quibble and alliteration could represent a biting irony that follows directly from the need to hide from Ophelia in the dangerous political environment of Elsinore.

Punctuation must also be considered here. The exclamation mark of the edition I have quoted is found in neither Good Quarto nor Folio. Both these texts have a comma and this may remind us that only the slightest pause is necessary after *now*. Further enquiry will tell us that the compositor who set the type for the Good Quarto from Shakespeare's manuscript was in the habit of adding to the punctuation of his copy, not lightening it.

So we may move on to the next questions, which must be 'Why *Nymph?*' and 'Why *orisons?*' Neither word was common in such a context, in theatrical or in everyday usage. Shakespeare used *nymph* in three ways: first, with reference to spirits, not mortals; second, in pastoral settings where a lover is totally enamoured of his lady; and thirdly, when he wished to suggest a strong and obvious sexual attraction. The last is the most unusual, but Hamlet's immediate reference to *sins* might imply that this is the sense required here, especially as Ophelia is no spirit and Elsinore no pastoral solitude. The sexual senses of *nymph* are found in the courtly settings of *Titus Andronicus*:

> To wanton with this queen,
> This goddess, this Semiramis, this nymph,
> This siren that will charm Rome's Saturnine,
> (II.i.21–3)

and in *Richard III*:

> and want love's majesty
> To strut before a wanton ambling nymph.
> (i.i.16–17)

Orisons is still more difficult to place exactly. By the year 1600 its archaic and poetic suggestions were already fairly established. Certainly Shakespeare used *prayers* rather than *orisons* on almost every occasion when both might have been suitable; and *devotions* is far more common in his plays than *orisons*. In association with *nymph*, some touch of unreality seems to be implied; but an alternative reading might find an edge of sarcasm in both words, especially since the syntax brings them together at the beginning of Hamlet's words to Ophelia, and the metre tends to distinguish them from the rest of the sentence. Shakespeare used *orisons* on four other occasions only, and in three of these the word is heavy with sarcasm or irony: when Queen Margaret taunts the Duke of York who is her prisoner and is being humiliated (*2 Henry VI*, i.ix.110); when Henry the Fifth taunts Sir Thomas Grey who has professed loyal piety as he prepares to assassinate his king (*Henry V*, ii.ii.53); and when Juliet pretends that she will pray before marrying Paris (*Romeo*, iv.iii.3). Only for Imogen's anxious fantasies about the absent Posthumous did Shakespeare use *orisons* without a clear edge of mockery, and here a measure of unreality is unmistakable. 'Nymph in thy orisons . . .' would be unique in Shakespeare's writings if it were a tender, heartfelt *and* real communication.

Word-order, syntax and metre are further important clues to dramatic meaning. Why start with the single word *Nymph*, why *orisons* so early and why *rememb'red* last? And why the passive construction? Does Hamlet think first of his own *sins*, and is this the reason why he speaks at all? Why is the rhythm of the concluding line controlled so firmly by the four leading monosyllables, with a regular iambic stress on *all* and *sins*? Why '*all* my sins'? Does Hamlet think of his sins because he supposes, either mockingly or tenderly, that Ophelia must be at her devotions in order to beg forgiveness for her own? Or for *his*?

These few words can suggest many and various enactments. For the moment, Hamlet could respond to Ophelia as an innocent and beautiful girl, and so speak gently and with reverence. The mellifluous phrasing and falling rhythms seem to support this. Or he could wince from the sight of her, suspecting some new corruption or deceit, and so speak scornfully and in self-defence. Biting stress on *'fair Ophelia'* and *'all* my *sins'*, which would chime with the first regular stresses of the iambic lines, could support this. It may be, however, that Hamlet is pretending to be mad, as he had promised that he would, and so expresses a distraction of his own mind in an exaggerated mixture of gentleness and sarcasm. Or, for the moment, does Hamlet stand quite lost?

Of course, the context of this encounter, and its place in a living performance of the play, will influence the meaning of this short speech. The physical distance between the two performers, their postures and relationships, will be important elements of this. Try calling these words as if communicating at some distance, and then speaking in a low voice as if Hamlet stands just behind a kneeling Ophelia. Speak them as you become suddenly tense, and then when you are excited; and then in a wholly relaxed state.

Perhaps the most persistent puzzle in Shakespeare's texts is the absence of stage-directions. An actor's position on stage can be crucial to the meaning of the words, and to the very action of the play. A crux of this importance occurs just before the passage we have been examining. The King is arranging with the Queen and Polonius for Hamlet to 'affront' Ophelia, and says

> Sweet Gertrude, leave us too;
> For we have closely sent for Hamlet hither,
> That he, as 'twere by accident, may here
> Affront Ophelia.
> Her father and myself – lawful espials –
> Will so bestow ourselves that, seeing unseen,
> We may of their encounter frankly judge,
> And gather by him, as he is behav'd,
> If't be the affliction of his love or no
> That thus he suffers for.
> (III.i.28–37)

Ophelia is on stage when all this is being spoken, but she could be out of earshot while the King speaks privately to the Queen: she might be engaged in talk with her father which no one else can hear. If the King's words do communicate to Ophelia, she will know that everything she says to Hamlet when they meet will be heard instantly by the King and her own father; then their encounter will be different from what it would be if she has not heard and does not know how she is being used to trap Hamlet. Does she think that

her father *is* 'at home' when she says he is? Or is she aware, at that
moment, that he is actually present and eavesdropping? Does the
brevity of her speeches indicate a full heart or a resolute deception?
How tender is her speech, how brave, how tentative or how hollow?
The mute language of the way she looks at Hamlet, when he speaks
to her, will have divergent meanings according to whether she does
or does not know that the King is there.

The text is not clear on this issue. The Queen continues:

> I shall obey you;
> And for your part, Ophelia, I do wish
> That your good beauties be the happy cause
> Of Hamlet's wildness.

All depends on whether Gertrude moves away from Claudius on 'I
shall obey you' and waits until she has reached Ophelia before
continuing with, 'And for your part, Ophelia', or whether she does
not move because Ophelia is so close that she has heard everything.
The fact that Polonius speaks next to Ophelia, and not to the King,
may indicate that the first alternative is correct and that he has
been standing aside with his daughter while Claudius has taken
Gertrude to the other extremity of the stage. The argument is nicely
balanced because Gertrude seems to continue a single line of thought
with 'And for your part, Ophelia . . .'. I do not know for sure which
stage-direction is required. I can only add that the part of Ophelia
is very difficult to play if she does, indeed, know everything.

For my present purpose the investigation of this short passage
has gone far enough, and perhaps too far. Only when a reader
explores a text for himself or herself, openly and in detail, asking
questions about the play in performance, seeing each part from
within and using his or her own imagination, will the worth and
excitement of such an exploration be established. What can appear
complicated and specialised is found then to be an adventurous
game, much more accessible than bridge, or crosswords, or learning
a foreign language. Our own creativity is set in action with
Shakespeare's text, under his instigation and guidance. Some simple
rules have to be followed and then all is open, and we can, if we
wish, use more sophisticated means of improving our play.

Very early in any investigation, a reader must enquire about the
authenticity of the text he is using. A good modern edition will

provide a textual introduction to each play explaining the nature of the 'copy' from which it was first printed, the differences between early editions where more than one exists, and how the modern editor has compiled his own text. If the reader uses a copy of the *Complete Works*, he should also consult a modern, single-volume edition for this information, although that will not explain his own editor's procedures. Alternatively, he should turn to Sir Walter W. Greg's *The Shakespeare First Folio: Its Bibliographical and Textual History* (Oxford 1955, and many times reprinted). More than twenty years' work of a whole school of 'bibliographical' textual scholarship is drawn together in this book which shows the varying authority of all the early editions. An excellent summary is provided on pages 426–32 and this should be studied to place the introductions of single-volume editions in a wider perspective.

In his life-time and in the years immediately following, Shakespeare's plays were printed from many different kinds of manuscript and from corrected or supplemented copies of earlier editions. The best of 'Good Quarto' editions and the best texts in the Folio Collected edition of 1623 were printed directly from his own manuscripts. These varied from comparatively rough drafts to careful 'fair copies'. Occasionally Shakespeare's manuscript was edited for the printer by some other hand, after comparison with a prompt-book or alternative version. A professional scrivener was sometimes used to make a new manuscript for the printer, from Shakespeare's papers or from the actor's prompt-book; this copyist might well punctuate to please himself or introduce new arrangements for the stage-directions or speech-prefixes. A few plays were printed from a prompt-book, or a transcript of one, and so record modifications that the players had introduced to Shakespeare's original. Six were first published in Quartos for which the printers used unauthorised versions taken down by dictation from actors and possibly augmented by shorthand or other notes taken during performance. Although these 'bad' texts are obviously deficient in sense and metre, they sometimes have illuminating stage-directions and alternative readings that correct errors in better texts. The Quartos of *Richard III* and *King Lear* are probably reconstructions, the former from the collective memory of the company of players and the latter from some careless or botched copy of authoritative papers. Numerous texts in the Folio were printed from copies of earlier Quarto editions which had been edited with or without reference to a prompt-book or some other manuscript version now completely lost.

The story of how Shakespeare's plays came to be printed is highly complicated and can never be fully known. In contrast to other dramatists (such as Ben Jonson and John Webster, who supplied authoritative manuscripts and visited the printing-house to check and correct the printing), Shakespeare seems to have taken very little trouble to ensure that his plays were published as accurately as possible. For each play a reader should enquire about its textual history and so understand how far the text he uses can be trusted, and what is the value of the alternative readings which he will find noted in the collations provided in most single-volume editions. When all allowances are made for the difficulties and accidents of Elizabethan publication, we and Shakespeare have been fortunate: within definable limits, when we read a modern text we are close to his manuscripts or some transcript of them.

Such reassurance can be taken only so far, however. We should be aware that there *are* many cruxes and some longer passages – and these in plays that are frequently performed and studied – where we can never be very sure of the text's authenticity. Moreover, in the last fifty years a great deal has been learnt about the compositors who set the original editions. As was mentioned earlier in this chapter in connection with the Good Quarto of *Hamlet*, we know now that, as a matter of course, they altered punctuation, and also spelling, to suit their own habits or convenience. We are thus now aware that we can never be sure of the authenticity of the original texts in these respects. Shortage of type – dramatic texts need many more marks of punctuation than others – or the need to fit 'copy' into a fixed number of pages, or the rapid correction of errors that were obvious on quick perusal of a proof sheet, or the misreading of 'copy', hasty work, carelessness, inexperience, bad light, broken type, faulty distribution of type, and many other accidents, would introduce further small alterations of this sort on almost every page. In ordinary circumstances, these minor changes introduced by compositors and chance would not be very significant, but for Shakespeare's plays, which must be searched for the tiniest clues of their implied stage-life, they are a continual source of insecurity and perplexity. The changes to punctuation, introduced by habit and error or for ease of working, throw a veil between a reader and Shakespeare's intentions that is always present and often inpenetrable. A great deal of work has been done on type-shortages, press-work and compositorial habits, but much more remains to be done, using computers and elaborate photographic devices, before any real progress can be achieved. For the present time and for years to come, a reader should maintain a total scepticism about the punctuation of any text he reads, whether original or edited. Metrical considerations can often show how faulty verse-lining or the confusion of verse and prose should be corrected, but there is little to help us to tackle the persistent problems of punctuation.

Modern editors usually punctuate to reveal the syntax as clearly as possible to a silent reader. This practice gives a cool and synthetic impression which is far from the dynamics of thought and speech. The experiment of reading aloud will show that the grammatical punctuation which is clear on the page can be laboured and metrically confusing in stage performance. Before rehearsals begin some theatre directors have the whole play typed out afresh, using only the very minimum of punctuation – chiefly full stops to separate the sentences – so that the actors will speak the text without interference from both the ancient and the modern punctuation which have replaced the dramatist's and removed it from our sight for ever. I recommend the exercise of making such a transcript as a means of becoming aware of this very pervasive problem. A highly dramatic episode or a long soliloquy offers the most revealing material. With the punctuation thus reduced to a minimum, a further exercise would be to speak the words in various ways so that they are metrically satisfying and make sense in the developing situation. Then new punctuation could be added to the transcript to represent the preferred reading.

Such work leads inevitably to a consideration of verse-lining, and here a reader is on surer ground. Infinite variations are possible in an actor's response to the metre, but the division of a text into lines is usually beyond reasonable doubt and provides most useful and continuous instruction for an actor. The importance of verse-lining is most obvious in the occurence of incomplete or half-lines which are the equivalent of stage-directions from Shakespeare himself indicating pauses or silences. Many modern editors have failed to grasp their significance and arrange the text on the printed page so that their presence is obscured, and some actors do not bother to follow their promptings. A few examples will show how verse-lining can help a reader's search for the stage-life of a play.

The Tragedy of Othello, with its intense and intimate scenes, illustrates this particularly well – for example, this exchange between Desdemona and Emilia:

EM.   Alas, what does this gentleman conceive?
       How do you, madam? How do you, my good lady?
DES.   Faith, half asleep.   *   *   *   *   *   *   *   *
EM.   Good madam, what's the matter with my lord?
DES.   With who?   *   *   *   *   *   *   *   *   *
EM.   Why, with my lord, madam.   *   *   *   *   *   *
DES.   Who is thy lord?
EM.   He that is yours, sweet lady.
DES.   I have none. Do not talk to me, Emilia;
       I cannot weep, nor answers have I none
       But what should go by water. Prithee, tonight
       Lay on my bed my wedding sheets – remember;
       And call thy husband hither.   *   *   *   *   *   *
EM.   Here's a change indeed!   *   *   *   *   *   *   *(*Exit*)
DES.   'Tis meet I should be us'd so, very meet. . . .
                                        (IV.ii.96–108)

I have marked incomplete lines with small asterisks; none of these lines has the ten syllables required to fill the pattern of an iambic pentameter. In this passage the text indicates how pauses could be sustained. At the start, Desdemona is 'half asleep': she does not know of whom Emilia speaks. Misunderstandings halt the talk until Desdemona asks a direct question. Then, as soon as she has said that she has no lord, she speedily seeks to stop further enquiry. The fourth line from the end – 'But what should go by water. Prithee, tonight' – could have two different metrical bases. With elision, it could be said without breaking the run of one verse-line; and so Desdemona's thoughts would seem to rush forward. But if no elision is permitted and a pause is taken at the full stop, the line could be read as two half-lines between which Desdemona does indeed weep or struggle against doing so. Desdemona's next unmistakable half-line shows that Emilia hesitates before she leaves on her errand. Then Emilia's concluding half-line shows that Desdemona is also silent before she speaks in soliloquy from the very depths of her being.

A useful way of exploring a text is to make a transcript which shows clearly all incomplete verse-lines, and then try to write in stage-directions that will account for the pauses that these indicate. It is an exercise that can lead on to a fuller examination of stage activity that would alert a reader to the absence of precise or complete directions in authoritative texts.

First, all entries should be rewritten so that their order and manner of moving are prescribed; if clothes have been changed since the last appearance, these should be noted. Next, exits should be described with similar care, noting speed, order, direction, manner. Then stage-directions should be added for all the actions that are implied in the dialogue, such as kneeling, weeping, kissing or touching. Whenever the words of the text state or imply that the persons on stage alter their positions, or that a figure crosses from one group to another or walks about the stage, those actions should be given precise and detailed stage-directions. If more than one reader undertakes this exercise, various additions to the text can be compared and differences of opinion investigated further. It is instructive to consult several printed editions to see if the various editors have added directions of the same kind and in the same places. Photographic reproductions of early printed editions may also be consulted, especially where more than one authoritative text exists. (But too great reliance should not be given to these, because – as we have already noted – Elizabethan compositors often misplaced directions in order to fit them into the space available on their pages.) Obviously texts printed from the author's own manuscript have especially valuable directions; but these are sometimes very incomplete, especially with regard to exits.

There will be many places in a text where stage-directions can never be formulated with certainty or precision. This is why most editors supply as few as possible, and those in the simplest of forms. But a reader should not be misled by this tactful and almost inevitable conspiracy of silence: a great deal of imaginative, inventive and tentative re-creation is required if the plays are not to flow past too easily in the mind, as words only, without regard for the living persons who speak them and who sustain them, or even counterstate them, by their actions.

Another passage in *Othello* will illustrate the need for this special vigilance with regard to stage-directions. In Act III, scene iii, most editions read more or less as follows:

OTH.   I have a pain upon my forehead here.
DES.   Faith, that's with watching; 'twill away again.
       Let me but bind it hard, within this hour

It will be well.   (*He puts the handkerchief from him, and she drops it*)
OTH.   Your napkin is too little.
Let it alone. Come, I'll go in with you.
DES.   I am very sorry that you are not well.   (*Exeunt*)

(ll. 288–93)

The moment is so crucial to the play's development that every reader should be warned that the stage-direction in this printed text has no authority whatever. Neither Quarto nor Folio text has any direction at this point. Most editors supply something similar to the words quoted here, and so indicate that the loss of the handkerchief is Desdemona's fault; the New Arden editor follows Nicholas Rowe's text of 1709 with a simple '*She drops the handkerchief*'.

But Othello might be responsible for the accident. He might snatch it away from her and let it fall himself. Desdemona could have fastened the handkerchief securely before Othello tears it off and throws it onto the ground. Or he could react so violently that Desdemona could have no responsibility for the accident; this is implied in the Signet editor's stage-direction: '*He pushes the handkerchief away, and it falls.*' On the other hand, Desdemona might never have got the handkerchief to Othello's head, the sight of it being enough to arouse his irritation; she might drop it in astonishment or because she is instantly more concerned for her husband's well-being than for any token. Emilia, it is true, tells Iago that Desdemona 'Let it drop by negligence'; but we do not know if she is right about this or how truly she speaks; and her words do not explain how or why or at what moment. As we have seen, editors have interpreted Emilia's words in many different ways.

A further question must then arise: How do Desdemona and Othello leave the stage? Are they together, or does he leave at once so that she has to hurry after? The only certain fact about the stage-action here is that neither of them stops because the handkerchief has been dropped; perhaps everything happens so quickly that the audience itself does not realise that the handkerchief has been left on the ground, until Emilia picks it up. In this case, the whole incident could be much lighter than most editors imply, and the peace between Desdemona and Othello seem stronger than any conflict or uncertainty. 'Let it alone. Come, I'll go in with you' could indicate that for the moment the Moor's wife has 'sung the savageness out of a bear' (IV.i.185–6).

This fatal moment in *Othello* illustrates what is true of every other moment in the plays: the words of the dialogue cannot tell us all, and printed stage-directions are always inadequate. Each text has to be imaginatively and responsibly explored in the light of a living performance of the drama.

A reader's exploration of a play will move from words to action and then back again, and so the process will continue. A discovery on one front leads quickly to questions on the other, because the division between words and actions exists only in our minds. Ideally both enquiries are one, and in our more instinctive responses they do proceed inextricably.

So far I have written most about the need to imagine the action of a play and to hear its words as part of a total performance, but I have no wish to undervalue the benefits of enquiring very closely into the meanings of words, their relationships, complexities and simplicities. I have been countering the tendency of many critics and almost all editors to limit their enquiry to *words*. While they ignore problems of punctuation and stage-directions, they retrieve meanings now lost in general usage and note multiple meanings, quotations from other writers, topical references, echoes from folk-lore and proverbs, and so on; they discuss fully every word that gives difficulty to a modern reader. All this can quicken our response to a text, but it is important to remember that the long and impressive notes of the Variorum, Arden, Oxford or Cambridge editions have great limitations, even in their chosen semantic emphasis.

Even the limited task of annotating the words of a text cannot be done satisfactorily without envisaging the play in action. For example, only a few editors gloss Othello's opening words in the last scene: 'It is the cause, it is the cause, my soul' (v.ii); and yet who can be sure what these words indicate about the great forces that are at full stretch within Othello? Is *the cause* an agent (perhaps in a bad sense), or the end (as in the 'final cause'), or the ground for action? Or is Othello referring to legal usage, whereby *the cause* signifies the subject for dispute or, even, the accusation? It is possible that here, as elsewhere, Shakespeare alludes to a late Latin usage, where *cause* means disease or 'that which has to be cured'.

Once a reader replaces the conventional questions of an editor, 'What are the difficulties in this passage, and what can the words mean?', with the theatrical question, 'Why does this person in the drama say this word at this moment?', the fullest page of annotations may become insufficient. In Othello's 'It is the cause, it is the cause . . .', we should ask: Why *It* and not 'This' or 'She'? Why *is* and not 'was'? Why the repetition? (Obviously this question goes beyond the meaning of words.) And what force does *soul* have here for Othello, and at this point in the play? All these questions are important for the actor of the part, and so they should be explored.

Can Othello be remembering 'O my soul's joy', the cry with which he greeted Desdemona upon their reunion in Cyprus (II.i.182)? Or his later realisation:

> Perdition catch my soul
> But I do love thee; and when I love thee not
> Chaos is come again.
> (III.iii.91–3)

Does *soul* mean the principle of life in Othello, his eternal being, or does it refer to the seat of his emotions? Of these two earlier passages, that in Act II suggests the first sense, the other the second. Moreover, we should notice that, 50 lines after the opening words of Act V, scene ii, Othello calls Desdemona 'sweet soul': is it possible that *my soul*, in the context of 'it is the cause, my soul', is also a term of endearment for Desdemona? (The very expression is used in *Twelfth Night*, I.v.253, in this manner – 'And call upon my soul within the house' – and in *A Midsummer Night's Dream* and *Cymbeline*.)

The questions raised by any line of text are far-reaching and delicate. In one way, obviously difficult words are the easiest to understand: a solution often clicks into place. Besides, we know that Shakespeare, in common with many contemporary writers, did coin new words and usages consciously, so that they would give pleasure as their meanings were recognised. (Bardolph's high-toned use of *accommodate*, when he is trying to impress Justice Shallow in *2 Henry IV*, III.ii.65–6, is a comical demonstration of this skill.) But Shakespeare's use of idiomatic words and phrases that are sometimes very simple to read, his echoing of proverbs, variations of normal grammatical usage and small modifications proper to a special trade, profession, culture, age-group, sex, social class or intimate relationship – these are all more difficult to perceive and trace. Constant vigilance is needed, and an essentially theatrical enquiry.

A student is often faced with two or more possible meanings – sometimes with contrary meanings. This is part of the richness of

Shakespeare's dialogue. If more than one interpretation of a word fits the context, all may be valid. Such ambiguities and double meanings are common in poetry and drama, and in the humour of all ages. They express minds in high excitement or deep involvement; and what may seem over-ingenious in explanation can be entirely lifelike in performance, as a natural overflow of sensation. The test must be whether complexity of meaning is appropriate to our sense of the dramatic moment for the person who is speaking.

A wider range of possible meanings than those quoted in any edition is easily discovered if the reader has access to two important publications. The first is the Oxford *New English Dictionary* (volumes published between 1888 and 1933) which enumerates and exemplifies all the meanings that its numerous compilers had recognised in books of the period. The second is a Shakespeare concordance. Computers are now producing replacements for John Bartlett's *Complete Concordance*, first published in London in 1894, but for most readers of Shakespeare this late-Victorian work is more than adequate and will be found in many libraries. Each citation is quoted at sufficient length to awaken a memory of its context. A reader should be warned, however, that Bartlett is really two concordances, the poems and sonnets having their own lists at the back of the volume. I find it hard to say which of these two publications is the more useful for an independent exploration of Shakespeare's text: the *New English Dictionary* can suggest meanings for any word, and the *Concordance* can reveal if any of these corresponds with Shakespeare's usage elsewhere in his works.

For the reader who has limited access to libraries and limited time, the best book to purchase as a supplement to Shakespeare's text is undoubtedly C. T. Onions's *A Shakespeare Glossary* (final revision, Oxford, 1953). Professor Onions was one of the editors of the *New English Dictionary* and in this small volume devoted to Shakespeare he has supplied

definitions and illustrations of words or senses of words now obsolete or surviving only in provincial or archaic use, together with explanations of others involving allusions not generally familiar, and of proper names carrying with them some connotative signification or offering special interest or difficulty in the passage in which they occur. (*Preface*)

Of course, the dangers of using this *Glossary* are that it is selective and that it does not list modern usages which were current –

sometimes surprisingly – in the sixteenth and early seventeenth centuries. But it contains much to awaken appreciation of Shakespeare's text and to recover what the passage of time has obscured.

SOURCE: Part of chapter 7, *Discovering Shakespeare: A New Guide to the Plays* (London, 1981), pp. 77–91 (slightly adapted by the author for this reprinting).

SUGGESTIONS FOR FURTHER STUDY

E. A. Abbott, *A Shakespearian Grammar* (London, 3rd ed., 1872): still very serviceable, especially as a means of finding parallel usages in Shakespeare's works.
G. L. Brook, *The Language of Shakespeare* (London, 1976).
E. J. Dobson, *English Pronunciation: 1500–1700* (Oxford, 2nd ed., 1968).
Sister Miriam Joseph, *Shakespeare's Use of the Arts of Language* (New York, 1947). A shortened version is available in paperback: *Rhetoric in Shakespeare's Time* (New York and London, 1962).
L. A. Sonnino, *A Handbook to Sixteenth-Century Rhetoric* (London, 1968).

Alexander Leggatt   The Extra Dimension: Shakespeare in Performance   (1977)

That Shakespeare's plays live in the theatre as well as in the study is now a commonplace; but it is a commonplace whose implications we are only beginning to come to terms with. Many scholars seem to regard a visit to the theatre as entering an enemy camp. Those who have written of their experiences have often done so under titles like 'For Jesus' Sake Forbear: Shakespeare *vs.* the Modern Theatre'[1] or, more mildly, 'Shakespeare on the Modern Stage: The Need for New Approaches'.[2] There are many reasons for their unhappiness with particular contemporary productions, and we need not dwell on them here; but one general factor is that actors and directors operate under a very different set of pressures from scholars. They have to produce, in a short time and with limited resources, a performance that will work for an audience composed largely of non-specialists. If they have to cut, decorate, or simply cheat to achieve this end, they generally will. The scholar, working for a readership of fellow specialists and taking his own good time, can speculate freely from a variety of angles. No one obliges him to bring his theory to a practical test before an audience; indeed, many approaches to Shakespeare (through the political thought of his time, for example) are by definition untestable in the modern theatre. Small wonder that when members of one group discuss the other a note of scorn is occasionally heard. And yet, radically different though the two enterprises seem to be, there is an obvious meeting ground in the plays themselves. And while the approaches of the performer and the critic can never be quite identical, it is simple common sense to expect some points of contact between them. In the last few years, actors and directors have been doing their homework, taking material from scholarship and criticism; and – more slowly and reluctantly, I think – scholars have been using theatrical performances as evidence for their own interpretations.

It is this latter point I wish to explore. There are certain features of a play in performance that any Shakespeare critic ought to be aware of, not just as a check on his more airy speculations, but as a source of fresh information that may lead to richer and more concrete interpretations. Basically stated, they are truisms; but their specific applications can be fascinating. One is that a performance is unstoppable: there will be pauses and silences, there will be an interval or two, but on the whole the continuity of the play is unbroken. It is not so in the study: the phone rings, lunch is ready – or, more dangerously, a point in the text convenient to the reader's interpretation is reached, and he stops to make a note of it. In *The Comedy of Errors* Adriana, meeting Antipholus of Syracuse for the first time and mistaking him for her husband, delivers a long speech about the closeness of the marriage bond, the identity of husband and wife:

> For know, my love, as easy mayst thou fall
> A drop of water in the breaking gulf,
> And take unmingled thence that drop again
> Without addition or diminishing,
> As take from me thyself, and not me too.
> (II.ii.124–8)

To the critic in the study, important thematic concerns are isolated
here – love, marriage, identity – and a serious statement is made,
one central to the play's vision. That is true, but it is not the whole
truth, as any one who saw this scene played by Alec McCowen and
Diana Rigg[3] will testify. The look of blank incomprehension on
Antipholus' face as the speech progressed, then the slow dawning
of an idea, and finally the shy delight of discovery in the question,
'Plead you to *me*, fair dame?' (ii.ii.146: my italics) – all this not only
brought down the house, but showed that Adriana's speech is not
just an idea, but an idea placed within a situation; and the idea and
the situation, as so often in Shakespeare, are ironically at odds. It is
a point easy to miss in the study, impossible to miss in the continuity
imposed by performance.

Similarly, the critic can isolate Hamlet's cool reflections about
the loss of reputation ('So, oft it chances in particular men. . .':
i.iv.23) and take them as a statement about the tragic flaw; in the
theatre we have to notice that Hamlet, waiting for his father's ghost
to appear, is allowing his mind to run off at a tangent; whatever the
speech tells us about reputation, or about how a personality can be
destroyed, its placement in the scene tells us even more about
Hamlet and the way his mind works. We can take certain speeches
from the finale of *Measure for Measure* and suggest that a miracle of
order, justice and mercy is being achieved, mysterious but compel-
ling; but in the theatre we cannot hush the voice of Lucio – heckling,
mocking, calling attention to himself even though the resolution has
nothing to do with him, and generally lowering the tone of the
occasion. We can isolate in the study the formal, playful beauty of
the dialogue on kissing that Romeo and Juliet share when they first
meet; but in the theatre we also notice how this beauty is sharpened
and made more vulnerable by the way it is placed, without
transitions, against the menaces of Tybalt and the cynical chatter
of the Nurse: 'I tell you, he that can lay hold of her Shall have the
chinks' (i.v.114–15).

It would of course be foolish to suggest that such effects are
apparent *only* in the theatre; a reasonably alert reading ought to
uncover them. But it is also true that when lecturing or writing
about Shakespeare we inevitably cut little pieces out of his text and
scatter them through our own, to prove what we want to prove. An
awareness of the continuity of performance should warn us against
doing this too crudely, and should suggest that many of the most

interesting and significant passages show effects pulling against each other – idea against situation, thought against character, style against style. The actor is as bound to run effects together as the critic is to isolate them; a concern with how one moment of his performance relates to another, and with how his work in a scene relates to that of his fellow performers, is basic to his work. If the critic can show a similar concern, discussing not just effects but particular combinations of effect, then his enterprise will touch on that of the actor, and he will have an idea of the sort of thing to look out for in performance. (And we might note that while the critic can relate effects within a structure of his own devising, the structure the actor is bound by is Shakespeare's.)

Some of the most significant combinations are tensions between what is heard and what is seen, and this leads to another fact about Shakespeare in performance that a critic needs to remember. Inga-Stina Ewbank writes of a 'purposeful dialectic between what is seen and what is said; between the power of words, on the one hand, and their impotence before a visually presented reality, on the other.'[4] Part of the effect of the balcony scene in *Romeo and Juliet* is the interplay of minds – tentative at first, then excited, then confident and assured. But another part is the physical separation imposed by the balcony itself. This has an emblematic force: the lovers are trying to reach each other across a barrier, and they never quite succeed. In Trevor Nunn's [1976] production the effect was under-lined by Romeo's comic, futile attempt to leap up to the balcony on 'O, wilt thou leave me so unsatisfied?' (II.ii.125). It was funny – some would say, too funny – but it was also a joke with a point.

The stage picture can also include characters whose mere presence carries a weight of unspoken commentary – Banquo at the discovery of Duncan's murder,[5] Iago at the reunion of Othello and Desdemona on Cyprus, Enobarbus almost any time. They may have asides that tell us their thoughts; but I think these contribute to the subtler and more powerful effect created by their silent, critical presence while the main characters are speaking. A particularly clear example of this effect – characteristic of the younger Shakespeare in its radicalism – occurs in *Titus Andronicus*. The single long scene that makes up the first act presents a complex but apparently completed action; practically all the main characters are involved, and the resolution achieved at the end of the act either satisfies them or wins their acquiescence. But throughout the scene Aaron is on stage.

Two things call our attention to him – he is black, and he is silent. We sense that he is an important character, and when the act achieves its resolution without a comment from him we have a nagging feeling of unfinished business. Then Act Two begins with a soliloquy by Aaron, and the main action is under way.

A play peculiarly rich in moments like this – moments of tension between the verbal and the visual – is *King Lear*. Edgar talks himself into a Stoic acceptance of his lot:

> Welcome, then,
> Thou unsubstantial air that I embrace!
> The wretch that thou hast blown unto the worst
> Owes nothing to thy blasts.
>
> (iv.i.6–9)

But just as he reaches this comforting conclusion, his father enters, blind and led by an old man, leading Edgar to exclaim. 'O gods! Who is't can say "I am at the worst"? I am worse than e'er I was' (iv.i.26–7). He creates for his father an experience of miraculous salvation, but we see the fall from the cliff taking place on a flat stage;[6] and as Edgar recommends 'free and patient thoughts' (iv.vi.80) Lear enters mad and crowned with flowers. As Lear offers to Cordelia his vision of innocent, child-like seclusion from the world – 'We two alone will sing like birds i'th' cage' (v.iii.9) – Edmund is standing beside him, and Edmund's army surrounds him. At this point in Grigori Kozintsev's film, as Lear and Cordelia gaze into each other's faces, sharing a private happiness, they are surrounded by a crowd that pushes them along and threatens to overwhelm them. In the last scene, there is much talk of order and justice – then Lear enters with the dead Cordelia.

But this effect is not restricted to the play's darker insights; it can pull us in the other direction. In the storm, in the hovel, and in the later scene with Gloucester, Lear offers some of his most powerful visions of the wretchedness and corruption of man. But as he does so he is surrounded by figures whose very presence expresses love and loyalty – the Fool, Kent, Gloucester, and – beneath the disguise of Poor Tom – Edgar. (It is one of the play's more intricate ironies that the ultimate *visual* image of human wretchedness, the naked lunatic, is a disguise adopted by the play's main spokesman for reason and hope. In reading and theorizing about the play, it is easy for Edgar to be submerged into poor Tom; in performance, the identity of the actor himself will always remind us of Edgar, and Shakespeare has given him enough asides to show that this is intentional.) These figures remind us that humanity cannot after all be summed up in lines like 'the usurer hangs the cozener' (iv.vi.163). Peter Brook's 1962 production for the Royal Shakespeare Company is best remembered for the bleakness of its vision; but there were many moments of another kind. As Lear pleaded with the unhearing gods, 'O, let me not be mad, not mad, sweet heaven! Keep me in temper; I would not be mad! (i.v.42–3), the Fool took his hand; for a moment the fear was shared, and the king and the fool were like two children admitting they were afraid of the dark. When in his later mad scene the king commanded, 'Pull off my boots; harder, harder' (iv.vi.173), the blind Gloucester obeyed the command, slowly, clumsily, and crying like a baby. Beneath the grotesque suffering was a simple visual image of loyalty, which led naturally to 'If thou wilt weep my fortunes, take my eyes. I know thee well enough; thy name is Gloucester' (iv.vi.177–8). Such moments are not sentimental; rather, they contribute to the toughness of the play's vision, which will not settle for an easy nihilism any more than for a simple affirmation. And one cannot approach the full range of that vision without noticing those times when a character's simple presence will carry a significance over and above his words.

The effects I have discussed so far are not peculiar to one production. They are, rather, built into the text, they ought to appear in any performance that respects the text, and a reader who takes the trouble to imagine a performance as he reads should be aware of them. But as I have suggested there are ways in which a particular production can give special emphasis to certain moments of this kind; and the emphasis may be selective according to the director's interpretation. Here we touch on the trickiest area of our topic. A theatrical interpretation, like a critical one, is inevitably selective. Many scholars have wished that it were not so, that we could have productions that gave us the full range of a play's possibilities. 'Any good production of *Measure for Measure*,' writes Kenneth Muir, 'would necessarily present us with the possibility that Duke Vincentio was a symbol of divine providence, or an earthly ruler who was God's steward, or a puppet-master, or a busybody. It is not the business of the director to choose one of these and exclude the others.'[7] Productions that seem comprehensive in this way do occur, though they are rare; but it is worth recalling

John Russell Brown's warning that 'even those rare productions, that seem on first viewing to fill a play to its very limits, will be thought in ten years' time to have missed whole areas of Shakespeare's invented world'.[8] The reason for this, quite simply, is that the range of possible interpretations for a Shakespeare play is constantly expanding. It is often the critics who appear most eccentric or single-minded – Wilson Knight, Harold Goddard, Jan Kott – who, without winning approval or agreement, can disrupt and re-shape our thinking about a play, leaving us annoyed with them but permanently in their debt. Similarly in the theatre, the directors who impose strongly personal visions on Shakespeare – directors like Tyrone Guthrie, Peter Brook and Robin Phillips – are often the ones from whom we learn most. Some 'controversial' interpretations turn out to be useless; every Shakespearean playgoer has his collection of horror stories. But some, while they may not win agreement, do provoke thought. We may complain, 'The productions are not myriad-minded; Shakespeare is not free';[9] but our awareness of how myriad-minded Shakespeare is depends in some measure on the insights of actors and directors who choose to light a play up from a special angle. Bearing in mind the two principles I stated earlier – the continuity of performance, and the supplementing of the text by visual effects – I would like to explore some examples, large and small, of particular theatrical interpretations that seemed to me to reveal something about the plays in question. Not many of them will seem at first glance outrageous; but for the most part they brought out a special feature of the text, not by giving it the 'straight' reading scholars are so fond of demanding, but by adding to it or interpreting it in a special way.

At the end of II.ii. of *A Midsummer Night's Dream* Lysander leaves the stage in pursuit of Helena, and Hermia wakes from a bad dream in which 'Methought a serpent eat my heart away, And you sat smiling at his cruel prey' (II.ii.149–50). In the text, she does not speak till he is offstage; but in Robin Phillips' 1976 production at Stratford, Ontario, Lysander was only just leaving as Hermia began to speak. She spoke out of her sleep, in a slow moan; he watched her as he left, and heard her first words, 'Help me, Lysander, help me; do thy best. To pluck this crawling serpent from my breast' (II.ii.145–6) – but they delayed him only a moment. The painfulness of the situation, the betrayal and desertion, were strikingly emphasized. The continuity of the play was actually strengthened, and a new visual effect was added, as the director kept the characters together a moment longer than Shakespeare had. One might protest that the moment was darker than Shakespeare had intended it to be; but the darkness is latent in the text, and to bring it out in this way suggested the real experience in which the play's seemingly artificial intrigue has its roots. A similar delayed exit for special emphasis was introduced by Peter Hall in his [1967] production of *Macbeth*. At the end of their first scene Macbeth and Lady Macbeth, standing near the front of the stage, embraced. The lights on them went out, and came up on the rear of the stage, where Duncan and his party were entering. As the next scene began – 'This castle hath a pleasant seat. . . .' (I.vi.1) – the dark silhouettes of Macbeth and his wife crossed the front of the stage, visually underlining the irony of Duncan's cheerfulness. In John Barton's *Twelfth Night*, [for the Royal Shakespeare Company, 1969] Sebastian's attempt to come to terms with Olivia's love – 'And though 'tis wonder that enwraps me thus, Yet 'tis not madness' (IV.iii.2–3) was accompanied by offstage cries from Malvolio, whose dark-room scene had just finished – 'Fool, I am not mad!' A Shakespearean text is full of significant juxtapositions; but in the cases referred to the director had selected a certain juxtaposition as particularly important, and underlined it in a distinctively theatrical way. In reading a play, it is tempting to pause and reflect at the end of a scene; but as these productions suggested, we may miss something important if the pause becomes a break.

It is also possible for a production to make connections between two scenes that are actually remote from each other, and in so doing to reveal implicit connections within the text. In Robin Phillips' production of *Antony and Cleopatra* [Stratford, Ontario, 1976] as Antony disarmed himself after the defeat of the third day's battle, on the words 'Off, pluck off' (IV.xiv.37) he suddenly tore off one wrist-piece as though it burned him; and we remembered that this piece had been put on by Cleopatra on the morning of the second battle. Hippolyta, in Peter Brook's 1970 *Midsummer Night's Dream* for the Royal Shakespeare Company, delivered her reaction to *Pyramus and Thisbe* – 'I am aweary of this moon. Would he would change!' (v.i.245) – as a sly mockery of Theseus; it became an ironic echo of Theseus' first speech in the play. In Clifford Williams' production of *The Merchant of Venice* [for the Royal Shakespeare

Company, 1965] Lorenzo's reference to 'The man that hath no
music in himself' (v.i.83) made Jessica look pensive and rather hurt;
evidently she was thinking of her father. Whether various parts of
The Winter's Tale can or should be connected in this way is debatable;
but John Barton made interesting efforts to do so in his production
for the Royal Shakespeare Company in 1976. Polixenes, playing
with Mamillius, pretended to be a bear; Leontes sang a lullaby to
his son, in which we recognized a line from one of Autolycus' songs,
('The pale moon shines by night'); in the background of the final
statue scene, we glimpsed shepherdesses from Bohemia. But it may
tell us something about this particular play that in this case the
connections were added to the text rather than drawn out of it; the
play seems to resist attempts to unify it in conventional terms.

With this exception, these were connections of a sort that a critic
might well want to make in the course of an argument about the
play. But in each case, the special language of the theatre allowed
the connection to be made with a directness and economy that the
critic might well envy. Similarly an actor can make his own critical
commentary on a character or scene, simply by the way he chooses
to perform it. He and his director have to make decisions about how
the character looks, speaks and moves, about what he does with his
hands and with the props he handles; such decisions, if sensitively
made, constitute interpretative criticism that deserves to be regarded
as seriously as the criticism of a writer, and to be used as supporting
evidence in any discussion of the play. In less time than it takes to
describe, Hume Cronyn[10] showed us how much Shylock was a
creature of the material world: his sudden reluctance to go to
Bassanio's feast was triggered by the weight in his hand of the key
he was about to give to Jessica. In the trial scene, he measured out
carefully the exact area of Antonio's chest he intended to carve; and
when Portia suggested a surgeon, he studied the bond for a painfully
long time to establish that this was not part of the agreement. Paul
Scofield's Coriolanus,[11] begging the 'voices' of the citizens, showed
his detachment from them by his effortless refusal to look any of
them in the eye. It is part of Scofield's special quality as an actor
that he seems to inhabit a private world; here this quality illuminated
the character admirably.

These touches brought out something distinctive about a character; but another kind of interpretative point that can be made by
the director, the actors, and sometimes the designer, is the way

different characters will form special unified groups, apart from the others. In John Barton's *Twelfth Night*, Viola and Sebastian wore a colour, dark green, worn by no one else – until the finale, when Orsino and Olivia appeared in the same colour. This established that a special group had been created with Viola and Sebastian (or Cesario, if you prefer) as its centre, and that this group was rather apart from the other characters. There was a similar use of colour in Robin Phillips and William Hutt's production of *The Tempest* [at Stratford, Ontario, 1976]. The court party wore a uniform rusty brown, worn by no one else – until the end, when Prospero, appearing not as a great magician but as Duke of Milan, wore the same colour. His return to normal humanity was economically established. If such groupings make individual characters seem to lose their individuality, that – especially in the comedies – is a characteristic Shakespearean effect. In Robin Phillips' production of *A Midsummer Night's Dream*, the lovers were treated in this way: the men were identically dressed, and so were the women; and at the end of the forest sequence both Puck and Oberon had some difficulty remembering which of the men was to be given the antidote. In all these cases, an interpretative point was being made, with a clarity and force that compelled attention.

As with the characters, so with the images of a play, both visual and verbal. David Warner's Richard II,[12] handing the crown to Bolingbroke – 'On this side my hand, and on that side thine' (iv.i.183) – suddenly turned it upside down. The crown became directly connected with the well and buckets of the following speech; and we were alerted to the absurdity of the whole situation, in which a crown is passed from one living king to another and is in grave danger of losing its significance in the process. Parolles, in the final scenes of John Barton's *All's Well That Ends Well*, [for the Royal Shakespeare Company 1967], carried a begging-box in the shape of a small drum, confirming his earlier plan for survival, 'Being fool'd, by fool'ry thrive' (iv.iii.315). The prop showed, rather more clearly than the lines do, that Parolles was indeed exploiting his disgrace. In other cases, the production can alert us to some special quality of the play's verbal images: the recurring sound of the sea in John Barton's *Twelfth Night* was not only evocative in itself but made us aware of how pervasive the sea-imagery is in the play's language. It was at first surprising when Robin Phillips presented the First Fairy, whose dialogue with Puck opens the second act of *A Midsummer*

Night's Dream, as a charlady scrubbing the stage. But then we noticed how much of the imagery of the scene is drawn from household chores and domestic life generally; a seemingly mischievous production decision had revealed something about the closeness of the fairies to ordinary mortals.

It is in this quality of the unexpected that the special interpretations offered in the theatre can be most valuable. We make habitual assumptions about the quality of certain scenes or speeches, and we need to be challenged by readings that pull against those assumptions. Kent's 'Vex not his ghost. O, let him pass!' (v.iii.313) used to be regarded as a gentle requiem or at most a mild reproach. Tom Fleming, in Peter Brook's production, delivered it as a flash of anger. Many in the audience were startled, even offended; but the reading alerted us to the absurdity and impertinence of conventional consolations in the play's last scene. In a similar moment of unexpected anger John Wood told us something about Brutus;[13] in the quarrel with Cassius, he showed some irritation but kept his dignity, as Brutus usually does. When, after the quarrel, the Poet burst into the tent Cassius (who had got rid of his anger) was merely amused, but Brutus flew into a startling rage and physically attacked the intruder; we saw then how much Brutus' attempt at Stoic calm as his world fell in ruins was costing him. We may think of Cleopatra's death as a dignified and exalted scene, in which the Queen rises above her former nature; she likes to see it that way herself. But Zoe Caldwell [at Stratford, Ontario, in 1967], on Cleopatra's reference to the dead Iras –

> If she first meet the curled Antony,
> He'll make demand of her, and spend that kiss
> Which is my heaven to have.
>
> (v.ii.299–301)

– gave a jealous pounce on '*my*' in the last line, and grabbed an asp out of the basket. We saw, in that moment, a flash of the old Cleopatra. Othello's speech to the Senate about his romantic past seems to require a grand-manner reading; but Brewster Mason, in a production set by John Barton in the nineteenth century, delivered the speech quietly, sitting in a chair and meditatively puffing a cigar.[14] The speech became an old soldier's nostalgia. Christopher Plummer [at Stratford, Ontario in 1957] did more with the comic side of Hamlet than most actors do: most revealingly, when he delivered 'Bloody, bawdy villain! Remorseless, treacherous, lecherous, kindless villain!' (ii.ii.575–6) not as direct passion but as a self-conscious and unsuccessful attempt to ape the style and gestures of the First Player. It was a shrewd comment on the precariousness of Hamlet's role as revenger. In every case the actor, doing some violence to traditional notions of tragic dignity, revealed something human and vulnerable in the character he was playing, and did so in a surprising and provocative way.

In creating this kind of effect the actor can work directly with the lines; more controversial, perhaps, is the role of the modern director in devising stage business, often quite elaborate business, which is not extrapolated from the text but frankly added to it. Sometimes the director is simply showing off; but at their best these additions too form a critical commentary of some value. In Peter Hall's production of *Hamlet* [1965], Fortinbras arrived to claim his inheritance by literally kicking the door down. The effect was surprising, and was meant to be; but one does not have to look very far in the text to see hints that Fortinbras is a brutal and dangerous opportunist, and that Hamlet's sanguine view of him is far from being the whole picture. In the last scene of his production of *Measure for Measure* [1975], Robin Phillips devised a staging at odds with tradition and with the apparent demands of the script. The scene began (again, this was a nineteenth-century setting) with jolly band music and much twirling of parasols to greet the Duke's return; with its colour and bustle, it looked like a conventional comic finale. As the scene advanced, and the revelations became more painful and complicated, business was contrived so that more and more characters left the stage and did not return. (At the scandalous accusations of the women against Angelo, a party of children was whisked off by their nursemaid.) Towards the end some half-dozen figures were left – and finally Isabella stood alone, tearing off her nun's headdress with an expression of bewilderment and dismay. The gradual filling of the stage, so basic to the traditional comic ending, was reversed; the effect was of deliberate parody, underlining the sense of unease, even failure, that lies beneath the apparent satisfaction of the scene as written.

In performance relationships between the characters can expand beyond what the dialogue suggests; here again the director can be helpful, devising business that provides a context for the characters' behaviour – even, at times, a whole social ambience. In John

Barton's production of *Love's Labour's Lost* [1965], the role of Boyet was built up from a few hints in the text so that he became an experienced senior advisor to a princess on her first diplomatic mission. He carried a small staff of office, and on the news of the old King's death he did a long, slow cross, knelt to the Princess, and delivered the staff to her. One of the concerns of the last scene is the experience of growing up; this moment gave that concern a political dimension, establishing a helpful context for the new dignity and seriousness of the Princess in the moments that followed, and suggesting the more serious world from which the world of courtship was finally just a holiday. One of the most directly helpful touches of this kind I can remember came in the last scene of Trevor Nunn's production of *The Taming of the Shrew* [1969]. As the women withdrew from the wedding feast, there was a collective masculine grunt of relief and satisfaction, a general unbuttoning, as chairs were pushed back and feet were placed on the table. Obviously the serious drinking was about to begin. In this context, the boasting and wagering on the absent wives was not an arbitrary way of ending the comedy but the natural expression of a rough, sporting, male-dominated world. In all these cases the hand of the director was felt most strongly in the last scene, giving us a final critical comment on the world of the play and the actions of the characters.

In this process of commentary and interpretation, the audience itself has a role to play, one which I can touch on only briefly here. An audience's reactions can be subtle, intangible, forbiddingly difficult to analyse. But certain broad effects, notably laughter, come through clearly. [I once] acted in a production of *All's Well That Ends Well*[15] in which, in addition to the usual rehearsals, we brooded over the play's problems in a number of seminars with local scholars. We kept coming back to Bertram's rejection of Helena, analysing its social and psychological dimensions, judging its rights and wrongs. But we made one of our most important discoveries only in performance. On the King's line 'Why, then, young Bertram, take her; she's thy wife' (ii.iii.103) Bertram looked around in a panic, mutely appealing to Parolles for help. There was a roar of laughter. Then, as Bertram began to defend his refusal, the laughter died, and on 'A poor physician's daughter my wife! Disdain Rather corrupt me ever!' (ii.iii.113–14) a chill crept through the house; at some performances one could hear gasps. Something important we had overlooked in our theorizing was the drama acted out by the audience itself: it reacts simply at first, seeing the absurdity of the King's order and recognizing the familiar comic figure of the young man afraid of marriage; then it is forced to look more closely, and to feel a little ashamed of itself, as it realizes the situation is more complex, human and painful than the first broad effect suggested.

In performances of the final romances the audience will acknowledge moments of self-conscious contrivance by laughter, often at points that do not seem paricularly funny in reading. In the finale of *Cymbeline*, Belarius' 'My boys, There was our error' (v.v.259–60) and Cornelius' 'O gods! I left out one thing which the Queen confess'd' (v.v.243–4) are traditional points of laughter; so is the pairing of Camillo and Paulina at the end of *The Winter's Tale*. When I saw Jean Gascon's 1973 production of *Pericles* at Stratford, Ontario, there was a loud and seemingly inexplicable burst of laughter on Cerimon's reference to the fainting Thaisa, 'O, she's but overjoy'd' (v.iii.21). Checking with friends who had seen other performances I discovered that there was always one such laugh somewhere in the last scene, but it was not always in the same place. It was not that the audience was unsympathetic – in fact the audience was profoundly moved. But at the same time it recognized something absurd in the happy ending, and that recognition had to find vent in laughter. It may indicate the extra sophistication of technique in *Cymbeline* and *The Winter's Tale* that the moments of laughter are predictable; Shakespeare allows for this recognition of absurdity, and has learned to place it at moments chosen by himself. The changing reaction of the audience, then, is an important part of the drama; critics need to be aware of it, as performers have always been. (I wonder how many playgoers realize that while they are analysing the actors the actors are analysing them?)

This is not to say that every performance of Shakespeare is a series of blinding revelations, or that actors, directors and audiences are endowed with a special wisdom that makes their interpretations authoritative. They are as prone to error and inattention as the rest of us, and they ride their own hobby-horses. But even from a flawed interpretation, one can learn much. I have referred several times to Robin Phillips' production of *A Midsummer Night's Dream* at Stratford, Ontario in 1976. The central device of this production was the sort of thing that sends academics swearing and muttering into the night. We were asked to imagine that the play was being performed by Queen Elizabeth and a group of her courtiers, with Elizabeth (Jessica

Tandy) doubling as Titania and Hippolyta. In passage after passage, the device was irritating, confusing and irrelevant. Yet there were moments when it allowed us to see the familiar text with fresh clarity. The doubling of the rulers of day and night did not, as in Peter Brook's production, suggest that the fairies were an aspect of the subconscious of the mortals; rather, it showed the fairies as a *court*, with all the tensions, squabbling and jealousy that a court can breed. Oberon's desire to torment his queen acquired an edge of angry excitement, for behind the figure of Oberon was a frustrated court favourite. Peaseblossom, Cobweb, Moth and Mustardseed were not capering children but adult courtiers, and when presented with Bottom as the new favourite they showed polite resentment. (We get so used to the play that the image of Titania courting Bottom seems natural and right; this was a salutary reminder of its comic and somewhat unsettling incongruity.) Finally Puck, restored to his mortal role as an elderly court jester, delivered his 'Now the hungry lion roars. . . .' (v.i.360), with its talk of ghosts and graveyards, to Elizabeth herself, as a reminder of her mortality. As the disembodied voices of Oberon and Titania spoke of bride-beds and children, we watched the old, solitary virgin queen slowly leave the stage. Of course this staging had nothing to do with the scene as Shakespeare wrote it. But through Puck's epilogue Shakespeare tells us that the play, ending and all, is a dream; and here its dream-like quality was underlined by suggesting its remoteness from the actual experience of the aged spinster who was Queen of England. And as Puck spoke his epilogue, the fairy charlady who had joined him in Act Two returned and started scrubbing the floor again. The courtiers had gone, the great hall was dark and empty, and the cleaning staff were at work. The play was over.

One went up the aisle thinking dark thoughts about directors who stick extra bits on to a perfectly shaped play; and yet one wanted to see the production again, and to think about it further. Phillips had revealed something about the recognizable human tensions that lie beneath the artifice of the play, and about the dark world of mortality that the play's poetry touches on at certain points and that makes the happiness of the ending at once precious and fragile. On paper, his interpretation would probably have collapsed at once; sustained by the resources of the theatre, it stayed alive long enough to provide a fitful but provocative commentary. It was commentary of a kind peculiar to the theatre – finding echoes, making connections, building a fully conceived life around the dialogue, giving the text an extra dimension.

SOURCE: Essay in *Mosaic: A Journal for the Comparative Study of Literature and Ideas*, X, 3 (1977), pp. 37–49.

NOTES

Abbreviated and renumbered from original by editor.

1. Alan S. Downer, in *Shakespeare Quarterly*, 13 (1962), 219–30.
2. Eric Salmon, in *Modern Drama*, 15 (1972), 305–19.
3. In Clifford Williams' production for the Royal Shakespeare Company in 1962.
4. 'More Pregnantly Than Words: Some Uses and Limitations of Visual Symbolism', *Shakespeare Survey*, 24 (1971), 15. See also John Russell Brown, *Shakespeare's Plays in Performance* (Harmondsworth, repr. 1969). p. 78.
5. See Brown, *Shakespeare's Plays*, p. 239.
6. See Ewbank, pp. 17–18.
7. 'The Critic, the Director, and the Liberty of Interpreting' in Joseph G. Price (ed.), *The Triple Bond* (University Park, Pennsylvania and London, 1975), p. 28.
8. *Shakespeare's Plays*, p. 208 (op. cit., Note 4).
9. John Russell Brown, 'Free Shakespeare', *Shakespeare Survey*, 24 (1971), 131. The argument, is expanded in Brown's, *Free Shakespeare* (London, 1974).
10. In Bill Glassco's production of *The Merchant of Venice* at Stratford, Ontario in 1976.
11. In Michael Langham's 1961 production at Stratford, Ontario.
12. In the 1964 Royal Shakespeare Company production, jointly directed by John Barton, Peter Hall and Clifford Williams.
13. In the Royal Shakespeare Company's 1972 production of *Julius Caesar*, directed by Trevor Nunn.
14. Royal Shakespeare Company, 1971. The cigar was cut later in the run.
15. Directed by Martin Hunter at Hart House Theatre, University of Toronto, 1976.

Bernard Beckerman   Explorations in Shakespeare's Drama   (1978)

There is evidence all around us that an important change has occurred in Shakespeare studies. Far from being supplemental and peripheral as in the past, analysis of Shakespeare through performance is now conceded to be a proper and perhaps central way of approaching Shakespeare. Something approximating what J. L. Styan terms a 'revolution' has occurred in the study and in the classroom.[1] At the same time, actors and directors are now meeting frequently with scholars, teachers, and critics, discussing Shakespeare in performance openly, critically, and fruitfully. So something equally significant seems to be taking place in the theatre.

But though there seems much to celebrate, there is also a need to take stock. It is one thing for us to attend a Shakespearean play, to enjoy and be thrilled by the actors, and to remember the performance as a special experience – after all, behind all our commentaries on Shakespeare, there should reverberate the memory of pleasurable playgoing. But the fact is we do not stop with playgoing alone. We also insist upon *speaking* about Shakespeare. It is not enough for us merely to attend performances, read plays, rehearse scenes, watch television productions, and keep quiet. Whether in classes or at conferences, in conversation or in journals, we delight in discussing performances: what they reveal of the text, how they compare to other performances, where they blaze new paths. Nor are our discussions merely social. Intellectually and educationally, we assume that by exploring the principles and processes of bringing Shakespeare alive in the theatre, we can more finely perceive the motions of his art.

Responding to a performance, however, and talking about either the performance or its text are two quite different activities. If one of us adores a production and another doesn't, there is very little to say. We can't argue with each other's feelings. But if we are going to explore the *nature* of performance and the relation of performance to text, then indeed we must talk to each other – that is, if we concur on *how* to talk to each other.

I

First, some ground clearing is necessary. The kind of talk we engage in will stem from the premises upon which we base that talk. One thing that seems terribly important, for instance, is how each of us connects Shakespeare to performance or performance to Shakespeare. Some people begin with Shakespeare and then proceed to a consideration of theatre. Allegiance for them is to Shakespeare, to his text and to his genius, which they find, or hope to find, illuminated by studying his theatre and the theatre in general. Other people proceed from the theatre to Shakespeare. That is, they are first engaged in theatre, they give it their first allegiance, and they therefore see Shakespeare as only a figure, albeit the premiere figure, in stage art.

The orientations of these two groups lead to contrary mental actions. Those who start with Shakespeare use him as a pole-star. They measure the theatre by how it clarifies or animates the potentiality of his text. They are astounded and delighted, but also dismayed, by the discovery that his words, when spoken, take on an unanticipated existence; the uncertainty of improvisation, the amplitude of motion and setting, the imperfection of the living moment. Their habit of referring their observations back to the text is fundamentally different from the approach of those with a theatrical orientation.

That difference is best summed up in a phrase widely used in the theatre. Often an actor or director, in assessing a scene, a speech, or a bit of business in rehearsal, will say that 'it works' or 'it doesn't work'. What does 'it works' really mean? One can hardly expect a literal or objective answer. There isn't any. The phrase 'it works' refers to some intuitive measure by which the actor or director recognizes that all the elements of a piece – word, gesture, thought – spring into imaginative life. The antennae of performers are so sensitized by experience, study, rehearsal, and – yes – prejudice, that they are keenly alert to that moment when all the parts of a scene come together. Admittedly, their intuition can mislead them as well as lead them to an inspired realization of the given material. Yet, setting aside the quality of the result, one must acknowledge that a theatrical orientation to a text is based on the assumption that its pole-star is an intuitive, imaginative awareness of when life fuses into style. Given such a theatrical assumption, Shakespeare is seen as subject to the imperatives of performance rather than performance as subject to the demands of Shakespeare.

Ideally, one would like to combine these two orientations, to allow both Shakespeare and the theatre their proper due. And perhaps now we are in a better position to do this than in recent years. The immediate past saw the theatre seize Shakespeare and make him march to the beat of mythic and social visions. In reaction partly to pointless historicism, partly to decorative realism, directors sought to evoke from the Shakespearean text a contemporary image, one that they hoped would penetrate to the core of an audience's being. They exploited analogies, symbols, vaudeville techniques, game plans, and a host of other devices in order to update Shakespeare. That, in the process, they often had to violate the explicit logic of the script was merely a casualty of theatrical adventuring.

Not that these adventures were inherently irresponsible. Quite the contrary. By being faithful to their own sense of life, actors and directors often discovered the pulse of life that beat most strongly in Shakespeare's work. Yet despite the obvious achievements of Peter Brook's *Midsummer Night's Dream*, for instance, or Michael Kahn's *Henry V*, we now witness in the theatre a decided reaction against what is viewed, in retrospect, as directorial abuse. For in practice it happened too frequently that in his search for relevance and immediacy, the director failed to distinguish his own diminished sense of existence from the expansiveness that Shakespeare demanded. A string of productions from Brook's *King Lear* to John Barton's *Richard II* illustrated that too programmatic and schematic a view of a play's significance could contract rather than enlarge the life-possibilities of the dramatic material. In short, although many people at the time felt that these productions 'worked', we now find that they 'work' only in the fashion of the times.

Symptomatic of the change in our current perspective is a shift from 'Director's Shakespeare' to 'Actor's Shakespeare'. Such a shift is reflected in John Russell Brown's plea to us to 'free Shakespeare'. It is embodied in director Terry Hands's stress on the actor's search for the poetry of the play. It is signalled by John Barton's claim that as a director he does little more than exercise a light, guiding touch upon a production.[2] In essence, we are seeing a return to the text of Shakespeare, or rather a renewed desire to let the text guide production more fully than it has in recent years. Not that the activity of the last twenty years can or should be erased. Not at all.

Rather, performers seem to be bringing all that they learned in that period – about how to mold theatrical images and how to contact audiences – into a new relationship with the plays.

It is important to note that this trend does not pertain solely to Shakespearean production. Rather, it is a general movement in the English-speaking theatre. The rich and chaotic sixties mounted an attack upon the verbal and rational elements of the theatre. Logic of action gave way to impulse and reaction. Gesture, we were told, was truer than language, spontaneity more honest than premeditation. Some of the most notable achievements in the theatre – e.g., the work of the Open Theatre in [the United States], the work of Peter Brook and Jerzy Grotowski [in Europe] – were directly or indirectly an outgrowth of this primal attitude toward theatre. Now, however, the impact of the movement of the sixties is waning. We have entered a new period of consolidation, and that period is characterized by a re-engagement with language.

There are many signs of this in the theatre. Playwrights are once again turning out realistic plays of conversation and confession. Acting schools, such as the one at Yale, are reorganizing their curricula to place renewed stress on textual study. Improvisers of the past, like Joe Chaikin of the Open Theatre, are now wrestling with literary texts. Thus, the change we see in Shakespearean production parallels and shares changes in theatrical production in general. For the two are just as inseparable now as they have always been. Sometimes Shakespearean production leads the way in innovation, sometimes it follows. But always in the theatre Shakespearean production is but a special instance of a general search for theatrical reality and excitement.

II

The re-engagement with the text that I describe seems to promise a bridging of the gap between theatrical and Shakespearean orientation. After all, have not many Shakespearean scholars clamoured for faithfulness to the text? But re-engagement with Shakespeare's text does not involve merely literal adherence to language. Instead it demands a vigorous searching of a play's dialogue in order to find its dramatic pulse. Fundamentally, this involves not only our way of reading and experiencing a play but also the principles underlying our way of reading. If we are to have Actor's Shakespeare, then the future quality of Shakespearean performance will depend on the quality of the actor's reading of Shakespeare.

Let us recall that we have had Actor's Shakespeare before – the Actor's Shakespeare of Henry Irving and Herbert Beerbohm-Tree, for instance. It was a Shakespeare reflective of the actor's ego and personality rather than of the text, a Shakespeare that Bernard Shaw mocked when he observed that 'more people to go the Lyceum Theatre to see Mr Irving . . . than to see Shakespear's plays'. Shaw went on to say that 'if Mr Irving were to present himself in as mutilated a condition as he presented King Lear, a shriek of horror would go up from all London'.[3] If we are to avoid such mutilation in the future and synthesize the scholar's and actor's views, it must be by the common foundation we all share as readers of Shakespeare.

Although it is pleasant to perpetuate the myth of the wholly individual reader, communication among us is only possible because reading is, in large measure, communal. On an imaginative level we practice the habits of reading that we have been led to admire; that is, we pay attention to what our culture considers significant. Where Shakespeare is involved, with the rich possibilities of reading he provides, we often concentrate only on those facets of his work that our local circle favours.

I am nowhere more cognizant of this fact than in my classes. Usually they contain both theatre and literature students. As one might guess, the two types of students read plays differently. Where the theatre student will read for situation, for stage business, for audience response, the literature student will read for symbolic significance, for thematic strands, for intellectual nuance. What is so rewarding in having these two kinds of reading intermix is that they complement one another marvellously. One way of reading feeds the other. At the same time, however, they share a common aspiration, for every type of reading seeks the same two ends. First, each type of reading seeks to put the reader in touch with the essential quality of a work, with that experience and those features which make each particular work a unique event. Second, each type of reading seeks to embrace the work as a whole, to enable the reader not only to taste the distinctive quality of the work but also to comprehend all the elements of it. As scholars and teachers, our goal is to encourage those habits which will enable the student to grasp the whole without losing the essence, and to become aware of the essential qualities without losing grasp of the whole.

For many of us this goal is best pursued through a theatrically sensitive reading of Shakespeare's text, through what J. R. Mulryne has termed a 'stage-centered' reading.[4] But, of course, each of us means something slightly different by a phrase of that sort. Scholars of the Elizabethan theatre, for example, almost always employ the word 'staging' to mean the way actors use the features of the physical stage – doors, stage traps, properties, and so forth. For me, on the other hand, while 'staging' includes the use of the physical stage, it also encompasses far more significant features such as actor relationships and performing rhythms.

When we mention the stage, we imply rehearsal, and rehearsal – at least rehearsal of Shakespeare's plays – begins with reading and re-reading. Even a beginning actor has to read and re-read, whether to memorize a speech or to know how to react to someone else's speech. This kind of rehearsing, re-reading, and re-saying only exemplifies in little that larger re-reading toward which we wish to move: a systematic re-reading, in sequence, of passages, scenes, and the play as a whole, a moving back and forth over the script, indeed a scanning of the script, as a means of 'living into' the flow of circumstances as the action unfolds. This larger kind of re-reading is aimed, not at securing data or determining theme, but at sensing vibrations in the text. And this kind of re-reading is fundamental because it recognizes that getting to an end is secondary. What is *primary* is the experience of moving toward an end.

III

Let us now look at what various other writers mean by a stage-centred reading. One matter currently receiving considerable attention is the non-verbal side of the Shakespearean text.[5] This involves culling clues in the dialogue in order to imagine the details of setting, costume, and movement – gestures implicit in the lines, for example, or symbolic uses of properties. That such visualization of the text is fundamental is beyond question. Seeing, no less than hearing, is central to the theatre. But we must keep in mind that attention to visual elements in a play is only a beginning, not an end in itself. Too often a theatrical reading is conceived primarily, if not entirely, as a matter of visualizing stage business. I would suggest a different emphasis. By becoming attuned, not only to the visual context of costume and properties, but also to the gestural language interwoven with the text, we can more acutely trace the essential action within the text.

Another aspect of stage-centered reading consists of bearing in mind that a dramatic text is full of choices. A dramatic text is, as is said so often, merely a pre-text. After being exposed to the impulses of all the words in the text, the actor must select from those impulses the ones that will guide him in creating a performance. In making each selection, the actor or the reader is not seeking the 'correct' choice so much as the most provocative choice – the choice most provocative of mental and emotional stimulation. To enable the student to engage directly in this kind of choice-oriented reading, some teachers, notably J. L. Styan, have advocated reading Shakespeare through rehearsal techniques.[6] A complementary approach is to encourage students to see and hear alternate performances of the same text. Both emphases are exciting and revealing – and they are not mutually exclusive. Once again, however, it is important to remember that they are only part of a more comprehensive reading. Ultimately, their value depends on other mental habits generated at the heart of rehearsal and playgoing.

Reading for visual clues and reading for dramatic choices are aspects of the effort to discern the *sensation* of living embodied in the text. That sensation is manifested in sequences of energy impulses, and such impulses are often conveyed by an incomplete contact between a thrust and its response. Sometimes we have the thrust without the response, sometimes the response without the thrust. Shakespeare's adroit use of mid-speech entrances frequently gives us a response without the thrust, as, for example, in the opening of *Othello*. Roderigo's line 'Tush, never tell me' obliges us to imagine the stimulus that produced such a response. This kind of dislocation between thrust and response is the common trade of all playwrights. What is exceptionally difficult, and what Shakespeare excels at, is to arrange a sequence of such units of energy into a meaningful whole, and even more, to arrange thrust and response in such a way as to surprise and satisfy us at the same time. When we still find ourselves surprised and satisfied even after we have come to know a work thoroughly, we experience the ultimate achievement of the dramaturgic imagination.

Inherent in what I am saying is a line of thought that not all theatrical people are prepared to accept. I would argue that in becoming attuned to the visual elements of a dramatic text and in weighing its choices, we are testing the limits of the play. Not all visual images are appropriate; not all choices are valid. In short, not all theatrical readings are defensible. Without always being able to set the exact limits of interpretation, we know that such limits exist. In my opinion, these limits are more readily perceived by examining the dramatic structure of a text than by any other means. The sequence of thrust and response that I mention here is the basis of that dramatic structure, a highly complex shape which is imprinted in the text like a fossil imprinted in a rock stratum. The better the dramatist, the more precisely is dramatic shape embedded in the language of the play. As readers or actors, we must learn to perceive the shape in the text. Earlier, I stressed reading and re-reading. This procedure enables the implicit shape to emerge from the text in all its complexity. A double process takes place. On the one hand, since every theatrical reading is provisional – that is, subject to change and revision – our experience of a work deepens. Yet on the other hand, since theatrical reading is also evolutionary – that is, subject to constant growth and refinement – our sense of the play develops by an accumulation of insights.

This type of process, which is what *I* mean by a stage-centered reading, may be best characterized as contextual, structural, dialectical. These adjectives are suggestive, rather than prescriptive. They emphasize one extremely important point about script reading, namely that it is relational in nature. Every word, every gesture, every sign takes on force because it is set off against some other word, gesture, or sign.

The compact and essentially objective nature of drama limits the discursiveness possible in a script. Dialogue and business must always be doing several things at once. And by relying on a direct presentation of the illusion of life, drama precludes any direct mediation of the dramatist's own sensibility. Even when Shakespeare presents a character speaking his inmost thoughts, therefore, we are aware not only of the thoughts themselves but also of the context within which the thoughts are uttered. For example, as we hear Henry the Fifth deplore vain Ceremony and envy 'the wretched slave' Who, with a body fill'd and vacant mind, Gets him to rest' (iv.i.264–66), we not only share his thoughts but weigh their worth, hearing them echo against his conversation with the common soldiers moments earlier.

As a result, then, of our contextual reading of a script, we attend simultaneously to three factors: (1) the impulse of the character who makes a scene happen, (2) the opposing thought or act against which that character projects his energy, and (3) the intangible interplay between the first two.

Being aware of visual elements is exceptionally important because they usually embody one of the first two polar forces. We can see this most obviously in *Hamlet* where the black suit of the prince shares stage with the wedding garments of the festive court. The visual contrast between prince and court embodies a lurking yet muted challenge by the prince to the court, one which the court at first chooses not to recognize. When Gertrude and Claudius eventually do face Hamlet's implied accusation, they do so with immense finesse, which accentuates all the more the awkwardness of the exchange between son and mother, nephew and uncle. It is therefore a highly complex dialectical interplay that the costumes set into motion.

Every element of the script, then, such as Hamlet's costume, needs to be read for its radiating qualities – that is, for the claims or assertions it might be making. Any every element is relational: making its claims or assertions in the face of an implicit or explicit contrast. Where the reading of a play script is tricky is that normally only one of the contributory elements, usually the one propelling the scene, is explicitly delineated in the dialogue or stage business. All the rest we must infer from the surrounding situation, the responsive lines, and the few stage directions the dramatist or prompter has included. A stage-centered reading, then, is designed to recover the implicit features of the context, in order that we may gain a full awareness of the action – the action not as a part of the narrative but as a working out of a human dialectic.

IV

The process is further complicated by the fact that as human beings we are both fickle and steadfast – and this paradox is embodied in our sensory system. We can only concentrate, perceptually and mentally, on one thing at a time. Yet, even when concentrating on a central stimulus, we do not lose complete awareness of subsidiary stimuli. In fact, we can only pay attention by focusing on one object which our senses have selected from a larger field. The focal range of our eyes, for instance, is severely circumscribed. But we have peripheral vision that enables us to subtend a wide arc of phenomena. Such a duality crucially affects our perception of dramatic events. We can concentrate on one thing on stage, but we are aware of that one thing as occurring within a context to which we are sensitive in a diffuse way. Thus, we see events in depth, as taking place in a larger world. This is true not only visually but mentally. In *Macbeth*, for example, we see Duncan approach Inverness lightheartedly, but we read the scene with peripheral awareness of his impending murder. And our awareness of his danger must remain peripheral, because if it were forced upon our attention focally, we would feel the connection to be heavy-handed and obvious.

This interconnection between what is focal and what is peripheral has been characterized in several ways. Elsewhere, following Gestalt psychology, I have spoken of a figure-ground configuration. In writing on the psychology of art, Rudolf Arnheim also speaks of figure and ground – or sometimes of foreground and background.[7] In his notes to *Caucasian Chalk Circle*, Bertolt Brecht refers to foreground and background relationships. And Erving Goffman, the sociologist, has recently stressed the notion of centered activity and a frame within which that activity is perceived.[8] All of these formulations have a common basis: as human beings we conceive of phenomena or events as focal-peripheral composites whereby one element is at the centre of our attention but always in relation to a less sharply defined context.

How does this affect our reading of Shakespeare's scripts? Because of the richness of the stimuli emitted by his work, it is possible – and we have examples of it everywhere – for readers and performers to respond to images and lines as though they were of focal significance when they may in fact be only peripheral. Thus, when John Barton, in the [1973] Royal Shakespeare production of *Richard II*, made Richard and Bolingbroke mirror images of each other, he was touching on some of the political overtones of the text; but these were overtones, not fundamentals. What was subsidiary he made central, and he justified it as a new interpretation when in reality it was nothing less than an adaptation. This example is not singular. We find criticism as well as theatrical production awash with reversals of figural and ground elements. For example, there are many studies of Elizabethan ideas as reflected in Shakespeare.

In writing on such a subject, it is extraordinarily important to discriminate between those ideas that merely serve as background and those that actively enter into the dramatic workings of that play. Much of the interpretive dispute over *Measure for Measure* has involved claims that Christian or Jacobean political doctrines were operative in the play. Corrective criticism has shown that these doctrines were at best tangential background ideas.[9]

How then, one might well ask, is a person to decide what in a Shakespearean play is focal and what is peripheral? Again, we have to rely on a contextual approach. Our first reading gives us impressions. We differentiate one aspect of the play from another. A re-reading tests our impressions, reorders our emphases, and opens new areas of exploration. A third reading, either of the whole or of parts, further enables us to let the play grow in us. Each reading, like each rehearsal, is an essay in distinguishing emphatic from subsidiary features of the work. When, in addition, that repetitive process is reinforced by a systematic way of assessing the dramatic totality, then we can begin to discern the potential shape imprinted in the text.

In the course of differentiating the focal from the subsidiary features of a play, we are actually engaged in separating what Yuri Lotman[10] calls the functional elements from the non-functional elements. The functional elements are those so central to a work that, were they removed, the work would cease to be what it is. The distinction is derived from linguistics. Linguists illustrate the difference between functional and non-functional sounds in the following manner. Let us take a word composed of four phonemes, the first of which is 'k', the third of which is the sibilant 's', and the last of which is 't'. We have k-st. The second phoneme, in English at least, must be a vowel. Suppose that vowel to be a flat or broad 'a'. Then we would have the word 'cast' or 'cahst'. In either instance the word would be the same, and it could be used in the phrase 'the "cast" [or "cahst"] of characters'. But were we to change the flat or broad 'a' to 'aw', then we would have the word 'cost', which is completely different. The shift from 'a' to 'ah' the linguist would call non-functional; the shift from 'a' to 'aw' he would call functional.

Now, I recognize that these shifts, if understood in a social context, can have other implications. Linguistically the difference between 'cast' and 'cahst' may be non-functional. For the student of dialect, however, it may be functional, serving to distinguish people by region or class. And at one time in the theatre it was of considerable importance whether one used the flat or the broad 'a'.

There are different kinds and degrees of significance, then, and distinguishing what is functional from what is non-functional may help us discriminate what is of prime importance in a play from what is secondary. That Hamlet is in black is functional; that his dress is Elizabethan or Cavalier is usually nonfunctional. Put him in a black tuxedo, however, and then the tuxedo as a sign becomes functional while the blackness of Hamlet's dress recedes into the background. In fact, the blackness loses its significance as a sign of mourning.

V

So far the examples I have been giving are isolated moments in the plays, and while selecting isolated moments is inevitable in such a brief presentation, it flies in the face of the kind of reading I am promoting. For above all else, a stage-centered reading is sequential. Scenes must be understood in terms of how they unfold one after another.

Stage-centered reading also stresses proportion. Each part has a graduated relationship to all other parts. The principle is the same as the one applied to vocal delivery of lines. Thus, one of the reasons we find John Barrymore's delivery of the line 'The play's the thing Wherein I'll catch the conscience of the king' so amusing is that for our ears his overemphasis on the word 'play' throws the line out of proportion.

Thus far I have been describing a stage-centered reading as contextual, structural, dialectical. But a stage-centered reading is also dynamic. It seizes on those portions of a work that convey significant interplay. It does not try to reduce a work to a central idea but to explore its motions.

And lastly, a stage-centered reading is detailed. It enables us to relate the smallest portion of a play to the most extensive, the word to the scene, the scene to the play as a whole. During at least part of our reading and re-reading we need to work with what I have elsewhere called the segment, what Emrys Jones has termed the scenic unit, and what is referred to by the post-Stanislavsky actor as the beat.[11] There is, it is true, some slight difference between

these first two terms and the term 'beat'. 'Beat' usually stands for a
section of a scene as perceived by the individual actor. It may or
may not coincide with the segment as organically formed by the
playwright and embracing all the actors who fall within it. This,
however, is not the place to dwell on fine distinctions. What matters
more is to note that common to all the terms is the treatment of a
text as a sequence of sub-units. These sub-units are organic phases
of the total work. Each has an immanent form that the production
or the imagination brings out. Each links with other sub-units to
make up the peculiar form and rhythm of a given play.

Before turning to a specific example, it might help to talk about a
segment in the abstract. I have already spoken of drama as
embodying a dialectic of thrust and responses.[12] What brings a
segment into being is some such initial assertion. It may take the
form of a character striving for an as yet unclear objective. It may
take the form of a character impressing himself on the audience, as
we find so often with the opening action of the Vice figures in Tudor
moral interludes. It may take the form of a character responding to
a shock of some sort. Whatever the initial force, the character's
impulse goes through phases of intensification and relaxation during
which a change comes about. For this to happen the initial force
must be set against some contrasting force so that the intensification
can be made manifest. That contrasting force need not take the form
of direct opposition. In the famous balcony scene, for example,
Romeo's longing for satisfaction is restrained by Juliet's apprehen-
sions even though, at a deeper level, they share the same aspirations.

VI

The dynamics of a segment in Shakespeare can perhaps be most
fully and economically illustrated by analysis of a scene from *Macbeth*.
I shall concentrate on the second half of Act I, scene vii, following
the soliloquy 'If it were done when 'tis done'. Lady Macbeth comes
from the banquet to seek her husband. He tells her he has decided
to go no further with the plot against Duncan. She goads and coaxes
him into proceeding with the murder. The scene is brief, only fifty-
five lines long, and on one level it has a simple structure.

As a type, the scene falls into the category of persuasion. Lady
Macbeth's appearance on stage exerts the initial force, to which

Macbeth offers at first evasive then direct opposition, saying 'We shall proceed no further in this business'. But Macbeth's opposition, firm at first, suddenly weakens. As Lady Macbeth attacks him for changing his mind and, by contrast to herself, failing to be a man, he first expresses his admiration for her ('Bring forth men-children only') and then yields ('I am settled'). On a primary plane, the tension between the two characters has been resolved and a new force set into motion as they go off to the murder.

Some comment about this primary plane is pertinent. The persuasion scene is one of drama's most common types of segments. It requires a character whose objective is to get another person to change his or her mind voluntarily. The crux of the encounter occurs when the person acted upon does or does not yield to the persuasion. The two dynamic elements of such a segment are the manner of persuasion and the quality of the resistance.

Oddly enough, the substance of persuasion – that is, the subject matter itself – falls into a few limited patterns. The persuader, as in the case of Lady Macbeth, may work upon the latent nature of the person to be moved. Calling Macbeth a coward arouses his pride as a man. Or the persuader may paint the horrors or the promises of the future. Lady Macbeth does the latter. Or the persuader may draw upon the past – as Lady Macbeth also does in small part. These three approaches tend to appear and reappear in one persuasion scene after another.

The quality of the resistance is difficult to make clear in a persuasion sequence. Logical argument is possible, but then the scene slips into debate. Normally, the playwright's objective is to suggest some deep-seated basis for the opposition to persuasion. As a consequence, the playwright usually avoids too explicit an articulation of the opposition. Its basis is hinted at rather than fully explored. In the *Macbeth* segment, Macbeth says much less than Lady Macbeth. He communicates his resistance more through silence than through anything said. Shaw uses a contrasting method in *Saint Joan*. When Joan tries to persuade Charles to be crowned at Rheims (scene ii), Charles's resistance, instead of taking the form of silence, assumes the form of unconventional responses. At one point Joan pleads with him, 'You have a little son. . . . Would you not fight for him?' Charles replies, 'No: a horrid boy. He hates me.' The unheroic response produces laughter, of course. In Shakespeare, on the other hand, Macbeth's silences encourage the audience to read into his response a mysterious agitation.

At this point we can move to a secondary plane of action. The underlying scheme of persuasion serves as the dynamic impulse for all the subsidiary movements of a persuasion scene. And these subsidiary movements consist of modulations in the main shape of action. In the *Macbeth* persuasion scene, modulations are of two sorts: first, those involving the exact way in which Lady Macbeth formulates her remarks; and second, those involving the precise path of Macbeth's response to her. Because Lady Macbeth is usually thought of as a powerful person and because she seems to overwhelm Macbeth in this scene, she is more often than not played as irresistibly dominant. But the success of the scene depends upon the actors' maintaining a careful balance between Lady Macbeth's urging and Macbeth's holding back. Shakespeare provides for this balance in the kinds of language he gives the performers. Lady Macbeth speaks forty-two lines. About half of them are cast in the form of questions. There is, moreover, an interesting arrangement of questions. Except for a line and a half, her first fifteen lines are all interrogative. Whether delivered in a probing or in a scornful manner, they undermine Macbeth's new-found determination. Amidst the questions there is the line and a half, a declarative statement, and it is dismissive. 'From this time, Such I account thy love.' The next nineteen or twenty lines are assertions, first offering a comparison of his behavior to hers, and then culminating in that deliberately shocking image of dashing out the brains of the babe that milks her. The grotesquerie of the image rather than its revealing psychology is what matters. When Macbeth shows the first signs of giving way, Lady Macbeth uses the bait of an easy crime to convince him, slipping from assertions to seductive questions in her last eight lines. These last questions are purely rhetorical, making evident how simple the murder can be. At the point when he is nearing acquiescence, Macbeth too slips into the rhetorical question. What does this syntactical arrangement tell us, and how does it relate to the underlying structure of the dramatic action?

In her first scene with Macbeth, Lady Macbeth coaches him by telling him how to behave before Duncan. His reply is cryptic: 'We will speak further'. When she seeks him out during the banquet, therefore, the matter of the murder is still unsettled as far as we know. And we cannot assume, merely because she persuades him by the end of the scene, that she is certain of success from the beginning. In other words, she may be less sure of herself than most actresses play her to be. The questions she poses certainly allow for a superior tone, it is true, but it may be more important that they allow for indirection. She has to approach Macbeth obliquely to determine how staunch his opposition is. Her use of questioning permits a range of intensity varying from understatement to hyperbole as she moves toward a direct attack. Obviously, an actress can try a number of approaches. But if she is to avoid the expected and the conventional, she has to make the struggle between Lady Macbeth and Macbeth a convincing one. Here the questions help. They are a retarding device. In such a scene as this, where the conclusion is too easily telegraphed from the beginning, the performer playing Lady Macbeth has to slow down the process of converting Macbeth so that the audience can feel the density of his resistance – feel it and think about it.

If we shift our attention now to Macbeth's resistance, we note that he makes an initial firm statement, establishing the terms of his opposition. He continues his resistance by telling Lady Macbeth to keep quiet and by defending his manhood. But by his next line he has begun to weaken. The text doesn't indicate just what line of hers has the most acute effect upon him or just why he gives way. And yet the focus of the scene is upon *how* he responds to her. What do we discover?

Despite the fact that Macbeth has talked himself into rejecting the murder for reasons of salvation or honor, something much cruder – and more trivial – still obsesses him. Lady Macbeth assaults him with her grotesque boast, and without an overt sign of reaction or transition comes his blunt question, 'If we should fail?' How should we take Macbeth's line? Is he simply revealing a deep-seated anxiety, a fear of failure? Or does he not know how to counter his wife's assertion?

In his response to the image of the babe's brains dashed out, Macbeth reveals his moral emptiness. No wonder he can then go on to admire Lady Macbeth's masculine virtues and gloat with her over the plans for the murder. At the end of the sequence, he appropriates her admonition from their first scene. Where she had warned him, 'To alter favour ever is to fear', he now replies 'False face must hide what the false heart doth know'. Thus, his resistance, expressed so firmly at the beginning, turns out to be a mere shell. The image of the babe propels the crux of the segment by breaking through Macbeth's shell and thereby freeing him to think the unthinkable.

This single scene cannot, of course, stand for the whole play. To comprehend *Macbeth* in a complete stage-centered reading, we would have to examine all of its scenes in detail and then link them to one another. But this exploration of one scene will, I hope, serve to illustrate a systematic way of studying the dynamics of a play script. Despite common misapprehensions, a close, systematic examination of a good text does not restrict the free play of the imagination or reductively limit the opportunities available for effective performance. Rather, it brings into more exciting relationship the most provocative features of a dramatic work.

Feeling at liberty to interpret a role or a scene in totally unlimited ways is not truly being free imaginatively. It is far more thrilling and emancipating to discover the limits within which a given work allows legitimate interpretation. Then one can focus upon how to convey, for instance, the feel, taste, and breath of Macbeth's bankrupt resistance. It is by conveying those sensations that one supplies the direct touch of life – that elusive life of Shakespeare's which we sometimes glimpse on the page and which we seek to experience nakedly in the theatre.

SOURCE: Essay in *Shakespeare Quarterly*, 29 (1978), pp. 133–45.

NOTES

Slightly abbreviated from the original by editor.
1. [Editor's note. See J. L. Styan, *The Shakespeare Revolution: Criticism and Performance in the Twentieth Century* (Cambridge, 1977).]
2. John Russell Brown, *Free Shakespeare* (London, 1974). The views I attribute to Terry Hands and John Barton were expressed, respectively, at the International Shakespeare Association Congress in Washington (April 1976) and at the International Shakespeare Conference at Stratford-upon-Avon (August 1976).
3. *Shaw on Theatre*, ed. E. J. West (New York, 1958), p. 45.
4. 'Students and the Stage-Centred Approach to Shakespeare: Some Queries.' Paper presented at the Symposium on Shakespeare in Performance, University of Illinois, 11 November 1977.
5. See Alan C. Dessen, *Elizabethan Drama and the Viewer's Eye* (Chapel Hill; Univ. of North Carolina Press, 1977).
6. See J. L. Styan, *Elements of Drama* (Cambridge, 1960) and *Shakespeare's Stagecraft* (Cambridge, 1967).

7. Bernard Beckerman, *Dynamics of Drama* (New York, 1970), pp. 137–44; Rudolph Arnheim, *Art and Visual Perception* (Berkeley, 1966), pp. 213–26 and 354–55; and *Visual Thinking* (Berkeley, 1969), pp. 283–86.

8. Bertolt Brecht, *Collected Plays*, ed. Ralph Manheim and John Willett (New York, 1974), VII, 296–97; Erving Goffman, *Frame Analysis* (Cambridge, Mass., 1974).

9. See especially Elizabeth Pope, 'The Renaissance Background of *Measure for Measure*', *Shakespeare Survey*, 2 (1949).

10. *Analysis of the Poetic Text*, ed. and trans. D. Barton Johnson (Ann Arbor, Michigan, 1976), pp. xiii, 11.

11. B. Beckerman, pp. 56ff.; Emrys Jones, *Scenic Form in Shakespeare* (Oxford, 1971), p. 3. 'Beat' is widely used in practice, but not in writing, it seems.

12. For a somewhat different and fuller treatment of dramatic energies, see my essay 'Shakespeare and the Life of the Scene' in *English Renaissance Drama*, eds. S. Henning, R. Kimbrough, R. Knowles (Carbondale, Illinois, 1976), pp. 36–45.

Grigori Kozintsev   On Directing
King Lear (1977)

I never regarded a new production as purely professional work. It was not just a question of applying my specialized knowledge or experience to the project. It meant somehow beginning to live all over again. Events and destinies, sometimes created centuries ago, would burst in on my life and occupy an increasingly large part of it. This would continue until the imaginary began to seem real: every day I would discover more and more completely realistic characteristics in this particular world, and in the people who lived in it.

Some alien person's life would merge with my own. This is how the flesh of the cinematographic forms would begin to take shape, and the words would become visible.

And then this most naturalistic art of photography would capture movements of life in full flight; they would be transferred from the pages of a book on to the screen.

And heaven knows what did not happen during this transition

and what did not get involved. I searched my memory: the books I had read, the countries I had visited, my childhood, arguments with friends or with myself; all these played some part.

I always had to find fault with past films or to argue with people who were no longer living. Professional practices and experience not only did not help, they hindered: I had to step beyond the bounds of the profession, to turn my experience upside down. I had to go back to school – indeed I was reduced to studying every day, taking lessons from experts who seemed to have no direct connection with my work – they taught me more than anything else. I had to do my homework and to swallow my disappointment when I got a bad mark for it: during this time I would give myself a bad mark for the same essay for which ten years ago I would have got the highest mark – or so it seemed.

A multitude of the most contradictory thoughts and feelings welled up inside me. But I – the person 'hereinafter named the director' (as contracts put it), and the organization 'hereinafter named the film studio' had entrusted a production to me. From a certain day onwards my thoughts and feelings were accounted for and programmed. The meter had begun to tick, the production had begun.

SOURCE: From the preface to *King Lear: The Space of Tragedy: The Diary of a Film Director* (London, 1977), p. xi.

SELECT BIBLIOGRAPHY

Books and articles excerpted or reprinted in this volume are not listed below; the reader is referred to the relevant Source citation.

Belsley, Catherine, *Critical Practice* (London, 1980): an introduction to new methods and theories.

Booth, Stephen, *'King Lear', 'Macbeth': Indefinition and Tragedy* (New Haven, 1983): a study of the changing impressions of character, theme and action received by audiences in the course of a play.

Culler, Jonathan, *The Pursuit of Signs: Semiotics, Literature, Deconstruction* (London, 1981).

Dollimore, Jonathan, and Sinfield, Alan, eds., *Political Shakespeare: New Essays in Cultural Materialism*, (Manchester, 1985).

Drakakis, John, ed., *Alternative Shakespeares*, (London and New York, 1985): an anthology introducing new modes of criticism.

Eagleton, Terry, *Criticism and Ideology: A Study in Marxist Literary Theory* (London, 1976).

Elam, Keir, *Shakespeare's Universe of Discourse: Language Games in the Comedies* (Cambridge, 1984).

Esslin, Martin, *The Field of Drama: How the Signs of Drama Create Meaning on Stage and Screen* (London, 1987).

Gardner, Helen, *The Business of Criticism* (Oxford, 1959).

Goldman, Michael, *Shakespeare and the Energies of Drama* (Princeton, N.J., 1972): a study of the histrionic elements in the plays.

Hawkes, Terence, *Shakespeare's Talking Animals: Language and Drama in Society* (London, 1973).

Hawkins, Harriet, *The Devil's Party: Critical Counter-interpretations of Shakespearian Drama* (Oxford, 1985): a discussion of conflicting views about individual plays.

Holderness, Graham, ed., *The Shakespeare Myth*, (Manchester, 1988): studies of Shakespeare's place in late twentieth-century culture, including ' "The Warrant of Womanhood": Shakespeare and Feminist Criticism', by Ann Thompson which is, probably, the best introduction to that branch of study.

Hunter, G. K., *Dramatic Identities and Cultural Tradition: Studies in Shakespeare and his Contemporaries* (Liverpool, 1978).

Levin, Richard, *New Readings vs Old Plays: Recent Trends in the Reinterpretation of English Renaissance Drama* (Chicago, 1979).

Ornstein, Robert, *The Moral Vision of Jacobean Tragedy* (Madison, Wisc., 1965).

Rabkin, Norman, ed., *Reinterpretations of Elizabethan Drama*, (New York, 1969): includes essays by Jonas A. Barish, Daniel Seltzer, Robert Hapgood

and Stephen Booth with 'shared assumptions [that] speak for what is
likely to be a period of rediscovery and of new understanding'.

Styan, J. L., *The Shakespeare Revolution: Criticism and Performance in the Twentieth
Century* (Cambridge, 1977).

Thomson, Peter, *Shakespeare's Theatre* (London, 1983): a volume in a series
of *Theatre Production Studies* which demonstrates how a knowledge of the
practicalities of Elizabethan theatre can illuminate the texts of the plays;
Shakespeare's works are also considered in two further volumes in the
series, on *Elizabethan Popular Theatre* and *Jacobean Private Theatre*.

Wells, Stanley, ed., *The Cambridge Companion to Shakespeare Studies*,
(Cambridge, 1986): a convenient reference book, in which new critical
approaches receive a separate treatment in a penultimate chapter.

Williams, R., 'Crisis in English Studies', *The New Left Review*, 129 (1981),
51–66.

NOTES ON CONTRIBUTORS

BERNARD BECKERMAN (died 1985): while Chairman of the Department of Drama and Speech at Hofstra College, he published *Shakespeare at the Globe* (New York, 1962) and directed an annual Festival of Shakespeare productions; he later became Professor of Theatre Arts at Columbia University, publishing on many aspects of theatre.

JOHN RUSSELL BROWN: Professor of Theatre at the University of Michigan and Director of Project Theatre, Ann Arbor, Michigan. He has published books on Shakespeare, Renaissance and Contemporary Drama, and Theatre. He is General Editor of *Theatre Production Studies*. From 1973 to 1988 he was an Associate of the National Theatre of Great Britain. He has directed numerous plays in professional and student theatres.

ROSALIE L. COLIE (died 1972): studied at Vassar and Columbia and taught at Barnard, Oxford, Yale, Toronto and Brown; latterly she was Chairman of the Department of Comparative Literature at Brown University. Her wide-ranging scholarship is exemplified in *The Resources of Kind: Genre-Theory in the Rennaissance* (Berkeley, Cal., 1973); it contains a critique of *King Lear*.

JONATHAN DOLLIMORE: teaches at the University of Sussex, in the School of England and American Studies. He is author of many essays and a joint-editor of *The Plays of John Webster* (Cambridge, 1984) and *Political Shakespeare: New Essays in Cultural Materialism* (Manchester, 1985). With Alan Sinfield, he is a General Editor of a series of studies, *Cultural Politics*.

E. A. J. HONIGMANN: Joseph Cowen Professor of English Literature at the University of Newcastle upon Tyne, taught previously at the Shakespeare Institute, Stratford-upon-Avon, and the University of Glasgow. He has edited *King John*, *Richard III* and *Twelfth Night* and is joint General Editor of The Revels Plays. He has written numerous books on Shakespeare's plays, his influence on other dramatists, the 'Lost Years' of his life, and on textual problems.

GRIGORI KOZINTSEV (died 1973): born in Kiev in 1905, he went to Leningrad at the age of nineteen to study under the theatre director, Meyerhold; he worked continuously in both theatre and film. His films of *Don Quixote*, *Hamlet* and *Lear* brought world-wide attention. His *Shakespeare: Time and Conscience* was published soon after the premiere of his *Hamlet*; in Russian its title was *Our Contemporary: William Shakespeare*. His study of *King Lear* has the subtitle, 'The Diary of a Film Director'.

ALEXANDER LEGGATT: Professor of English at University College, the University of Toronto. He has published books and essays on Shakespeare and Jacobean theatre; he was a major contributor to volume III of *The Revels History of Drama in English*, dealing with the years 1576 to 1613. His *Shakespeare's Comedy of Love* (London, 1974) benefits from the author's detailed knowledge and appreciation of the plays in performance.

MAYNARD MACK: Professor Emeritus of English, Yale University; he has published books on both Alexander Pope and Shakespeare and is editor of the standard edition of Pope; *King Lear in Our Time* (Berkeley, Cal., 1965) was followed by *Killing the King: Three Studies in Shakespeare's Dramatic Structure* (New Haven, 1973).

NORMAN RABKIN: Professor of English at the University of California, Berkeley, was editor of an important collection of essays for the English Institute, New York, *Reinterpretations of Elizabethan Drama* (1969), which heralded a 'marked shift in approach'. His own books are *Shakespeare and the Common Understanding* (New York, 1967) and *Shakespeare and the Problem of Meaning* (Chicago and London, 1981).

INDEX